Ethnoarchaeology

Implications of Ethnography for Archaeology

Ethnoarchaeology

Implications of Ethnography
for Archaeology

Carol Kramer, Editor

Columbia University Press/New York

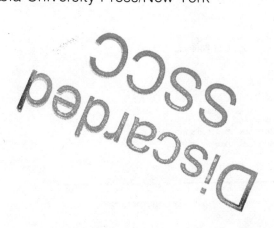

Library of Congress Cataloging in Publication Data

Main entry under title:

Ethnoarchaeology.

  Includes bibliographies and index.
  1. Ethnology—Addresses, essays, lectures.
2. Archaeology—Addresses, essays, lectures.
I. Kramer, Carol, 1943–
GN325.E78   301.2   78-10357
ISBN 0-231-04183-7

Columbia University Press

New York   Guildford, Surrey

Copyright © 1979 Columbia University Press

Printed in the United States of America

Contents

Ethnoarchaeology

Implications of Ethnography
for Archaeology

Introduction

Carol Kramer
Department of Anthropology
Lehman College,
City University of New York

Ethnoarchaeology has emerged as a useful approach to the study of archaeological remains.[1] The following prefatory remarks outline some of its basic assumptions and objectives, cite some examples of recent work in the field,[2] and suggest some lines along which future ethnoarchaeological research might be pursued.

Ethnoarchaeology: Basic Assumptions

Like other publications on ethnoarchaeology, the articles in the present volume reflect several assumptions shared in varying degree by most archaeologists. It is assumed that some behavioral elements of sociocultural systems have material correlates; if they are incorporated in the archaeological record, such residues may be used to develop inferences about the behaviors with which they were associated. Observations of contemporary behavior can facilitate the development and refinement of insights into past behaviors, particularly when strong similarities can be shown to exist between the environments and technologies of the past and contemporary sociocultural systems being compared. Ethnoarchaeological research investigates aspects of contemporary sociocultural behavior from an archaeological perspective; ethnoarchaeologists attempt to systematically define relationships between behavior and material culture not often explored by ethnologists, and to ascertain how certain features of observable behavior may be reflected in remains which archaeologists may find. Such research is therefore relevant to the collection, analysis, and interpretation of archaeological remains. The utility of insights into past behavior derived from observations of contemporary behavior is greatest when they can be framed as hypotheses and tested.

The assumptions outlined above are fundamental to the somewhat diverse ideas and methods subsumed in the term "ethnographic analogy." A number of recent publications have discussed the limits of analogical reasoning in archaeology; Binford (1967, 1972), among others, has provided examples of its applications. In his seminal paper on the subject, Ascher (1961) distinguished between the "folk-culture" or "direct historical approach" to analogical reasoning, in which behavioral continuities from prehistoric to historic periods within a given region can be documented or reasonably assumed, and the "new analogy"—Chang's (1967) "general comparative" analogy—which involves selecting analogs not necessarily restricted to the same geographic area as the archaeological data with which they are compared. This distinction continues to be used by many anthropologists.

It cannot be assumed that all past behaviors have analogs available for observation today; conversely, we cannot assume that all forms of cultural behavior which may be observed today have analogs in the past. Because pre-*sapiens* populations differed physiologically from *Homo sapiens sapiens,* it may be assumed that biologically determined aspects of hominid behavior prior to the late Pleistocene differed in some respects from that of modern forms (see S. Binford 1968). However, it seems unnecessary to dismiss analogical reasoning as totally irrelevant to the interpretation of the archaeology of early hominids. It has, for example, been argued that some of the variables affecting pre-*sapiens* behavior (such as species exploited) are available for analysis today (Binford 1977). Some of the constraints affecting subsistence, settlement pattern, and variation in local group size of earlier hominids are therefore amenable to analysis and thus to the interpretation of their archaeological remains (see Martin 1973; Speth and Davis 1976; Wilkinson 1972).[3] Further, there seems reason to expect that insights into the behavior of pre-*sapiens* populations will continue to be gained by developing and testing models emerging in the proliferating recent research in primate and carnivore ethology, and from the increasing application of more general ecological concepts pertaining, for example, to human responses to resource distributions and costs of travel and resource procurement (cf. Harpending and Davis 1977; Jochim 1976, among others).

Even in the case of *Homo sapiens sapiens,* we cannot assume that all forms of cultural behavior which existed in the past are available for observation in the present. This point, discussed by Freeman (1968) and others, is perhaps particularly clear in the case of contemporary hunter-gatherers, who occupy a more restricted range of habitats than did those foraging Pleistocene populations known through decades of archaeological research. Further, our perceptions of both contemporary and archaeological hunter-gatherers may be limited by a tendency to treat them as behavioral isolates, and to ignore the fact that in the past as in the present hunting groups articulated not only with other hunter-gatherers but also with social groupings characterized by greater institutional complexity. Possibly, too, anthropologists are sometimes prone to develop modal descriptions of hunter-gatherer behavior, rather than attempting to observe, describe, and explain behavioral variability. Archaeologists utilizing data reflecting such methodological and theoretical shortcomings are in danger of reconstructing a distorted archaeological record (cf. Wobst 1978).

Much recent ethnoarchaeological research has in fact focused on hunter-gatherers. (One practitioner of ethnoarchaeology, Peterson [1971:239], has gone so far as to define it as the study of hunter-gatherers.) Archaeologists' active interest in contemporary hunter-gatherers is, in part, based on the fact that for most of the several million years during which hominids have evolved, they were foragers rather than food producers. Further, collecting adaptations are currently near extinction; there is thus considerable justification in the argument that those few groups still functioning as foragers be studied systematically before they are either decimated or even further integrated into more complex societies, radically modifying their subsistence and settlement strategies and concomitantly altering their technologies and sociopolitical institutions.

The current geographic distribution of hunter-gatherers has led to a bias in favor of research in Alaska (Ackerman and Ackerman 1974; Binford 1976; Binford and Bertram 1977; Binford and Chasko 1976; Oswalt and VanStone 1967), Africa (Yellen 1976, 1977), and Australasia (Gould 1968, 1971, 1973, 1974; Jones 1971; Schrire 1972; White and Peterson 1969). These studies address a wide range of problems (examining, for example, tool manufacture, use, and curation; reconstructing subsistence and settlement systems; describing butchering and the modification and redistribution of animal bone by non-human agents). This research has in some cases involved the explicit integration of archaeological, ethnohistoric, and ethnographic data (see, for example, Allen 1974; Campbell 1968; Jones 1971; Oswalt and VanStone 1967; White and Peterson 1969).

The authors of these and other ethnoarchaeological studies do not necessarily assume that all past behaviors (whether of pre-*sapiens* or *sapiens* populations) have analogs available for observation today; indeed, such a position is untenable on logical grounds alone. Their work is based on the premise that ethnoarchaeological research can provide valuable empirical information about classes of data, and relationships between data sets, not yet described in the literature. It would be fatuous to repudiate completely data bearing on the behavior of contemporary hominids in attempting to understand the past behavior responsible for archaeological residues, since these are the only culture-bearing animals available to us for observation and questioning.[4] Observations of contemporary cultural behavior and its material correlates can suggest relationships among archaeological data which are not immediately apparent; the utility of such observations to archaeologists is greatest when their collection and analysis are designed to result in the formulation of hypotheses which may be tested against independent sets of archaeological and ethnographic data (cf. L. Binford 1968).

Ethnography for Archaeology: Objectives of Ethnoarchaeology

The term "ethnoarchaeology" has most often connoted problem-oriented ethnographic research conducted by anthropologists trained as field archaeologists.[5] It is designed to meet the special needs of archaeologists, who can rarely question informants about the remains with which they work. Like much ethnographic fieldwork, ethnoarchaeological research often involves the use of participant observation and interviewing. However, in contrast to much sociocultural anthropology, ethnoarchaeology usually involves the explicit integration of ethnographic and ethnohistoric data with archaeological data. In that it entails fieldwork with contemporary populations, ethnoarchaeology provides substantive empirical data which supplement those available in the published ethnographic record. More importantly, such data are often collected in order to evaluate hypotheses derived initially from interpretations of archaeological data, as well as from independent ethnographic observations.

Archaeologists seek to comprehend relationships between cultural behaviors and their associated material residues. Many ethnographers have not, in recent decades, provided systematic documentation of material culture in the societies which they describe, whereas it is precisely this which constitutes the bulk of archaeological remains. The ethnoarchaeologist thus frequently seeks to compensate for this difference in focus, investigating details observed but not necessarily systematically described by the sociocultural anthropologist.

The recent literature reflects the wide range of problems and geographic regions with which archaeologists are concerned. Ethnoarchaeological work has been done not only among hunter-gatherers, but in more complex societies as well. Studies of fishermen in Mexico (Ascher 1962, 1968), of nomadic pastoralists in East Africa (Gifford 1976; Robbins 1973) and Southwest Asia (Hole 1975), of agriculturalists in Africa (David 1971; David and Hennig 1972; McIntosh 1976), Melanesia (Cranstone 1971; Heider 1967; White 1967), South America (DeBoer 1974, 1975), and Southwest Asia (Watson 1966, 1978; Ochsenschlager 1974a, 1974b), and in industrial North America (Ascher 1968; Rathje 1974) address a wide range of topics. Examples of the kinds of issues investigated in recent research include the relationships between activities and objects functionally specific to them (cf. Krotsker 1974; Peterson 1968; Yellen 1976), relationships between variability in objects and the social groups which make them (David and Hennig 1972; Stanislawski 1974a), relationships between the size and composition of local groups and the structures which they inhabit (David 1971; Bonnichsen 1973; Lange and Rydberg 1972; Longacre and Ayres 1968; Yellen 1976), and relationships between particular classes of object and their manufacturers' and archaeologists' systems of classification (Arnold 1971; Gould 1974; White and Thomas 1972). Much recent ethnoarchaeological work thus treats aspects of contemporary material culture and the internal organization of sites; some studies investigate selected features of subsistence, demography, and social organization (Binford and Chasko 1976; David 1971; Martin 1973; Yellen 1976, and others). Some of the works cited claim only to be relevant to the interpretation of specific archaeological data sets; others have implications for understanding broader processes of culture change. It is noteworthy that many of the works cited here have moved beyond the rather bleak level of the "cautionary tales" of Cranstone (1971) and Heider (1967) to express optimism about increasing the reliability of inferences about past behavior based on material remains, some even suggesting ways in which meaningful elements of material culture may be monitored in archaeological sampling, analysis, and interpretation (Binford 1976; David 1972; DeBoer 1974; McIntosh 1976).

The papers in the present volume reflect the range of issues currently being explored in ethnoarchaeological research.[6] They focus on objects (Carneiro, DeBoer and Lathrap, Ebert, Hardin, Messer), and associations between objects (DeBoer and Lathrap, Jochim, Messer), settlements (Hole, Jacobs, Kramer), land use, subsistence, and settlement patterns (Carneiro, Hole, Jochim, Lees, Messer), aspects of demography (Jacobs, Jochim, Kramer, Sumner), and political organization (Lees). Hole, Lees, and Jochim are explicitly concerned with the analysis of data from a regional perspective. Watson provides a discussion of the individual papers and their implications, and makes more general observations about the utility and limitations of ethnoarchaeology. On the cultural level, hunter-gatherers, agriculturalists, pastoralists, and state societies are represented here; on the geographical level, the volume includes cases from South America, Mesoamerica, Europe, Southwest Asia, and Africa. In providing studies focusing on subsistence, settlement pattern, and long-term regional change, and in suggesting some implications for archaeological research design, the present collection complements and extends some of the earlier emphases of ethnoarchaeological research.

Ethnoarchaeology and Archaeological Data and Problems

In contrast with ethnographic data, archaeological data do not derive from the direct observation of human behavior; rather, they consist of a wide variety of excavated and unexcavated remains. Many of the studies cited above are oriented to the investigation of excavated archaeological materials. However, a substantial body of archaeological data is obtained in surface surveys. In such cases the raw data consist of artifacts and their distributions on sites, the sites themselves, their locations with respect to one another and to topographic features, and changes in site size and morphology through time. Recent studies of archaeological settlement patterns have utilized a regional framework to infer changes in land use patterns, population size and distribution, economic organization, and sociopolitical organization. Much of the methodology and theory on which such studies have drawn comes from geography (cf. Johnson 1977). Ethnoarchaeological research can make useful contributions at the regional level, just as it can at both the level of the individual community and at the artifactual level. Given the diachronic and regional concerns of many archaeologists, it is appropriate that ethnoarchaeology is beginning to move beyond the level of the individual house or settlement. Ackerman and Ackerman (1974), Campbell (1968), Gould (1968), Hole (1975), Jochim (1976), Lauer (1971), Peterson (1971), Stanislawski (1974b), White and Peterson (1969), and Yellen (1976) are among those whose work clearly reflects a regional orientation.

As a research strategy, ethnoarchaeology need not be restricted to the collection of empirical data designed to "fill gaps" in the current ethnographic literature. Such research may also be designed with a view to aiding in the collection and analysis, as well as in the interpretation, of archaeological remains.[7] During the course of obtaining, recording, and analyzing both excavated and surface materials, archaeologists constantly contend with issues of typology, spatial analysis, chronological control, stratigraphy, and the selection of appropriate strategies for sampling and data analysis. While archaeologists usually seek to explain artifactual remains in terms of human behavior, they are forced to work toward this objective by retrieval and analysis of fragmentary samples of variable, changing, and now extinct cultural systems. The archaeologist also attempts to discriminate between cultural behavior and those noncultural processes which may have affected the archaeologically-retrieved byproducts of human activities.

In analyzing a collection of excavated ceramics, for example, the archaeologist usually attempts to define and interpret the range of formal variability observed; archaeological classification facilitates the measurement, description, analysis, and comparison of archaeological assemblages. Is the apparent ceramic variation a reflection of functional differences, stylistic differences, exchange, chronological change, or perhaps small-scale motor variability among manufacturers? Does artifacts' spatial distribution within a site or group of sites reflect different activity sets, different social groupings, or some other phenomena? Does the variation in numbers, types, and sizes of pot sherds reflect variations in vessels' longevity, their numbers in the original community, or ethnic, demographic, or economic variation in the population using the vessels? Foster (1960), David and Hennig (1972), Krotsker (1974), Pastron (1974), and others have provided data bearing on these questions.

In recording and analyzing archaeological data, archaeologists must consider which might be the most appropriate units and measures of analysis. As in any research, the analytic units used vary with questions asked; the archaeologist's observation of contemporary behavior may suggest that some analytic units and measures are more appropriate to his task than others. In dealing with an excavated collection of sherds, for example, the archaeologist must decide whether to count anything and, if so, what to count (all sherds, decorated sherds, rim sherds, or perhaps a proportion of the total sherdage) and what to measure (sherd size, sherd weight, rim diameter, sherd length, width of painted lines, etc.). Some recent ethnoarchaeological research with ceramics (Arnold 1971; David 1972; Friedrich 1970) and chipped stone (Gould 1974; Gould, Koster and Sontz 1971; White and Thomas 1972) and other objects (cf. Binford 1976) have interesting ramifications for the manipulation and interpretation of archaeological data, and the findings of these and other studies might usefully be incorporated in archaeological research designs.

Archaeologists are not only concerned with patterned behavior as it affects the nature and numbers of objects and structures, and their spatial and temporal distributions in ongoing cultural systems. They are also interested in the behavior of artifacts after they cease to be used. To what extent does the archaeological context of pot sherds reflect such primary cultural behavior as the manufacture, use, exchange, and numbers of ceramic vessels, and to what extent is it a function of secondary usage, of disposition after breakage, of spatial rearrangement and comminution as they are trampled and incorporated in the stratigraphic record? To what extent are the contexts of these sherds the result of stratigraphic redistribution resulting from the actions of burrowing animals, erosional agents, and subsequent inhabitants?

Ethnoarchaeology can provide a useful approach to the investigation of these and other questions. Common sense may structure an appreciation of the roles of some processes of residue formation; these can, however, be more fully illuminated when observed in contemporary settings. Ascher (1961) has noted the desirability, if not the necessity, of archaeologists examining living communities; he has emphasized (1968) that all living communities are constantly in process of discarding and decomposing, forming cultural residues which misleadingly appear to reflect a single point in (archaeological) time. This issue is also discussed by Schiffer (1976), who distinguishes between behavioral or cultural transformation processes contributing to the archaeological record ("C-transforms"), and post-depositional changes caused by non-cultural processes ("N-transforms"). Insofar as we need to understand the behavior of objects, as well as of the people who manufactured, used, and discarded them, taphonomy (the study of death assemblages, most often treated as a branch of paleontology but relevant to archaeology as well; cf. Gifford 1976) clearly merits further investigation.[8] Some recent studies of butchering practices, and of modification and dissemination of animal bones by scavengers and geological agents (cf. Binford and Bertram 1977; Crader 1974; Isaac 1967) have potential applications in the analysis and interpretation of archaeological faunal residues. Studies of ceramic vessel longevity (David 1971; DeBoer 1974) suggest new approaches not only to the estimation of site population and duration of occupation, but to the recording and analysis of archaeological ceramics. Studies of decay processes of building materials (McIntosh 1974, 1977) and of the post-abandonment behavior of house structures (Lange and Rydberg 1972; McIntosh 1976), like those of faunal remains and ceramic longevity, shed light on some of the non-cultural processes affecting cultural materials and the formation of the archaeological record.

Future Research: Suggested Problems and Approaches

Additional ethnographic data bearing on relationships between culturally-patterned behaviors and their material correlates, collected to explore explicitly defined relationships, and used to test specific hypotheses, can only add to the general fund of anthropological knowledge. Having developed out of a growing desire on the part of archaeologists to explore more systematically relationships between behavior and archaeological remains, ethnoarchaeology reflects a perspective sometimes lacking in more traditional approaches to material culture (such as largely descriptive studies of ancient iconography, and of such contemporary items as fishhooks and hammocks). Rather than argue that it is either "sites" (Gould 1974) or "regions" (Peterson 1971) which constitute the most appropriate units of study, it is suggested that in ethnoarchaeology, as in any anthropological research, subjects should reflect the questions asked, just as methods and field localities legitimately vary with research problems. In concluding these introductory remarks, some of the many additional issues which might be addressed in future ethnoarchaeological research are suggested.

Additional empirical documentation of ethnographic variability, at virtually any level of observation, should facilitate the initial selection of archaeological samples. To take but one example, all settlements (or sites) are internally subdivided; ethnographic models can provide bases for formulating sampling designs, which vary with archaeological objectives (e.g., to obtain analytically meaningful samples of objects, activity areas, burials, and/or houses, in order to investigate specific problems). Similarly, familiarity with ranges of variation in a contemporary annual round should facilitate the prediction of archaeological site locations and functions, and permit the refinement of sampling design, particularly where data on paleo-environments are available and can be utilized in conjunction with relevant environmental data for the ethnographic present. Observation of contemporary processes of residue formation, both cultural and non-cultural, should provide greater insight into the nature of excavated remains; taphonomic studies should be of interest to archaeologists, who have limited chronological control over highly compressed stratigraphic phenomena but who wish to distinguish the culturally relevant from secondary or non-cultural archaeological manifestations.

Additional empirical data on population size and composition, and their relationship to site size, house size, and number of household objects, are sorely needed, as are data on the nature, causes, and consequences of population stability or change, and variations in rate of change, particularly in non-industrial societies. Archaeological settlement pattern data might be made even more meaningful if integrated with additional information on "sustaining areas" for various population sizes, subsistence strategies, and exploitative technologies, and with additional information about ways in which different land use strategies may be employed by contemporaneous populations within a single regional framework. Information about ranges of variation in communities within a region, the material correlates of interactions between such communities, and ways in which historical relationships between settlements may be reflected in settlement pattern, would prove relevant to a number of archaeological problems. The investigation of relationships between the areal size of settlements and their functional size should further illuminate economic and political relationships between ancient sites,[9] and complement and extend recent work by geographers.

In order to better understand relationships between archaeological remains and culturally patterned behavior, we also require the more thorough delineation of material correlates of variation in socioeconomic rank (cf. Peebles and Kus 1977); of variation in mortuary practices (Binford 1971; Ucko 1969); of seasonal variations in botanical and zoological, as well as artifactual, remains; and of material correlates of intra- and inter-regional exchange systems (Earle and Ericson 1977; Pires-Ferreira and Flannery 1976; Sabloff and Willey 1975; Wilmsen 1972).

Additional information concerning the social functions of style is also needed (cf. Sackett 1977). Stylistic variation may reflect not only variation in residence rules, but ethnicity, social and economic pressures for conformity, market demand, and a number of other variables. One of the basic assumptions of much interesting recent archaeological writing—that there are positive correlations between residence rule and degree of stylistic homogeneity and/or continuity (Deetz 1965; Hill 1970; Longacre 1970, among others)—might usefully be tested against additional ethnographic as well as archaeological data sets (see Longacre 1974). Archaeologists, with their interest and experience in typological analysis, are perhaps uniquely suited to examine stylistic variation in ethnographic contexts, and could usefully analyze variability in undecorated as well as decorated ceramics, and in a range of non-ceramic objects (cf. Wobst 1977). If archaeologists conducting ethnographic research are able to suggest appropriate material measures of selected features of social organization, and to operationalize them for the analysis of archaeological data, it is likely that their work will contribute substantially to discussions of the evolution of social organizational features (see Allen and Richardson 1971; Deetz 1968; Dumond 1977; Ember 1973; Hunter-Anderson 1977; Whiting and Ayres 1968).

Like ethnological research, ethnoarchaeology of necessity investigates sociocultural behavior over the short term, and may therefore pertain primarily to specific chronologically and spatially restricted archaeological data sets considered comparable to those observed in the present. Nonetheless, archaeologists may take to the ethnographic field because they view the available literature for their particular areas as restricted by previous investigators' topical interests and chronological coverage. For example, a year-long study of one community may not provide data bearing on the variability and change in material culture in which the archaeologist is interested. Future ethnoarchaeological research might address the issue of variability in contemporary behavior as it affects variability in potential archaeological residues. The archaeologist doing ethnographic fieldwork can utilize a comparative framework in order to elucidate some of the processes and material correlates of cultural changes. In view of their overriding interest in the processes of change, archaeologists can apply the time-honored methods of controlled comparison to the study of contemporary societies at different levels of sociocultural complexity, as well as to the selection for investigation of societies in transition. Regardless of the research problem investigated, it should be incumbent on archaeologists doing ethnographic research to suggest means of converting their observations of contemporary behavior and its associated material correlates to operational measures which may be applied to the analysis and interpretation of archaeological remains.

Notes

1. The term "ethnoarchaeology" is used here because it appears to have somewhat wider currency in the anthropological literature than some alternate terms. These include "action archaeology" (Kleindienst and Watson 1956), "living archaeology" (Gould 1974), "archaeoethnography" (Oswalt 1974), and "ethnographic archaeology" (Pastron 1974). For brief discussions of the development of the subfield, the reader is referred to Gould (1974), Oswalt (1974), and Stiles (1977). Stiles, whose recent article (1977) appeared after the writing of this introduction, also discusses

some of the points raised here. For their critical comments on earlier drafts, the author thanks Janet Chernela, Sheila Dauer, Ann Farber, Lee Horne, Gregory A. Johnson, Steve Kowalewski, Brian Spooner, and Harvey Weiss.

2. The bibliography is not, of course, an exhaustive listing of publications treating ethnoarchaeological research.

3. Such interpretation would be predicated on the assumption that we can control for possible divergences of those ancient environmental variables (such as animal behaviors) from their modern counterparts.

4. One can of course additionally argue that if one aim of archaeology is to generate law-like propositions, then they must account for both contemporary and past situations (see Binford 1976:299).

5. This has come to be so for a variety of historical reasons, perhaps most obviously the nature of graduate anthropology programs in North America.

6. Earlier versions of some of the articles in this volume were presented at the seventy-fifth annual meeting of the American Anthropological Association (November 1976, Washington, D.C.).

7. Cross-cultural research and experimental archaeology (see Coles 1973; Ingersoll, Yellen, and MacDonald 1977) are additional approaches which may be well suited to certain problems not easily tackled singlehandedly by an ethnoarchaeologist. Neither ordinarily involves fieldwork with contemporary populations, yet each can be used to investigate relationships between cultural behavior and material remains. Such sources for cross-cultural research as the Human Relations Area Files, however, encompass a wide and heterogeneous range of data collected over many years; this variability imposes certain limitations on those utilizing HRAF and comparable sources.

8. The paleontological analysis of death assemblages begins with species buried in the same locality. These species did not necessarily live together, however. Through study of the kinds, conditions, and associations of bones, the species themselves, and their geological context, the taphonomist reconstructs the processes which brought the specimens to the burial site. Similar principles may be applicable to the analysis of discarded cultural items found in archaeological contexts.

9. Functional size refers to the number of different kinds of activities carried out within a settlement.

References Cited

Ackerman, Robert and Lillian Ackerman
    1974. "Ethnoarchaeological Interpretations of Territoriality and Land Use in Southwestern Alaska." *Ethnohistory* 20:315–34.
Allen, Harry
    1974. "The Bagundji of the Darling Basin: Cereal Gatherers in an Uncertain Environment." *World Archaeology* 5:309–22.

Allen, William L. and J. B. Richardson III
    1971. "The Reconstruction of Kinship from Archaeological Data: The Concepts, the Methods, and the Feasibility." *American Antiquity* 36:41–53.
Arnold, Dean
    1971. "Ethnomineralogy of Ticul, Yucatan Potters: Etics and Emics." *American Antiquity* 36:20–40.
Ascher, Robert
    1961. "Analogy in Archaeological Interpretation." *Southwestern Journal of Anthropology* 17:317–25.
    1962. "Ethnography for Archaeology: A Case from the Seri Indians." *Ethnology* 1:360–69.
    1968. "Time's Arrow and the Archaeology of a Contemporary Community." In K. C. Chang, ed., *Settlement Archaeology*, pp. 43–52. Palo Alto: National Press Books.
Binford, Lewis R.
    1967. "Smudge Pits and Hide Smoking: the Use of Analogy in Archaeological Reasoning." *American Antiquity* 32:1–12.
    1968. "Methodological Considerations of the Archeological Use of Ethnographic Data." In Richard Lee and Irven Devore, eds., *Man the Hunter*, pp. 268–73. Chicago: Aldine.
    1971. "Mortuary Practices: Their Study and Their Potential." In James A. Brown, ed., *Approaches to the Social Dimensions of Mortuary Practices*, pp. 6–29. Memoirs of the Society for American Archaeology, No. 25.
    1972. "Archaeological Reasoning and Smudge Pits—Revisited." In *An Archaeological Perspective*, pp. 52–58. New York: Seminar Press.
    1973. "Interassemblage Variability—the Mousterian and the 'Functional' Argument." In Colin Renfrew, ed., *The Explanation of Culture Change: Models in Prehistory*, pp. 227–54. Pittsburgh: University of Pittsburgh Press.
    1976. "Forty-Seven Trips: A Case Study in the Character of Some Formation Processes of the Archaeological Record." In Edwin S. Hall, Jr., ed., *Contributions to Anthropology: The Interior Peoples of Northern Alaska*, pp. 299–351. National Museum of Man, Mercury Series. Archaeological Survey of Canada, Paper 49. Ottawa: National Museums of Canada.
    1977. "General Introduction." In Lewis R. Binford, ed., *For Theory Building in Archaeology*, pp. 1–10. New York: Academic Press.
Binford, Lewis R. and W. J. Chasko, Jr.
    1976. "Nunamiut Demographic History: A Provocative Case." In Ezra B. W. Zubrow, ed., *Demographic Anthropology: Quantitative Approaches*, pp. 63–143. Albuquerque: University of New Mexico Press.
Binford, Lewis R. and Jack B. Bertram
    1977. "Bone Frequencies—and Attritional Processes." In Lewis R. Binford, ed., *For Theory Building in Archaeology*, pp. 77–153. New York: Academic Press.
Binford, Sally R.
    1968. "Ethnographic Data and Understanding the Pleistocene." In Richard Lee and Irven DeVore, eds., *Man the Hunter*, pp. 274–75. Chicago: Aldine.

Bonnichsen, Robson
  1973. "Millie's Camp: An Experiment in Archaeology." *World Archaeology* 4:277–91.
Campbell, John M.
  1968. "Territoriality among Ancient Hunters: Interpretations from Ethnography and Nature." In Betty Meggers, ed., *Anthropological Archeology in the Americas*, pp. 1–21. Washington, D.C.: Anthropological Society of Washington.
Chang, Kwang-chih
  1967. "Major Aspects of the Interrelationship of Archaeology and Ethnology." *Current Anthropology* 8:227–43.
Coles, John
  1973. *Archaeology by Experiment*. New York: Scribners.
Crader, Diana C.
  1974. "The Effects of Scavengers on Bone Material from a Large Mammal: An Experiment Conducted among the Bisa of the Luangwa Valley, Zambia." In Christopher B. Donnan and C. William Clewlow, Jr., eds., *Ethnoarchaeology*, Monograph 4, pp. 161–73. Los Angeles: University of California, Institute of Archaeology.
Cranstone, B.A.L.
  1971. "The Tifalmin: A 'Neolithic' People in New Guinea." *World Archaeology* 3:132–42.
David, Nicholas
  1971. "The Fulani Compound and the Archaeologist." *World Archaeology* 3:111–31.
  1972. "On the Life Span of Pottery, Type Frequencies, and Archaeological Inference." *American Antiquity* 37:141–42.
David, Nicholas and Hilke Hennig
  1972. "The Ethnography of Pottery: A Fulani Case Seen in Archaeological Perspective," pp. 1–29. McCaleb Module in Anthropology 21. Reading, Mass.: Addison-Wesley.
DeBoer, Warren R.
  1974. "Ceramic Longevity and Archaeological Interpretation: An Example from the Upper Ucayali, Peru." *American Antiquity* 39:335–43.
  1975. "The Archaeological Evidence for Manioc Cultivation: A Cautionary Note." *American Antiquity* 40:419–33.
Deetz, James
  1965. *The Dynamics of Stylistic Change in Arikara Ceramics*. Illinois Studies in Anthropology, No. 4. Urbana: University of Illinois Press.
  1968. "The Inference of Residence and Descent Rules from Archeological Data." In Sally R. Binford and Lewis R. Binford, eds., *New Perspectives in Archeology*, pp. 41–48. Chicago: Aldine.
Dumond, Don E.
  1977. "Science in Archaeology: The Saints Go Marching In." *American Antiquity* 42:330–49.
Earle, Timothy K. and J. E. Ericson, eds.
  1977. *Exchange Systems in Prehistory*. New York: Academic Press.

Ember, Melvin
　　1973. "An Archaeological Indicator of Matrilocal versus Patrilocal Residence."
　　American Antiquity 38:177–82.
Forbes, Mary H. Clark
　　1976. "Farming and Foraging in Prehistoric Greece: A Cultural Ecological Per-
　　spective." In Muriel Dimen and Ernestine Friedl, eds., *Regional Variation in*
　　Modern Greece and Cyprus: Toward a Perspective on the Ethnography of
　　Greece, pp. 127–42. *Annals of the New York Academy of Sciences,* vol. 268.
　　New York: New York Academy of Sciences.
Foster, George
　　1960. "Archaeological Implications of the Modern Pottery of Acatlan, Puebla,
　　Mexico." *American Antiquity* 26:205–14.
Freeman, Leslie G., Jr.
　　1968. "A Theoretical Framework for Interpreting Archeological Materials." In
　　Richard Lee and Irven DeVore, eds., *Man the Hunter,* pp. 262–67. Chicago:
　　Aldine.
Friedrich, Margaret Hardin
　　1970. "Design Structure and Social Interaction: Archaeological Implications of
　　an Ethnographic Analysis." *American Antiquity* 35:332–43.
Gifford, Diane P.
　　1976. "Site Taphonomy at East Lake Turkana, Kenya." Paper prepared for
　　participants in Burg Wartenstein Symposium No. 69: Taphonomy and Ver-
　　tebrate Palaeoecology: With Special Reference to the Late Cenozoic of Sub-
　　Saharan Africa, July 2–11, 1976. New York: Wenner-Gren Foundation for An-
　　thropological Research. Mimeo.
Gould, Richard A.
　　1967. "Notes on Hunting, Butchering, and Sharing of Game among the Ngatat-
　　jara and Their Neighbors in the Western Australian Desert." *Kroeber Anthro-*
　　pological Society Papers 36:41–66.
　　1971. "The Archaeologist as Ethnographer: A Case from the Western Desert of
　　Australia." *World Archaeology* 3:143–77.
　　1973. "Australian Archaeology in Ecological and Ethnographic Perspective,"
　　pp. 1–33. Warner Modular Publications. Module 7. Andover, Mass.
　　1974. "Some Current Problems in Ethnoarchaeology." In Christopher B. Don-
　　nan and C. William Clewlow, Jr., eds., *Ethnoarchaeology,* Monograph 4, pp.
　　29–48. Los Angeles: University of California, Institute of Archaeology.
Gould, Richard A., D. A. Koster, and A. H. L. Sontz
　　1971. "The Lithic Assemblage of the Western Desert Aborigines of Australia."
　　American Antiquity 36:149–69.
Harpending, Henry and Herbert Davis
　　1977. "Some Implications for Hunter-Gatherer Ecology Derived from the Spa-
　　tial Structure of Resources." *World Archaeology* 8:275–86.
Heider, Karl G.
　　1967. "Archaeological Assumptions and Ethnographical Facts: A Cautionary
　　Tale from New Guinea." *Southwestern Journal of Anthropology* 23:52–64.

Hill, James N.

1970. *Broken K Pueblo*. Anthropological Papers of the University of Arizona, no. 18. Tucson: University of Arizona Press.

Hole, Frank

1975. "Ethnoarcheology of Nomadic Pastoralism: A Case Study." Paper prepared for School of American Research Seminar on Ethnoarcheology, Santa Fe, New Mexico, November 17–21, 1975. Mimeo.

Hunter-Anderson, Rosalind L.

1977. "A Theoretical Approach to the Study of House Form." In Lewis R. Binford, ed., *For Theory Building in Archaeology*, pp. 287–315. New York: Academic Press.

Ingersoll, Daniel, John Yellen, and William MacDonald, eds.

1977. *Experimental Archeology*. New York: Columbia University Press.

Isaac, Glynn

1967. "Towards the Interpretation of Occupation Debris: Some Experiments and Observations." *Kroeber Anthropological Society Papers* 37:31–57.

Jochim, Michael A.

1976. *Hunter-Gatherer Subsistence and Settlement: A Predictive Model*. New York: Academic Press.

Johnson, Gregory A.

1977. "Aspects of Regional Analysis in Archaeology." In Bernard J. Siegel, ed., *Annual Review of Anthropology* 6:479–508. Palo Alto: Annual Reviews, Inc.

Jones, Rhys

1971. "The Demography of Hunters and Farmers in Tasmania." In D. J. Mulvaney and Jack Golson, eds., *Aboriginal Man and Environment in Australia*, pp. 271–87. Canberra: Australian National University Press.

Kleindienst, Maxine and Patty Jo Watson

1956. "Action Archaeology: The Archaeological Inventory of a Living Community." *Anthropology Tomorrow* 5:75–78.

Krotsker, Paula H.

1974. "Country Potters of Veracruz, Mexico: Technological Survivals and Culture Change." In Christopher B. Donnan and C. William Clewlow, Jr., eds., *Ethnoarchaeology*, Monograph 4, pp. 131–46. Los Angeles: University of California, Institute of Archaeology.

Lange, Frederick W. and Charles R. Rydberg

1972. "Abandonment and Post-Abandonment Behavior at a Rural Central American House-Site." *American Antiquity* 37:419–32.

Lauer, Peter K.

1971. "Changing Patterns of Pottery Trade to the Trobriand Islands." *World Archaeology* 3:197–209.

Longacre, William A.

1970. *Archaeology as Anthropology: A Case Study*. Anthropological Papers of the University of Arizona, no. 17. Tucson: University of Arizona Press.

1974. "Kalinga Pottery-Making: The Evolution of a Research Design." In

Murray J. Leaf, ed., *Frontiers of Anthropology,* pp. 51–67. New York: Van Nostrand.

Longacre, William A. and James E. Ayres
1968. "Archeological Lessons from an Apache Wickiup." In Sally R. Binford and Lewis R. Binford, eds., *New Perspectives in Archeology,* pp. 151–59. Chicago: Aldine.

Martin, John F.
1973. "On the Estimation of the Sizes of Local Groups in a Hunting-Gathering Environment." *American Anthropologist* 75:1448–68.

McIntosh, Roderick J.
1974. "Archaeology and Mud Wall Decay in a West African Village." *World Archaeology* 6:154–71.
1976. "Square Huts in Round Concepts: Prediction of Settlement Features in West Africa." *Archaeology* 29:92–101.
1977. "The Excavation of Mud Structures: An Experiment from West Africa." *World Archaeology* 9:185–99.

Ochsenschlager, Edward
1974a. "Mud Objects from al-Hiba." *Archaeology* 27:162–74.
1974b. "Modern Potters at al-Hiba, with Some Reflections on the Excavated Early Dynastic Pottery." In Christopher B. Donnan and C. William Clewlow, Jr., eds., *Ethnoarchaeology,* Monograph 4, pp. 149–57. Los Angeles: University of California, Institute of Archaeology.

Oswalt, Wendell H.
1974. "Ethnoarchaeology." In Christopher B. Donnan and C. William Clewlow, Jr., eds., *Ethnoarchaeology,* Monograph 4, pp. 3–11. Los Angeles: University of California, Institute of Archaeology.

Oswalt, Wendell H. and James W. VanStone
1967. *The Ethnoarchaeology of Crow Village, Alaska.* Washington, D.C.: Bureau of American Ethnology, Bulletin 199.

Pastron, Allen G.
1974. "Preliminary Ethnoarchaeological Investigations among the Tarahumara." In Christopher B. Donnan and C. William Clewlow, Jr., eds., *Ethnoarchaeology,* Monograph 4, pp. 93–114. Los Angeles: University of California, Institute of Archaeology.

Peebles, Christopher S. and Susan M. Kus
1977. "Some Archaeological Correlates of Ranked Societies." *American Antiquity* 42:421–48.

Peterson, Nicolas
1968. "The Pestle and Mortar: An Ethnographic Analogy for Archaeology in Arnhem Land." *Mankind* 6:567–70.
1971. "Open Sites and the Ethnographic Approach to the Archaeology of Hunter-Gatherers." In D. J. Mulvaney and Jack Golson, eds., *Aboriginal Man and Environment in Australia,* pp. 239–48. Canberra: Australian National University Press.

Pires-Ferreira, Jane W. and Kent V. Flannery
1976. "Ethnographic Models for Formative Exchange." In Kent V. Flannery,

ed., *The Early Mesoamerican Village,* pp. 286–92. New York: Academic Press.

Rathje, William
    1974. "The Garbage Project." *Archaeology* 27:236–41.

Robbins, L. H.
    1973. "Turkana Material Culture Viewed from an Archaeological Perspective." *World Archaeology* 5:209–14.

Sabloff, Jeremy A. and C. C. Lamberg-Karlovsky, eds.
    1975. *Ancient Civilization and Trade.* Albuquerque: University of New Mexico Press.

Sackett, James R.
    1977. "The Meaning of Style in Archaeology: A General Model." *American Antiquity* 42:369–80.

Schiffer, Michael B.
    1976. *Behavioral Archeology.* New York: Academic Press.

Schrire, Carmel
    1972. "Ethno-archaeological Models and Subsistence Behaviour in Arnhem Land." In David Clarke, ed., *Models in Prehistory,* pp. 653–70. London: Methuen.

Speth, John D. and Dave D. Davis
    1976. "Seasonal Variability in Early Hominid Predation." *Science* 192:441–45.

Stanislawski, Michael B.
    1969. "The Ethno-archaeology of Hopi Pottery Making." *Plateau* 42:27–33.
    1974a. "The Relationships of Ethnoarchaeology, Traditional, and Systems Archaeology." In Christopher B. Donnan and C. William Clewlow, Jr., eds., *Ethnoarchaeology,* Monograph 4, pp. 15–26. Los Angeles: University of California, Institute of Archaeology.
    1974b. "Ethnoarchaeology and Settlement Archaeology." *Ethnohistory* 20:375–92.

Stiles, Daniel
    1977. "Ethnoarchaeology: A Discussion of Methods and Applications." *Man* 12:87–103.

Ucko, Peter J.
    1969. "Ethnography and Archaeological Interpretation of Funerary Remains." *World Archaeology* 1:262–80.

Watson, Patty Jo
    1966. "Clues to Iranian Prehistory in Modern Village Life." *Expedition* 8:9–19.
    1977. "Design Analysis of Painted Pottery." *American Antiquity* 42:381–93.
    1978. *Archaeological Ethnography in Western Iran.* Viking Fund Publications in Anthropology, no. 57. Tucson: University of Arizona Press.

White, Carmel and Nicolas Peterson
    1969. "Ethnographic Interpretations of the Prehistory of Western Arnhem Land." *Southwestern Journal of Anthropology* 25:45–67.

White, J. Peter
    1967. "Ethno-archaeology in New Guinea: Two Examples." *Mankind* 6:409–14.

White, J. Peter and David H. Thomas

  1972. "What Mean These Stones: Ethno-Taxonomic Models and Archaeological Interpretations in the New Guinea Highlands." In David Clarke, ed., *Models in Prehistory,* pp. 275–308. London: Methuen.

Whiting, John and Barbara Ayres

  1968. "Inferences from the Shape of Dwellings." In Kwang Chih Chang, ed., *Settlement Archaeology,* pp. 117–33. Palo Alto: National Press Books.

Wilkinson, P. F.

  1972. "Ecosystem Models and Demographic Hypotheses: Predation and Prehistory in North America." In David Clarke, ed., *Models in Prehistory,* pp. 543–76. London: Methuen.

Wilmsen, Edwin N., ed.

  1972. *Social Exchange and Interaction.* Museum of Anthropology, Anthropological Papers, no. 46. Ann Arbor: University of Michigan.

Wobst, H. Martin

  1977. "Stylistic Behavior and Information Exchange." *Michigan Anthropological Papers* 61:317–42.

  1978. "The 'Archaeo-Ethnology of Hunter-Gatherers' or the Tyranny of the Ethnographic Record in Archaeology." *American Antiquity* 43:303–9.

Yellen, John E.

  1976. "Settlement Patterns of the !Kung: An Archaeological Perspective." In Richard Lee and Irven DeVore, eds., *Kalahari Hunter-Gatherers,* pp. 47–72. Cambridge, Mass.: Harvard University Press.

  1977. *Archaeological Approaches to the Present.* New York: Academic Press.

1 / Tree Felling with the Stone Ax: An Experiment Carried Out Among the Yanomamö Indians of Southern Venezuela

Robert L. Carneiro
Department of Anthropology
American Museum of Natural History

In this study in experimental archaeology, Carneiro discusses the felling of a tree by a contemporary Venezuelan Yanomamö. In contrast with much experimental research, Carneiro's project involved the observation of a native's activities. Focusing on the utilization of a single tool type, rather than on an entire tool assemblage such as those discussed below by Ebert, Carneiro provides a detailed description of the methods and materials employed in hafting a stone ax, and the process of chopping a tree. On the basis of this experiment, he develops a formula which may be used in future attempts to estimate time and manpower expenditures in both primary- and secondary-forest clearance. This subject is of considerable interest not only to those studying contemporary systems of shifting cultivation, but to archaeologists concerned with the early phases of food-producing systems in many areas of the world.

The felling of a tree with a stone ax was a common occurrence over much of the world during Neolithic times. Indeed, because of its frequency and importance in preparing land for cultivation, it can almost be thought of as the hallmark of Neolithic life.[1] Yet, as commonplace as it once was, it is an event that has rarely been witnessed by ethnologists. Even explorers and early travelers seem seldom to

The expedition that provided the background for this paper was supported by the National Institute of Mental Health under grant SSR 5 RO1 MH26008. The line drawings in the present article were prepared by Nicholas Amorosi of the American Museum of Natural History.

have observed it, and when they did so, paid little attention to it. In fact, so far as I know, not a single detailed account of just how a tree was felled with a stone ax has ever been published for South America, even though this is the continent where the stone ax remained in use the longest (see Carneiro 1974:107–8).

In April of 1975, while a member of an expedition to the Yanomamö Indians of the Upper Orinoco, I had the opportunity to witness such a felling. I would like to describe here the circumstances under which it occurred and exactly how it was done. Then I would like to consider what light this case may shed on Stone Age tree felling, not only in Amazonia but in the Neolithic world generally.

For a number of years I have been very interested in the stone ax. In a recent article (Carneiro 1974) I described the use of this implement by the Amahuaca of eastern Peru as told to me by informants who either had seen it used when they were children, or else had heard firsthand accounts of its use from their elders. In the same article I quoted the few brief passages I was able to find in the ethnographic literature purporting to describe how the stone ax was used by several Amazonian tribes. The observations I made among the Yanomamö in 1975 will augment and, in certain respects, correct what I said on the subject in 1974. They will also lead me to question some of the statements on the use of the stone ax appearing in the published literature.

The Yanomamö and the Stone Ax

Let me begin by sketching the background to the Yanomamö stone ax experiment. Several years ago Napoleon A. Chagnon showed me some stone ax heads he had obtained in Yanomamö territory. Older informants told Chagnon that when they were young men, the Yanomamö lacked steel axes, and in felling trees they had used the stone ax, which they called *pore poo* (Chagnon 1968:33). Similarly, Daniel de Barandiaran (1967:25–26), writing about the Sanemá-Yanoama, indicated that older informants remembered the time when they felled trees with stone axes. And mention of the stone ax recurs in Yanomamö myths (Lizot 1975a:18, 91).[2]

Nowadays, though, the stone ax is no longer used as a cutting tool by any Yanomamö group.[3] Thus, Kenneth Taylor (1974:41) has written of the Sanumá subgroup of Yanomamö in northern Brazil: "I neither saw nor heard anything of the polished stone ax heads which both Barandiaran and Chagnon mention as being occasionally found in the forest, but not in current use."

The Yanomamö are fairly recent migrants into the territory in which Chagnon obtained his stone ax heads. It is uncertain, therefore, if the ax heads in his possession were made by the Yanomamö themselves or by earlier occupants of the area. In any case it is probable that the type of stone ax once used by the Yanomamö was the same as that collected by Chagnon, namely a full-grooved ax. Thus it differs from the ungrooved celt typical of most of central and eastern Amazonia.

In March 1975 an expedition led by Chagnon, of which I was a member, began field work among the Yanomamö in southern Venezuela.[4] Prior to the start of the expedition it occurred to me that I might be able to persuade a Yanomamö to haft a stone ax and cut down a tree with it. Even though none of the Yanomamö I was likely to encounter would himself have ever used the stone ax, all Yanomamö are highly skilled in using the steel ax, and I thought that this skill would be "transferrable." At any rate, it seemed to me that the results of an experiment in which a modern-day Yanomamö felled a tree with a stone ax, if not a perfect replication of aboriginal tree felling, would nevertheless shed light on it.

Being uncertain that I could locate a stone ax blade in the field, I asked Chagnon if I could use one from his collection, and he very kindly agreed.

The Experiment

The experiment I am about to describe took place in April of 1975 in the Yanomamö village of Hasuböwateri, located close to the south bank of the upper Orinoco River, roughly halfway between the rapids known as Guaharibo and Peñascal. On the evening of March 31, shortly before his departure from this village, Chagnon spoke with Dobrabewä, a young Yanomamö about nineteen years old, about my interest in seeing a tree felled with a stone ax. Dobrabewä offered to do so, and I promised him a machete in payment.

The following morning Dobrabewä appeared at the house the

Yanomamö had built for us and I handed him the ax head.[5] It was a fully grooved ax, but while the notches at the top and bottom were fairly deep, the grooves along the sides of the blade were quite shallow.

Other than to tell him to haft the ax and cut down a tree with it, I purposely gave Dobrabewä no instructions. I wanted to see his native reaction to all aspects of the problem.

Hafting the Ax

The first thing Dobrabewä did was to fell a sapling of a tree called *washamonamá*, and cut a handle from it for the ax. This handle was 23 inches long and 1⅛ inches in diameter. After splitting it down the middle for some 9 inches Dobrabewä pulled the split halves apart slightly and inserted the stone ax head between them. He then started lashing the head to the handle with some split lengths of *masi masi*, a kind of vine the Yanomamö use in house construction.[6]

In the reading I had done on the hafting of full-grooved axes I had not come across any reliable accounts of this type of "cleft-stick" hafting. Grooved axes are generally hafted by splitting a branch or a withe, heating a split half until pliable, bending it around the groove in the ax head, and wrapping it tightly where the bent halves of the handle come together just below the ax head. This is the way the Tuparí (Snethlage 1937:172) and the Nambikuara (Carneiro 1974:120c) hafted their stone axes, and I expected Dobrabewä to do the same. So here, then, was my first surprise.

Perhaps I should not have been so surprised since Barandiaran (1967:27, figures 2 and 4) shows a Yanomamö hafting a stone ax head in this way. However, one of the stone axes he illustrates (1967:27, figure 5) has the blade hafted tangentially against an unsplit handle, and I had been very skeptical (as I continue to be) that this flimsy mode of hafting, which could not keep the blade rigid, was really aboriginal (Carneiro 1974:116, n. 7). And I was also skeptical of the cleft-stick type of hafting shown in Barandiaran's photograph. Thus, when I saw Dobrabewä hafting the blade in this way I felt that this could not be the native way of doing it.[7] Moreover, I seriously doubted that this mode of hafting would be able to hold the ax securely in place when he began to use it. But I kept my peace and continued to watch.

With the blade held in the split cleft, Dobrabewä wrapped the *masi masi* vine around the divided handle several times, both above and below the ax head, and also criss-crossed the lashings back and forth diagonally across the blade. The hafted ax looked pretty makeshift, as if it would not stand up to heavy use. But since it was not a propitious moment to begin the experiment in tree felling, I put the ax away till a more opportune time.

Three days later, on the afternoon of April 4, Dobrabewä appeared at our house, ready to work. In the intervening days, however, the vine lashings had come unwound, so Dobrabewä proceeded to remove the old *masi masi* lashings and relash the ax using a different type of vine. The vine he used this time was unsplit, but had the bark peeled off. Dobrabewä wound this vine around the handle in the same way as he had the *masi masi* lashings except that this time he wrapped the vine a few turns around the butt end of the ax.[8]

When Dobrabewä had finished hafting the ax, I asked him to follow me up the trail toward the village. A short distance from my house, in a small clearing next to the trail, I selected a tree and asked him to fell it. The tree, which Dobrabewä identified as an *ashawa*,[9] was 12.5 inches in diameter—big enough, it seemed, to provide him with a real test, but not so big that he would tire of the work and quit before completing the experiment. Moreover, the tree had hard wood and was thus typical of primary forest trees. (Later, when I placed a fresh-cut chip of wood from the *ashawa* into water, it sank, showing that the specific gravity of the wood, while still green, was greater than 1.)

Satisfied that conditions were favorable for the experiment, I handed Dobrabewä the stone ax and asked him to begin. He started chopping, but in less than a minute the strands of vine wrapped around the poll of the ax broke. Dobrabewä agreed that the material he had used for lashing was no good, but said that suitable vines were not available nearby.

Knowing that most Amazonian tribes, including the Yanomamö, make their strongest and heaviest cord from the shredded inner bark of the *Cecropia* tree (*shīkī* in Yanomamö), I suggested to Dobrabewä that instead of trying vines again he make use of this kind of cordage.[10] He indicated he would do so, but told me to *waiha*—wait.

Early next morning (April 5), Dobrabewä appeared at the house but said he had no *Cecropia* cord. And he seemed disinclined to get more *masi masi*. As he had done once before, he asked me for some manufactured cord to use in lashing the ax, and it was only with some difficulty and with the help of my field partner, Kenneth Good, that I was able to convince Dobrabewä that, for my purposes, the ax had to be lashed with native materials. Finally, around 8:15 A.M., he went off to get some, taking the ax head and handle with him.

Two and a half hours later I met Dobrabewä on the trail coming toward our house. In addition to the ax head and the handle, he was carrying a length of *Cecropia* cord about 5 or 6 feet long which was obviously an old bowstring. He also carried a lump of black beeswax.

We went back to the house and there Dobrabewä began to haft the ax again. First he rubbed the lump of beeswax, unheated, back and forth along one end of the cord to make it sticky. Next he placed the waxed end of the cord into the cleft in the handle and pushed it down about as far as it would go to secure it in place, and wrapped the string around the handle tightly a couple of times so it would not continue to split below this point.

Dobrabewä then sat down facing the wall of the house. He took the remaining length of cord which dangled from the handle and wrapped it one turn around the lower part of a house post, tying the free end around his instep.

Having anchored the lashing cord in this way, Dobrabewä then pulled the split halves of the handle apart slightly and inserted the ax head into the slot. When he released his hold on them the two halves of the upper part of the handle accommodated themselves in the shallow grooves along each side of the blade. Dobrabewä then pushed the ax head down as far as he could into the cleft. The cord he had previously wrapped around the handle just below the lower end of the cleft did indeed keep the handle from splitting further despite the downward pressure Dobrabewä exerted on the ax head.

The split ends of the handle now protruded an inch or so above the ax head. Dobrabewä put them in his mouth and using his jaws as a vise bit down hard on them in order to bring them as close together as possible above the blade. This was done to make it easier for him to wrap the cord around the split ends. So great was the force he applied with his teeth that he succeeded in bending the ends toward each other and even slightly cracked one of them.

Next Dobrabewä carried the cord from just below the ax head, where he had wrapped it a couple of times, to just above it, and there wrapped the cord around the split ends of the handle several times. Before doing so, though, Dobrabewä first waxed the string with the lump of beeswax, making it tackier so the lashings would have greater friction and would not slip. As he proceeded to lash the blade in place, Dobrabewä carried the string diagonally across it on either side. He also wrapped the cord three times around the poll.

I was very much struck by the fact that the technique he was using for wrapping the cord around the ax enabled Dobrabewä to pull back on it with both hands. Actually, it is more accurate to say that he wrapped the ax around the cord than the cord around the ax. The distal end of the cord was not free, but had been wound once around a house post and then attached to his foot. Thus there was no free end to wrap around the ax; instead, the ax was twisted and turned and wound onto the cord.

The fact that the cord was wound around the house post made it possible for Dobrabewä, as he sat on the ground, to pull back against it, not only with both hands but with the weight of his upper body as well. He could thus lash the ax much tighter than if he had merely held it in one hand and wound the cord around it with the other. Tightness of lashing is of great importance in making the stone ax an effective cutting tool, and I strongly suspect that Dobrabewä's technique was not his own invention but an established mechanical principle in Yanomamö culture which no doubt had been used aboriginally in hafting stone axes.

The Chopping Resumed

Once Dobrabewä had finished lashing the ax (see figure 1.1), I led him back up the trail to the *ashawa* tree he had begun to cut the previous day, and at 11:14 A.M. he started cutting it again. As he had done earlier, he chopped using only one hand. Indeed, not once during the experiment did he ever attempt to use both hands.[11]

After some 6 or 8 minutes of chopping, though, Dobrabewä was forced to stop because two of the three strands of cord he had wound around the poll of the ax had broken. At first he had merely wrapped the broken ends of the cord around other strands that were still intact and resumed chopping. But finally he had to stop altogether because the successive blows had forced the ax head back through the slit in the handle until only an inch or so of the cutting edge protruded in front.

This backward slippage of the ax head was most likely due to the breaking of the two cords. Although to the eye the lashing appeared tight except near the place where the cord had broken, probably the tension on the lashing had been significantly diminished over much of the blade. That the *Cecropia* lashing had broken twice in only 6 or 8 minutes I attributed partly to its age. I could tell the cord was old not only because it was dirty, but also because it was only about ⅛ of an inch in diameter. A new *Cecropia* bowstring is about ¼ of an inch in diameter, but continued stretching under the tension of the bow eventually reduces it to half that thickness. Nevertheless,

Figure 1.1 Dobrabewä holding the stone ax hafted with *washamonamá* wood and an old bowstring of *Cecropia* fiber.

at this point in the experiment it seemed to me that even a new
Cecropia cord wound around the poll could not have withstood the
shock of repeated heavy blows for very long.

The cut Dobrabewä had made in the tree during the 6 or 8 minutes he chopped was about 9 inches long, 2 to 3 inches wide, and
about 1½ inches deep (see figure 1.2). Dobrabewä's stroke remained
pretty nearly at right angles to the trunk of the tree. This was another
surprise. I had expected a steeper angle, perhaps as much as 45
degrees from the horizontal. Amahuaca informants had told me in
1961 that when their ancestors cut down a tree with a stone ax they
chopped at a steep angle. In fact, referring to blows delivered at right
angles to the trunk of a tree, one Amahuaca informant had said, "No

Figure 1.2. Cut made in the *ashawa* tree by Dobrabewä after some 6 or 8 minutes of
chopping with the stone ax.

entra, dice,'' meaning that he had heard that such a blow would not penetrate the trunk.

After this second session of cutting had come to·an end I examined the cutting edge of the ax and noted that very tiny chips had already begun to come off. Moreover, the handle had split nearly 15 inches down from the upper end, almost three-quarters of its length. Still, the split halves were holding together pretty well thanks to the cord wrapped around them 3 inches below the head.

Despite the failure of the ax to hold up, Dobrabewä did not seem discouraged. Indeed, he appeared to have developed a certain interest in the project beyond that of earning a machete. So next afternoon, around one o'clock, he reappeared with a new handle for the stone ax. The old handle had been of relatively soft wood, but the new one was made from the sapling of a tree called *payoarikohi,* which Dobrabewä said was harder.[12] It measured $1^{13}/_{16}$ of an inch in diameter.

Borrowing my saw, Dobrabewä cut the handle to a length of 16¾ inches. This was more than 6 inches shorter than the first handle, and when I pointed this out to him, he indicated he had done so intentionally. Using a machete he partially sharpened one end of the handle and then scraped off the thin bark from its entire length.

In addition to a new handle, Dobrabewä had brought along another piece of *Cecropia* bowstring. This one had also been used and had even broken and been knotted in a couple of places, but it still looked newer than the first one. Taking one end of the cord, he wrapped it several times around the new handle about 5 inches below the end he had sharpened. With his machete he then carefully split the handle down to the point he had just wrapped. Dobrabewä had brought along the old handle and he now split it in half. Using one of the halves as a wedge, he inserted it into the cleft of the new handle and used it to pry the split ends apart.

Leaving the wedge in place to keep the ends separated, Dobrabewä pushed the ax head into the cleft, hammering it down with a piece of wood until it reached a point near the cord wrapping, about 6 inches below the upper end. When he had forced the blade down as far as it would go in the handle, he pulled out the wedge. He then wound the cord once around a house post and attached its free end to his foot, as he had done before.

Rubbing successive lengths of the string with beeswax as he went along, Dobrabewä proceeded to lash the ax head to the handle.

The extra friction imparted by the beeswax was of considerable help in keeping newly lashed segments of the cord from slipping when, as he did on occasion, Dobrabewä temporarily relaxed some of the tension on it.

Every time he wrapped the cord another turn around the ax, Dobrabewä pulled back against it as hard as he could, grunting as he did so. He was trying to lash the blade in place as tightly as possible, apparently to prevent it from slipping back through the cleft as it had done before.

In lashing the ax Dobrabewä extended the cord diagonally across the handle from a point below the ax head to a point just above it. He again wound the cord around the poll of the ax, but while previously he had done so three times, now he did it seven times. This was also intended to prevent the blade from working its way back through the cleft in the handle.

When the ax was lashed to his satisfaction, Dobrabewä cut off the extra cord, placed the freshly cut end under a loop, took hold of it between his teeth, and pulled it as hard as he could in order to keep it from slipping.

After some 50 minutes of work, Dobrabewä had finished hafting the ax (see figure 1.3) and I led him back up the trail to the *ashawa* tree and motioned for him to resume cutting.

At 1:55 P.M. Dobrabewä began chopping, once more holding the ax with one hand. Despite the shortness of the handle he did not hold it at the very end but choked up on it about 5 inches. His strokes,

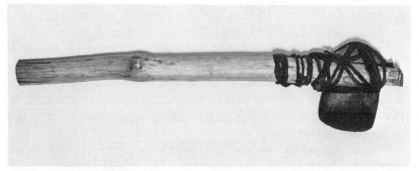

Figure 1.3. Stone ax hafted with handle of *payoarikohi* wood and lashings of newer *Cecropia* fiber. Photographed after its use in felling the *ashawa* tree. Note that the ax blade has rotated downward slightly in the handle.

which were delivered a little below chest height, were short, and he did not reach back to deliver them. The strokes started out hard and solid, and remained that way throughout the cutting. While not delivered with full force, they probably were as hard as was compatible with hitting the desired spot on the tree. Certainly Dobrabewä did not curb the force of his blows to spare the ax. Being made of andesite, a tough stone, the ax blade seemed able to withstand the blows without danger of breaking.

Dobrabewä's cutting had a definite rhythm. He chopped in short bursts of some 10 to 14 strokes delivered rapidly at a rate slightly faster than one per second. Between bursts of chopping he rested briefly for something like 10 or 12 seconds. This tempo was maintained throughout the experiment.

During the previous day's cutting Dobrabewä had directed his blows pretty much at right angles to the trunk, but now, as he began cutting again, the blows were delivered a bit more steeply, at an angle of about 20 degrees to 30 degrees above the horizontal. The earlier blows had made the initial cut in the tree; now the slightly oblique blows seemed designed to remove more wood. Most of the chips were small (see figure 1.4) and flew off fast, often spraying several feet in various directions. Occasionally a bigger one was dislodged, but never one that approached in size an ordinary chip cut with a steel ax.

After he had cut an inch or two into one part of the trunk, Dobrabewä moved a short distance around the tree in a clockwise direction and began chopping at a different spot in order to extend the cut laterally. He continued to do this for about 10 minutes. By 2:04 the arc of the trunk he had cut into was about 160 degrees.

Just then I discovered, much to my dismay, that in order to make his task easier, Dobrabewä had cut halfway through the other side of the tree with a steel ax! Knowing that I would have vetoed the idea, he had done so without telling me. But, hesitant to jeopardize a project which already had had so many false starts, I decided to let Dobrabewä continue working on the *ashawa* rather than insisting that he start on a new tree.

After extending the cut in a clockwise direction, Dobrabewä backtracked and started chopping a fresh section of the trunk counterclockwise from the spot where his cutting had begun. By 2:08, when he stopped for a brief rest, he had chopped almost 180 degrees around the tree, not counting the section he had cut with the steel ax. When he resumed work a minute or so later, he tried to deepen the cut he had already made. However, given the relatively narrow width of the cut and the thickness of the ax blade, he had cut into the trunk about as deeply as he could. In order to deepen the cut further he first had to widen it. This he did by starting to cut a new "tier" of wood just above the cut he had already made (see figure 1.5).

Dobrabewä would first chop at an angle of about 30 degrees to 45 degrees, which would begin to loosen a large chip. Then he would cut more or less horizontally into the cleft in order to cut away the wood he had just loosened, which usually flew off in several pieces. This mode of cutting produced larger chips than had come off when

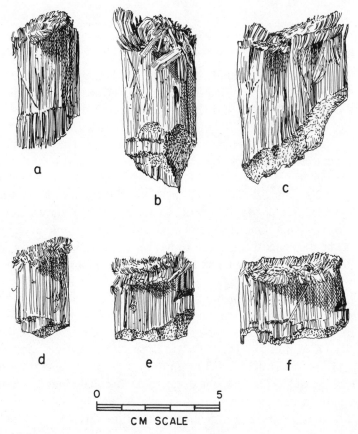

Figure 1.4. Drawing of some wood chips cut by Dobrabewä from the *ashawa* tree with the stone ax.

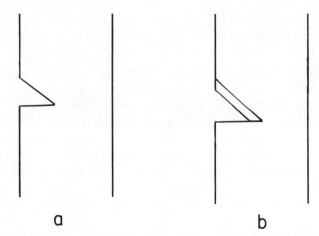

a   b

Figure 1.5. Schematic representation showing (a) the appearance of the *ashawa* tree after Dobrabewä had cut into the trunk as deeply as he could, and (b) the "tier" of wood he had to cut away before he could deepen the cut further.

he had chopped at right angles to the trunk. Sometimes Dobrabewä pulled off a large chip he had loosened instead of cutting it. He did this to clean out the cleft and also to save himself a few strokes.

Around 2:14, some 20 minutes after he started cutting, Dobrabewä stopped for a brief rest. I had promised him a machete for felling the tree and he took this opportunity to ask me if he was really going to get it.

By 2:20, after 25 minutes of chopping, the cut was about 4 to 5 inches wide and nearly 2 inches deep. Figure 1.6 shows how it looked at this time. One can see that the cut was now wide enough so it could be deepened further before having to be widened again, and at 2:30, after an 8-minute break for me to get my camera, Dobrabewä began to do just that.

It seemed clear from the way Dobrabewä was cutting that the aboriginal method of felling a tree with a stone ax involved cutting it entirely around the trunk. This contrasts, of course, with the way it is done with a steel ax, in which a notch is first made on one side of the tree, and the tree is then felled by cutting as deeply as necessary into the opposite side. The thought occurred to me that ringing the tree completely in cutting it with a stone ax, as Dobrabewä was doing, would have made it more difficult to control the direction in which it fell.

At 2:36, after Dobrabewä had been cutting for 33 minutes, I

took a close look at the ax. To my considerable surprise, the lashings were holding up well, and the blade had moved only slightly in the handle. The cutting edge, though, showed slight nicks which no doubt somewhat diminished its effectiveness.

By 2:38 Dobrabewä was cutting into the deepest part of the cleft and said something which indicated he thought the tree would fall soon. As he continued to cut, only small chips flew out. The cut was now 3 inches deep in places and looked quite clean. Constricted as it was by the relatively narrow sides of the deepening cleft, the stone ax was unable to cut large chips. However, although Dobrabewä was not getting out much wood, he kept chopping into the cleft, hoping the tree would fall. But the tree stood firm.

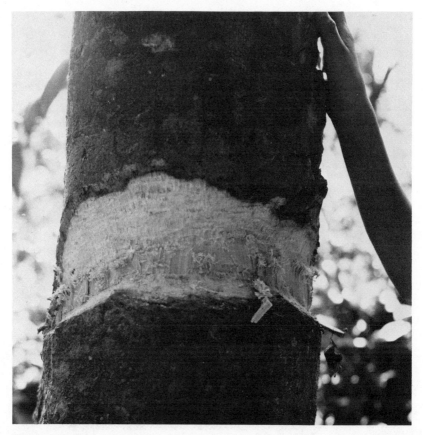

Figure 1.6. The *ashawa* tree as it looked after Dobrabewä had been chopping at it for 25 minutes.

The "mangling" often mentioned in ethnographic descriptions of aboriginal tree felling, to which I will return later, was to be seen in this experiment only in the deepest part of the cut. Here the edge of the ax blade was striking at right angles against a narrow, constricted area of wood. As a result, chips could not readily be cut, and those that did fly out were relatively few, small, and looked somewhat more bruised and less cleanly cut than had the others.

At 2:43 Dobrabewä began extending the cut laterally in a clockwise direction, hoping this would cause the tree to fall. When it did not, he began to cut above the cleft, getting a few more chips to fly off. But the tree still stood. Two minutes later he decided that the reason the *ashawa* would not go down was that a branch of an ad-

Figure 1.7. Dobrabewä cutting into the *ashawa* tree. Photograph taken 48 minutes after beginning of chopping.

jacent tree was propping it up, and sent a boy up to the village to bring his machete so he could cut down the nearby tree. He put his ear to the trunk of the *ashawa* to listen for cracks, but apparently heard none.

For 10 or 12 minutes Dobrabewä had been trying to get the tree to fall by deepening the cut without widening it further. But he had now cut as deeply into the cleft as the thickness of the ax blade would allow. Finally he realized he could get no further this way and decided to widen the cleft again preparatory to deepening it some more. At 2:47 he began chopping slightly above the cleft, directing his strokes at an angle of about 20 to 30 degrees above the horizontal.

At 2:51 Dobrabewä told me to move out of the way because the tree would fall across the trail at the spot where I was standing. Then he proceeded to cut deeper into the tree above the cleft (see figure 1.7).

Three minutes later he again put his ear to the trunk, listening for cracks that would tell him that his work was finally over and that he should get out of the way. He looked up at the surrounding trees trying to make up his mind which way the *ashawa* was going to fall, and this time decided it would fall up the trail instead of across it. Then he resumed cutting, widening and deepening the cleft still more.

At 2:57 I noticed that one strand of the lashings near the poll had broken, and pointed this out to Dobrabewä. He merely tucked the loose ends under some strands that were still intact, said "good," and continued chopping.

Two minutes later he stopped cutting briefly and tried unsuccessfully to push the tree over with his hands. Then he moved to a different spot on the tree and resumed chopping. He stopped momentarily to blow out wood dust and tiny chips from the deepest part of the cleft and listened again for cracking noises. By this time he had cut an arc about 200 degrees around the tree, not counting what he had cut with the steel ax.

At 3:03 Dobrabewä began cutting at one end of the cleft, and about 30 seconds later the first real crack was heard. But the *ashawa* still would not go down when he again tried to push it over. Dobrabewä then paused briefly and inspected two bigger trees growing up the trail, trying to determine what would happen if the *ashawa* hit them as it fell.

Figure 1.8. The ashawa tree lying on the ground showing the contrast between the side cut with a steel ax (*left*) and that cut with the stone ax (*right*).

Figure 1.9. Close-up of the butt end of the *ashawa* trunk showing the marks produced by cutting with a stone ax.

By 3:07 Dobrabewä had deepened the cleft as much as he could without cutting yet another tier of wood, but the tree still would not go down. He asked me to let him use a steel ax to finish the job, but I refused.

After chopping a little more, Dobrabewä turned to the small tree that was helping hold up the *ashawa* and with his machete cut it down. With this support gone, the *ashawa* finally gave way and came crashing to the ground, falling away from the trail in a direction Dobrabewä had not anticipated. The time was 3:14 P.M. The total time Dobrabewä had spent wielding the stone ax was 78 minutes.

As the *ashawa* lay on the ground, its butt end in the sunlight, it was easy to see the contrast between the part Dobrabewä had cut with the stone ax and that he had cut with the steel ax (see figure 1.8). Suffering what may have been a twinge of conscience at having used a steel ax on part of the trunk, Dobrabewä began hitting this part with the stone ax in order to roughen it and give it more the appearance of having been cut with the stone ax. But this was a mere token gesture which he soon gave up.

General Observations

The results of this experiment in tree felling with a stone ax invite comparison with the few other such studies that have been made.[13] Best known of these is the experiment carried out in Denmark in 1952 in which two acres of a mixed oak forest were cleared by a small team of loggers and archaeologists using Neolithic flint axes. Describing this experiment, Johannes Iversen (1956:37–38) wrote:

> When the party attacked the trees, it soon became apparent that the usual tree-chopping technique, in which one puts his shoulders and weight into long, powerful blows, would not do. It often shattered the edge of the delicate flint blade or broke the blade in two. The lumberjacks, unable to change their habits, damaged several axes. The archaeologists soon discovered that the proper way to use the flint axe was to chip at the tree with short, quick strokes, using mainly the elbow and wrist.

I have already noted that although Dobrabewä chopped with only one hand and used relatively short strokes, his blows were hard and he made no effort to spare the ax. The difference between the strength of Dobrabewä's strokes and those employed by the Danish archaeologists surely is due to the difference in toughness of the respective stone axes. Flint is hard but very brittle; a thin cutting edge will smash under the force of a heavy blow. Andesite, on the other hand, is tough, and can withstand a succession of hard blows without breaking. Tiny spalls do come off the cutting edge with continued use, but major fractures are relatively rare.[14]

Since ground stone axes were much more commonly made of tough igneous rocks than of flint, it is probably safe to conclude that Dobrabewä's hard blows were more typical of Neolithic practice than were the lighter blows of the Danish archaeologists. The use of one hand instead of two in wielding the ax, though, would depend on the length of the handle rather than on the kind of stone used for the blade. And I am not prepared to say whether, in Neolithic times, short handles were more common than long ones.

One of the surprising results of the experiment for me was that the trunk of the *ashawa* looked *cut*. Only deep in the cleft did it looked *bruised*. An Amahuaca informant (though not an eyewitness himself) once told me that a tree cut with a stone ax looked *raspado*, that is, scraped. And in the ethnographic literature for Amazonia I had found several statements by purported eyewitnesses that the stone ax "mangled," "lacerated," "crushed," "broke," and "chewed up" the wood in felling the tree (see Carneiro 1974:112–13). But none of these words would, I think, aptly describe the appearance of the felled *ashawa* (see figure 1.9).

I might add here that a relatively clean cut rather than a mangling or bruising is what appears in a photograph of a tree felled by a Héta Indian reproduced in Carneiro (1974:122). Had I given more weight to this piece of visual evidence and less to verbal references to "mangled" tree trunks, the results of Dobrabewä's work would have surprised me less.

Having examined the felled tree, my next concern was: How had the stone ax fared? Again, to my surprise, it had survived the experiment very well. Except for the one strand that had broken, the *Cecropia* bowstring, old as it was, had stood up to the shock of many repeated blows. The blade had rotated some 12 degrees downward (see figure 1.3), but it had not been forced back through the cleft in the handle as had happened in the earlier trial. The cleft-stick technique had proved to be perfectly feasible and had produced a stone ax quite capable of felling a tree. It was obvious, though, that in order for this method to work, the blade had to be lashed very tightly to the handle. Dobrabewä's strenuous efforts in this regard had been entirely warranted.

Looking closely at the bit of the ax (see figure 1.10) one could see that a number of tiny fragments had been chipped or abraded from the dark greenish cortex of the stone and that the cutting edge had been roughened back about $^3/_{16}$ of an inch. The ax had thus been significantly dulled. And if 1 hour and 18 minutes of use had dulled the stone ax to this extent, 3 or 4 hours would surely have made resharpening it a necessity. This is confirmed by the experiment carried out by William H. Townsend (1969:201) among the Heve of New Guinea in which a stone adze used in felling trees was deemed sufficiently dull after 3 hours and 49 minutes of use to require sharpening.

These results lend credence to something I was told by an Amahuaca informant, namely, that aboriginally, when the forest was being cleared for garden plots, men had to sharpen their stone axes every morning. Indeed, I suspect that when the stone ax was in heavy use, Neolithic peoples may have had to sharpen the implement more than once a day.

After he had felled the *ashawa,* Dobrabewä wanted to sharpen the stone ax, but I asked him not to do so since I wanted to preserve the worn edge for future study. Thus I do not know how long it

Figure 1.10. Enlarged photograph showing the wear produced on the edge of the stone ax after 78 minutes of use in felling the tree.

would have taken him to resharpen it. However, in the Heve experiment cited above (Townsend 1969:201), resharpening a stone adze took about an hour, and that figure is probably not far from the general average.

That in Neolithic times stone axes were subjected to repeated sharpening is demonstrated by the many archaeological specimens which show considerable evidence of being ground down. One stone ax blade collected for me by the Amahuaca, for example, had been sharpened so many times that it had been reduced to perhaps one-third of its original size (see Rydén 1941:128; Lathrap 1970:62).

A Formula for Tree Felling Time

The results of the experiment described above have implications that go beyond the individual case. For example, they can be used to construct a formula predicting the time it will take to fell a tree of a given diameter by means of a stone ax. The problem, though, is not a simple one. It involves several steps and a number of assumptions, idealizations, and simplifications. Let us begin by considering something of the geometry of the problem.

As we have seen, in felling a tree with a stone ax it seems to be the common practice to cut it all the way around the trunk instead of notching it on one side and then cutting it through on the opposite side.[15] The volume of wood cut away from a tree is essentially a disc of the shape shown in figure 1.11. In our experiment with the *asha-*

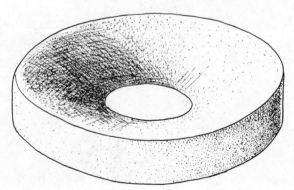

Figure 1.11. Schematic drawing of a disc representing the volume of wood that is cut out of a tree in felling it with a stone ax.

wa, the base of this "disc" was not really flat, but curved down somewhat at the outer edge. However, it seemed to me that the ideal cut Dobrabewä aimed at was that shown in figure 1.12a rather than in figure 1.12b, and that therefore the closest relatively simple geometric shape representing it is the disc shown in figure 1.11.

The first step in calculating the time required to fell a tree of a given diameter is to determine the volume of wood of the shape of this disc that has to be cut out of it. Having found this, we must next ascertain the time it takes to cut out a specified volume of wood, say, one cubic inch, and then multiply the time required per cubic inch by the number of cubic inches that must be cut away.

How can we find the volume of this disc? We can think of the disc as being the lower half of a ring (shaped like a pineapple ring) that has been sliced diagonally all the way around, the upper half of which looks like figure 1.13. The two discs produced by this "slicing" are not exactly the same in volume; the lower one is somewhat larger than the upper one. However, they are near enough in volume that for our purposes we can consider them equal in size. All we need to do, then, to obtain the volume of the lower disc is to calculate the

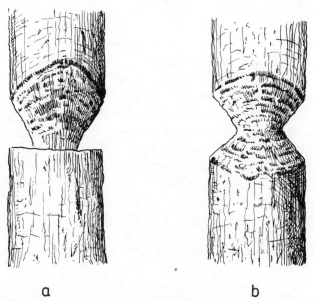

      a   b

Figure 1.12. Sketch contrasting, in idealized form, (*a*) the cut made by Dobrabewä in felling the *ashawa* tree and (*b*) the "beaver-gnawed" type of cut, not employed by him.

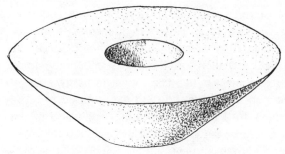

Figure 1.13. Upper half of the "pineapple ring" of wood, the lower half of which is shown in figure 1.11.

volume of the entire ring and divide by 2. The formula for the volume of a ring is:

$$V = \frac{\pi}{4} h (D^2 - d^2) \tag{1}$$

where D is the outside diameter, d the inside diameter, and h the height (or thickness) of the ring. The formula for the volume of our diagonally sliced disc would then be:

$$V = \frac{\frac{\pi}{4} h (D^2 - d^2)}{2} \tag{2}$$

In applying this formula to tree felling, the outside diameter of the ring, D, is simply the diameter of the tree at the height it is cut. But how are we to obtain the inside diameter? This dimension will depend on how far in toward its center the tree must be cut in order to fall. To estimate this we must examine the one case available to us. In felling the *ashawa*, Dobrabewä cut about 4 inches into the trunk on the side that he chopped with the stone ax, and he probably would have cut in as deeply around the entire circumference of the tree had he used the stone ax for the whole operation. Since the *ashawa* was 12.5 inches in diameter, cutting 4 inches into the side of it means cutting the trunk a total of 8 inches of its diameter. The inner core of wood left uncut at the center of the tree was thus 4.5 inches in diameter. If we were applying formula (2) to the *ashawa*, D would be 12.5 and d, 4.5.

It would be more convenient, though, if we could recast the formula so that d, the diameter of the uncut inner core of wood, were expressed as a percentage of D, the overall diameter of the tree. In the case of the *ashawa*, for which $D = 12.5$ and $d = 4.5$, this percentage would be $4.5/12.5$, which is 36 percent, or in decimal form, $.36D$. I will assume that this relationship holds true in the felling of any tree; that is to say, that a central core of wood $.36$ of the diameter of the tree remains uncut and simply breaks when the tree falls.[16] If we use the symbol d (instead of D) to represent the diameter of the tree, the formula now reads:

$$V = \frac{\frac{\pi}{4}h\,[d^2 - (.36d)^2]}{2} \tag{3}$$

Next, let us consider h, the height or width of the cut. As we noted in describing Dobrabewä's felling of the *ashawa*, the height of the cut will vary with its depth. In order to deepen the cut beyond a certain point, it must first be widened. Moreover, there is probably a nearly constant ratio between the height of the cut and its depth. And if this is so, then we can express h in terms of d, which would simplify our formula still further.

Consider the diagram (figure 1.14), a schematic representation of the cut through the *ashawa* just prior to its falling. Since Dobrabewä cut some 4 inches into the side of the tree, $a = 4$. But now a is $4/12.5$ of d, which is the same as $.32d$. Thus, in our calculations the depth of the cut just before the tree falls can be taken to be $.32$ of the diameter of the tree.

Next we need to express h in terms of d. The angle of the cut in the *ashawa* just before it fell, labeled i in figure 1.14, was about 40

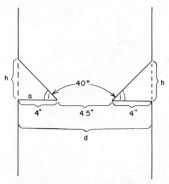

Figure 1.14. Schematic representation of the cut made in the *ashawa* tree as it looked just prior to the tree's falling, showing the relationship between the height (*h*) and depth (*a*) of the cut and the diameter of the tree (*d*).

degrees. Assuming that this angle is pretty much the same for all trees felled with a stone ax, the ratio of h to a is given by the tangent of the angle i, 40 degrees, which is .8391. So the numerical value of h is .8391a. However, since a is 4/12.5 or .32 of the diameter of the tree, then $h = .8391 \times .32d$. This is equal to .2685d, so that the formula becomes:

$$V = \frac{\frac{\pi}{4}.2685d\,[d^2 - (.36d)^2]}{2} \tag{4}$$

Still another simplification can be made. Since $\pi/4$ is a constant whose value is .7854, we can multiply .2685d by .7854, getting .21d. The formula now reads:

$$V = \frac{.21d\,[d^2 - (.36d)^2]}{2} \tag{5}$$

As it stands, the formula gives the volume of wood (in cubic inches, say) that must be cut out of a tree of known diameter in order to make it fall.

The next step in our mathematical treatment of the problem is to expand the formula so it will yield the *time* required to fell a tree of a given diameter. In order to do so we must return again to the observations made during the felling of the *ashawa*. It will be recalled that Dobrabewä spent 78 minutes chopping at the tree with the stone ax before it fell. If we can calculate the total number of cubic inches of wood he cut out of the trunk during this time, we can compute how long it took him, on the average, to cut out each cubic inch.

Dobrabewä did only about half the cutting with the stone ax, the other half being done with a steel ax. Thus, in order to determine how much wood he chopped out with the stone ax we simply calculate the total volume of wood he would have had to cut in order to fell the tree, and take half of it. We do this with formula (5):

$$V = \frac{.21d\,[d^2 - (.36d)^2]}{2} \tag{5}$$

Substituting 12.5 for d, the diameter of the *ashawa*, we have:

$$V = \frac{.21 \times 12.5\,[12.5^2 - (.36 \times 12.5)^2]}{2} \tag{6}$$

Solving the equation we get $V = 178.5$ cubic inches, half of which is 89.25 cubic inches. Thus, in the 78 minutes he wielded the stone ax

Dobrabewä cut some 89.25 cubic inches of wood. This works out to .8739 minutes, or .0146 hours, per cubic inch of wood. The time, in hours, required to fell a tree, then, is given by the formula:

$$t = .0146 \frac{.21d\,[d^2 - (.36d)^2]}{2} \tag{7}$$

Let us apply this formula to a few examples. How long would it take, for instance, to cut down a tree 1 foot in diameter? Converting feet to inches we have $d = 12$, and inserting this number into the equation gives us:

$$t = .0146 \frac{.21 \times 12\,[12^2 - (.36 \times 12)^2]}{2} \tag{8}$$

Working the equation through yields an answer of 2.3 hours. Now, if we compute the felling time of a tree 2 feet in diameter the answer comes out $t = 18.4$ hours, and for a tree 3 feet in diameter, $t = 62.3$ hours.

With these figures in hand we can simplify our formula very drastically. Plotting these felling times against tree diameter on logarithmic graph paper we get the results shown in figure 1.15. The

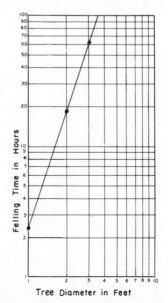

Figure 1.15. Graph with logarithmic scales, showing the relationship between diameter of tree and felling time when the cutting tool is a stone ax. Based on experiment with Dobrabewä.

equation for the regression line of the graph is of the type $y = ax^b$. The value of a, the intercept, is 2.3 hours because this is the value of y when $x = 1$ foot. The value of the exponent, b, is obtained by measuring the slope of the regression line, which turns out to be 3. Accordingly, our new formula reads:

$$t = 2.3d^3 \tag{9}$$

That is to say, with a stone ax as the cutting tool, the time, in hours, that it takes to fell a tree is obtained by cubing the diameter of the tree, in feet, and multiplying the cube by 2.3.

That our more cumbersome equation (7) should be reducible to this simpler form should not surprise us. It is a well-known geometric fact that the volume of a solid, including our "diagonally sliced disc," is proportional to the cube of its linear dimensions. Thus, we should expect that as the diameter of a tree is doubled, the volume of wood that must be cut out of it in order to fell it will increase 8 times. And indeed this is reflected in the fact that the 18.4 hours we calculated as being required to fell a tree 2 feet in diameter is precisely 8 times the 2.3 hours required to fell a tree 1 foot in diameter.

There are several advantages to having the equation in the form $t = 2.3d^3$. For one thing, it makes calculating the value of t much easier. Moreover, since this equation is based on the fundamental geometric relationship that volume increases as the cube of the linear dimensions, we can be reasonably sure that the *form* of the equation is correct. If other experiments with the stone ax reveal felling times significantly different from those presented above, one should be able to adapt the formula to fit the new data by simply changing the value of a, the intercept. Thus, if another Neolithic people were found to take 1.8 hours, instead of 2.3, to fell a tree a foot in diameter, then all we would need to do in order to determine felling time for trees of other diameters among that group would be to alter the formula to read $t = 1.8d^3$.

Having raised the possibility that the formula would have to be modified for use with different groups, let us see what factors might require this.

First of all, despite all the mathematical gyrations we went through in constructing formula (9), we cannot be sure how accurate it is, even for the Yanomamö. After all, our figures are based on only a single felling; indeed, on only *half* a felling, since Dobrabewä "cheated" in cutting the other half of the *ashawa*. And since Dobrabewä was improvising in using the stone ax rather than repeating something he had done all his life, his manner of working might have been more aberrant than typical of aboriginal Yanomamö tree felling. It is quite possible, for example, that Dobrabewä took longer to fell the tree simply because he was unaccustomed to using a stone ax. I would not, however, stress this point since he was certainly skilled in using a steel ax, and much of this skill no doubt carried over to his use of the stone ax.

Nonetheless, Dobrabewä did spend some fairly unproductive time trying to deepen the cleft in the trunk when it was too narrow to permit the ax to cut much wood out of it. Had he recognized earlier that he had to widen the cut before he could deepen it, several minutes of cutting might have been saved. An experienced stone ax user would no doubt have known this.

It should be evident that various characteristics of the stone ax will affect felling time: the weight of the blade (a heavier blade cutting deeper than a light one);[17] a broad cutting edge as opposed to a narrow one; a handle long enough to permit wielding the ax with both hands instead of just one. Dobrabewä's ax was light, weighing only 15 ounces in all, the cutting edge was small, measuring only 2.5 inches,[18] and the handle was short, so he could not chop with two hands. Since the amount of wood cut out by each stroke is directly proportional to the force of the blow, a wider, heavier blade, a stouter handle, and a two-handed swing would surely have dislodged more wood per stroke.

On the other hand, heavier blades are generally thicker too, and the width of the cleft that would have to be made in the tree in order to cut as deeply as necessary might well have been greater. This would certainly be true, for example, if one were using the stone ax of the Héta, which is of the "embedded celt" type (Carneiro 1974:120a), and has an enlargement of the upper part of the handle fully 4 inches in diameter. The effect of this bulbous head would be to diminish some of the saving in cutting time that its greater weight made possible.

It should then be clear that since stone axes vary in size, weight, shape, cutting edge, thickness, toughness, mode of use, etc., no one formula may be applicable to them all. It may well be necessary to modify formula (9) to take account of these and other variables.

However, the beauty of the problem is that the many factors involved in tree felling, however numerous and varied, and whatever their respective magnitudes, all have their effects funneled into and expressed through a single parameter: cutting time. Accordingly, all we have to do to adapt formula (9) for the conditions of tree felling prevailing among any Neolithic group would be to pick out 3 or 4 trees exactly one foot in diameter, have them felled with the stone ax used by the group, and average their felling time. We would then substitute this figure for 2.3 as the value of a in the formula, and with this substitution made, we would be ready to predict the felling time of trees of any other diameter.

There is still another variable affecting felling time, which is probably more important than any of the rest. Moreover, it is one

Table 1.1 Actual and Expected Cutting Times for Selected Trees Felled with a Stone Adze by the Heve of New Guinea

Diameter of tree *	Actual time required to fell *	Felling time predicted by formula
9.3 in.	30 mins.	62 mins.
11.3 in.	41 mins.	116 mins.
11.6 in.	74 mins.	126 mins.
15.4 in.	119 mins.	292 mins.

*Townsend 1969:203.

which requires special mathematical treatment. The effect of this variable began to emerge when I compared the results of the Yanomamö experiment with those of one conducted by William Townsend (1969) among the Heve of New Guinea. Table 1.1 presents Townsend's (1969:203) figures for the time taken by the Heve (using a stone adze) in cutting down the four largest trees felled during the experiment. Next to these figures I have entered the predicted felling time for trees of these diameters as given by our formula, $t = 2.3d^3$.

It is clear from these figures that the Heve took substantially less time to fell trees of various diameters than our formula predicted. Their cutting time was, in fact, only about half of that we would have expected. Why the discrepancy?

First of all, is it possible that the stone adze might be a more efficient cutting tool than the stone ax? I frankly doubt it. Even though the Heve wield the adze with both hands, their overhead stroke delivered at head height or higher would seem not to allow them to apply as much force as the level stroke of an ax delivered at chest height. Moreover, to judge from one of Townsend's drawings (1969:202), the way the Heve use the stone adze seems to involve cutting more wood out of the tree than did Dobrabewä's mode of cutting. Thus I think we can dismiss the differences between the ax and the adze as significant factors in explaining the differences in felling time.

The Heve's greater experience with stone cutting tools likewise does not seem to me to be the answer. True, the Heve used them until shortly before Townsend's arrival, but their greater skill in the use of the adze cannot account for a ratio of almost 2 to 1 in relative cutting time. Some other factor must be at work.

The most likely answer to why the Heve fell trees faster must involve differences in hardness of wood. The *ashawa* Dobrabewä felled was relatively hard. Fresh chips cut from it sank when placed in water. Air dried chips were later determined to have a specific gravity of about 0.76. Now the question arises, how hard were the four trees felled by the Heve?

Unfortunately, Townsend does not answer this question. He says only that "the trees were selected to cover a representative range of varieties, sizes, and hardness of wood" (1969:201). However, he adds that of the 91 trees cut down, 31 were of the family Burseraceae, which he notes (1969:201) is "the most common type" of tree in Heve territory. Townsend says nothing further about the trees of this family, but we can add some relevant information.

The family Burseraceae is not restricted to the western Pacific; it is also represented in tropical America. In the standard reference work, *Timbers of Tropical America,* Record and Mell (1924:339) give the specific gravity (oven-dried) of one species of this family, *Bursera simaruba,* as 0.3, which is very light.[19] Moreover, the authors say that in the border area between Guatemala and Honduras *Bursera* sp. is "abundant in the second-growth forests" (1924:338). It appears, then, that the area in which the Heve experiment was carried out was a secondary forest, and that "a representative range of . . . hardness of wood" for such an area would not include trees as hard as those of primary forest, where trees with a specific gravity of 0.8 or higher are not uncommon. The consistently lower cutting time for trees felled by the Heve thus appears to be explained by the fact that they were felling soft-wooded trees.

This immediately suggests that in order to make our formula for felling time more accurate, and to make results obtained from various areas of the world more comparable, we must incorporate into it some measure of the hardness of the tree being felled. How is this to be done? Forestry laboratories measure the hardness of wood by determining the weight required to imbed a 0.444-inch steel ball one-half its diameter into the wood being tested (Record 1914:40). Clearly, this test is impracticable for the anthropologist to carry out. However, an indirect measure of hardness is obtainable with relative ease. The hardness of a given wood is closely related to its density, and its density can be found by determining its specific gravity.[20]

As closely as I could determine it, the specific gravity of the *ashawa* felled by Dobrabewä was 0.76. Now if the four largest trees felled by the Heve belonged to the family Burseraceae, and if they had the same specific gravity as the American representative of that family, *Bursera simaruba,* namely, 0.3, then the ratio of the specific gravity of these trees to that of the *ashawa* is 1 to 2.53. From the data in table 1.1 we can calculate the ratios between the actual felling times of these trees and the felling times predicted for them by formula (9). The results of this calculation will enable us to see if these ratios are anything like the ratios between their relative hardness and that of the *ashawa*.

Using formula (9) we find that the ratios of actual to predicted felling times for these four trees are 1 to 2.07, 1 to 2.8, 1 to 1.7, and 1 to 2.45. The average of these ratios is 1 to 2.26, which is quite close to the ratio of 1 to 2.53 in the relative hardness between them and the *ashawa*. These figures strongly suggest that felling time is directly proportional to the first power of the hardness of a tree. Accordingly, if we expand our formula to take account of hardness, we should be able to predict felling time much more accurately.[21]

The simplest way to incorporate hardness into the formula would be to multiply the right-hand side of the equation by the specific gravity of the wood in question. And had the *ashawa* tree, which served as the standard for our formula, happened to have a specific gravity of exactly 1, this is all we would have had to do. However, since its specific gravity is 0.76, we must multiply this figure by 1.3 in order to raise it to 1. So our formula now reads:

$$t = 2.3d^3 \times 1.3h \qquad (10)$$

where h is the hardness of the wood as measured by its specific gravity.

Let us apply this formula to the four largest trees felled in the Heve experiment to see if the results come closer to actual felling times than those predicted by formula (9). The largest of these trees measured 15.4 inches in diameter, which is 1.283 feet. Its specific gravity we are taking to be 0.3. Thus, in our revised formula, $d = 1.283$ and $h = 0.3$. Substituting these values into the equation we have

$$t = 2.3 \times 1.283^3 \times 1.3 \times 0.3. \tag{11}$$

Solving the equation we get $t = 1.89$ hours, or 1 hour and 54 minutes, compared to the actual felling time of 1 hour and 59 minutes. Thus the new formula comes within 5 minutes of predicting the actual felling time of this tree, whereas the old one was off by 173 minutes.

When formula (10) is applied to the other three trees, the same marked improvement in prediction is observed. For the tree 9.3 inches in diameter the prediction made by the new formula is 27 minutes closer than that made by the old one; for the tree 11.3 inches in diameter it is 71 minutes closer; and for the tree 11.6 inches in diameter it is 27 minutes closer. The average deviation between predicted and actual felling times for the four trees is now only 14 percent, which seems to me to be a relatively close fit.

Of course the figures obtainable through these calculations do not tell the whole story of the time taken in Stone Age tree felling. Neolithic farmers in Amazonia, and undoubtedly elsewhere, found two major ways of saving labor when they cleared a tract of forest. One of them was to use fire as an adjunct in felling the larger trees. Firewood, brush, or bark was piled against the tree and set afire. The fire burned part way into the trunk, and the charred wood, which was softer than the green wood, was then hacked out with a stone ax. The process was repeated until the tree fell. This alternate burning and chopping allowed a tree to be felled with a much smaller expenditure of effort than if the green trunk had had to be cut through entirely by hand.

Another labor saving practice of Neolithic peoples was the driving tree fall. Several small trees standing in the expected direction of fall of a larger one were notched, and when the larger tree was felled, it brought down with it the smaller ones in its path. This method saved a great deal of cutting: 6 or 8 fair-sized trees might easily be toppled by a large one.[22]

Any careful estimate of Neolithic forest clearing time must therefore take account of such auxiliary techniques. Still, dozens of trees were probably always felled with the stone ax alone, and the time required for this felling is the largest single factor in estimating total forest clearing time. The final version of our formula, with whatever modifications are needed to allow for local differences in cutting tools and techniques, can be applied to any Neolithic group to provide a reasonable approximation of forest felling time.

Of course, in order to do this, data on the size of forest clearings, the range in diameters of the trees to be felled, and the hardness of the various species of trees must be available. However, these values can probably be estimated from the published literature and, especially, from field measurements made specifically for the purpose. Indeed, future field work on this problem should be directed at arriving at typical numerical values for these factors for primary and secondary forests in both temperate and tropical areas.

Any calculation we might make with these data would of course not be an end in itself. It would be but a means to an end. And that end would be to gain a more precise notion of the expenditure of labor required of Neolithic man in clearing the forest prior to planting his gardens and raising his crops. Such information would help us not only to reconstruct the culture history of a particular group, but also to elucidate the general relationships that have obtained between environment, technology, subsistence, labor, and society. And that, as becomes clearer every day, is the common objective toward which ethnologists and archaeologists are rapidly converging.

Notes

1. This has not always been recognized, however. As recently as 1945, Grahame Clark found it necessary to marshal the arguments against the prevailing view of European prehistorians that Neolithic man in northern Europe had stuck pretty much to unwooded areas in making his gardens and villages because he was incapable of clearing the forest with the stone tools available to him (Clark 1945).

2. The stone ax was not always used unaided in felling trees. Chagnon (1968:33) writes that the Yanomamö "had to kill the big trees by cutting a ring of bark off

around the base of the stump, using a crude stone ax, piling brush around them, and burning them.'' Barandiaran (1967:26) indicates that to burn the ring around the trees the Yanomamö first applied a layer of resin to it.

3. The only use now made of stone ax heads by the Yanomamö is to grind seeds of the *Piptadenia peregrina* tree to make snuff.

4. This expedition included, besides Chagnon, Eric Fredlund, Kenneth R. Good, and Raymond Hames, with William T. Sanders and myself serving as consultants.

5. I occupied this house for one month with my field partner, Kenneth R. Good, who remained at Hasuböwateri doing field work until May 1977.

6. *Washamonamá* (or *wēshēmonama*, as he writes it) is identified by Jacques Lizot (1975b:94) as *Amphirrox latifolia*, the common Venezuelan name for which is "patagrulla.'' Kenneth Good informs me that the wood of this tree is often used by the Yanomamö to haft a *haowa,* a "machete-ax'' described in note 7. The *masi masi* vine is identified by Lizot (1975b:49) as *Hetropsis jenmanii,* but he gives no common name for it.

7. I was not then aware of the existence of a Yanomamö cutting tool called a *haowa,* still used today in felling trees when a steel ax is not available. It consists of a piece of broken machete blade, sharpened at one end, inserted into a split wooden handle and tightly lashed to it. Kenneth Good (personal communication) suggests that the "cleft-stick'' method Dobrabewä used in hafting the stone ax was a direct imitation of the way in which the *haowa* is hafted. And he further suggests that the way in which the *haowa* is hafted may in turn be an imitation of the way in which the stone ax was once hafted. Thus, while Dobrabewä had never seen a stone ax being hafted, the way he did it may well have been the aboriginal Yanomamö way of doing so. Moreover, I have recently found an actual description, brief as it is, of what appears to be the "cleft-stick'' type of hafting among the sixteenth-century Tupinambá: "cortam suas madeiras e paus com pedras como cunhas, metidas em um pau entre duas talas, mui bem atadas e por tal maneira que andam fortes'' (Vaz de Caminha 1943 and earlier editions, quoted in Pinto 1938:143).

8. That Neolithic peoples sometimes passed the lashings around the poll of a grooved ax is suggested by the fact that a few stone axes found archaeologically have a distinct notch in the poll along which the lashings could be wound with little likelihood of their slipping off. Earl Morris (1939: Plate 152, *c* and *d;* Plate 154, *c* and *d*) illustrates several such poll-notched axes from the Southwest, and a Taíno stone ax head I have recently seen has such a notch.

9. I do not, however, have a botanical identification for this tree.

10. *Cecropia* cordage is the almost universal choice of Amazonian Indians for bowstrings, and is very often used for making hammock ropes as well. Moreover, the Amahuaca told me in 1961 that their ancestors had hafted their T-shaped stone axes with *Cecropia* cord. In central and eastern Amazonia, where the embedded stone celt was the usual form, no lashings were used. The celt was either rammed tightly into the socket gouged out for it in the upper part of the handle, or else was cemented in place with resin (see Kozák 1972:22).

11. This was no doubt related to the short length of the handles he used. Shortness of handle may well be a common feature of aboriginal stone axes. According to Ivan Schoen (1969:18), the short-handled stone axes used by the Akuriyo of Surinam are "only long enough to be held in one hand." One ax illustrated by Schoen (1969:14), and the only one whose dimensions he gives, had a handle 17 inches long. The shortness of the charred remains of handles found on archaeological stone axes from the Southwest convinced Earl Morris (1939:136–37) that they must have been wielded with only one hand.

12. *Payoarikohi* is probably the same tree that Lizot (1975b:6) gives as *bayoarima* in his Yanõmamɨ-Spanish dictionary, and which he identifies botanically as *Rinorea* sp. From its wood the Yanomamö also make the hard plugs inserted into the nock ends of arrows to help keep them from splitting.

13. For a reference to some of the earlier experiments along these lines see Clark (1945:68).

14. Broken stone ax heads of tough stone certainly do occur archaeologically, and indeed I have collected a broken Amahuaca ax head on the upper Inuya River in eastern Peru. But such breaks might be due to small, unperceived flaws that existed in the stone before it was ground into shape rather than being a necessary consequence of use.

15. This is also the technique used by the Heve of New Guinea in felling a tree even though they used stone adzes instead of axes (Townsend 1969:202).

16. Of course, this will not always hold true. What percentage of the trunk will have to be cut through is influenced by such factors as the hardness of the wood; the inclination the tree might have away from the vertical; an asymmetrical crown weighting it in one direction; the presence of adjacent trees whose branches might serve to support the tree being cut; and lianas which might attach the crown of the tree to that of others, which also would give it extra support. But certain simplifying assumptions must be made if a formula is going to be worked out at all.

17. The effect of weight of ax on cutting time was shown in experiments carried out by Halvor L. Skavlem, scion of a pioneer Norwegian family in southern Wisconsin. Using a stone ax of his own manufacture, Skavlem cut down a dogwood tree 4 inches in diameter in 10 minutes. Later he worked over the ax head so that while the cutting edge remained unaltered, the blade was trimmed down to make it more symmetrical and to reduce its weight. A second tree (presumably of about the same diameter and hardness as the first) was then felled with the ax and the time required for this second felling proved to be twice that of the first (Pond 1930:94).

18. A Taíno stone ax head from Haiti I have examined has an edge 6.75 inches long measured along the curve.

19. By way of comparison, balsa wood, the world's lightest wood, ranges in specific gravity from 0.12 to 0.2 when oven dried (Record and Mell 1924:426). White oak, on the other hand, has a specific gravity of 0.59 (Record 1914:56).

20. How this can be done is described in detail in Record (1914:136–37). The specific gravity of a sample of wood will vary, of course, depending on whether the

chip is fresh, air dried, or oven dried. Air dried chips seem to me to be the most appropriate for the experiment.

21. An incident I witnessed among the Yanomamö brought home to me the difference that hardness can make in felling time. A man who had been felling primary forest trees for me with a steel ax as part of another experiment told me he was tired and wanted to quit. I said all right, expecting him to lay down his ax and head for home. I was surprised, therefore, when he suddenly began to chop at another tree, 8.25 inches in diameter, that lay just outside the experimental plot. However, the tree proved to have very soft wood and, despite its girth, in 1 minute and 32 seconds it was on the ground.

22. The driving tree fall has been retained by slash-and-burn cultivators even after adopting the steel ax. To the best of my knowledge, though, the practice of alternately charring and chopping the trunk of a large tree in felling it is invariably abandoned once the steel ax has replaced the stone one.

References Cited

Barandiaran, Daniel de
1967. "Agricultura y recolección entre los Sanemá-Yanoama, o el hacha de piedra y la psicología paleolítica de los mismos." *Antropológica* 19:24–50.

Carneiro, Robert L.
1974. "On the Use of the Stone Axe by the Amahuaca Indians of Eastern Peru." *Ethnologische Zeitschrift Zürich* 1:107–22.

Chagnon, Napoleon A.
1968. *Yanomamö, The Fierce People.* New York: Holt, Rinehart, and Winston.

Clark, Grahame
1945. "Farmers and Forests in Neolithic Europe." *Antiquity* 19:57–71.

Iversen, Johannes
1956. "Forest Clearance in the Stone Age." *Scientific American* 194:36–41.

Kozák, Vladimír
1972. "Stone Age Revisited." *Natural History* 81(8):14, 16, 18–22, 24.

Lathrap, Donald W.
1970. *The Upper Amazon.* New York: Praeger.

Lizot, Jacques
1975a. *El hombre de la pantorrilla preñada, y otros mitos Yanōmami.* Caracas: Fundación La Salle de Ciencias Naturales.
1975b. *Diccionario Yanōmami-Español.* Roberto Lizarralde, trans. Caracas: Universidad Central de Venezuela, Facultad de Ciencias Económicas y Sociales, División de Publicaciones.

Morris, Earl H.
1939. *Archaeological Studies in the La Plata District, Southwestern Colorado and Northwestern New Mexico.* Washington, D.C.: The Carnegie Institution of Washington.

Pinto, Estevão
1938. *Os Indígenas do Nordeste,* vol. 2. Biblioteca Pedagógica Brasileira, Brasiliana, vol. 112. São Paulo: Companhia Editora Nacional.

Pond, Alonzo W.
1930. "Primitive Methods of Working Stone Based on Experiments of Halvor L. Skavlem." *Logan Museum Bulletin,* vol. 2, no. 1.

Record, Samuel J.
1914. *The Mechanical Properties of Wood.* New York: Wiley.

Record, Samuel J. and Clayton D. Mell
1924. *Timbers of Tropical America.* New Haven: Yale University Press.

Rydén, Stig
1941. *A Study of the Siriono Indians.* Göteborg: N.J. Gumperts Bokhandel A.-B.

Schoen, Ivan L.
1969. "Contact with the Stone Age." *Natural History,* 78(1):10–18, 66–67.

Snethlage, Emil Heinrich
1937. *Atiko y.* Berlin: Klinthardt & Biermann.

Taylor, Kenneth I.
1974. *Sanumá Fauna: Prohibitions and Classifications.* Fundación La Salle de Ciencias Naturales, Monografía No. 18. Caracas.

Townsend, William H.
1969. "Stone and Steel Tool Use in a New Guinea Society." *Ethnology* 8:199–205.

Vaz de Caminha, Pero
1943. *A Carta de Pero Vaz de Caminha.* Jayme Cortesão, ed. Rio de Janeiro: Editora Livros de Portugal.

2 / An Ethnoarchaeological Approach to Reassessing the Meaning of Variability in Stone Tool Assemblages

James I. Ebert
Department of Anthropology
University of New Mexico, Albuquerque

Ebert's fieldwork, like that discussed by Hole and by DeBoer and Lathrap, entailed both archaeological and ethnographic research. His observations of the activities, toolkits, and sites of contemporary Botswana Bushmen form the basis for his comments regarding the analysis and interpretation of archaeological lithic assemblages. Focusing on the mobility of hunter-gatherers and the sizes of their tools and energy expended in their manufacture, Ebert suggests that the sizes and variety of tools in a given sample is a more useful index of group mobility, tool curation, and site activities than are type counts or percentages. His theoretical argument is illustrated with a comparison of assemblages from different sites, an approach also utilized by Jochim. The approach to the analysis of lithic assemblages advocated by Ebert has potential applications in a wide range of geographic and temporal settings, and might also be attempted with other classes of archaeological artifact.

Notwithstanding the great variation in archaeological method and theory apparent in the literature today, it is probably safe to say that all archaeologists would agree that the data of anthropology and archaeology—the ethnographic record and the archaeological record—can be brought to bear logically on one another. This realization has led, in recent years, to the development of ethnoarchaeology; recent

The data and ideas which are discussed in this paper were developed under the support of the National Science Foundation (grant SOC 75-02253); the opinions and conclusions expressed are those of the author alone, however.

ethnoarchaeological research has taken archaeologists to such diverse hunter-gatherer groups as the Western Desert Aborigines of Australia (Gould 1971), the Eubid Agta of the Philippines (Griffin n.d.), the !Kung Bushmen of the Kalahari Desert (Yellen 1974), and the Nunamiut Eskimos of Alaska (Binford 1976). All of these investigations have a common aim: to increase our understanding of the material correlates of human behavior, both in the past and the present.

During the course of these and many other considerations of ethnoarchaeological method, however, doubts as well as hopes have been raised. A persistent echo in the ethnoarchaeological literature urges caution in comparing past and present behavior and material correlates. Such warnings range from the optimistic and well-considered (Gould 1971, 1973; David 1971; White 1967; White and Thomas 1972) to the absurd, culminating in the declaration that ethnographic analogy is so "dangerous" that it should not be attempted except under certain circumstances (Johnson 1972). Much of this seems to spring from a feeling that, as archaeological materials and human behavior become farther removed in time, the chances of incorrect interpretation increase (Chang 1967). What many archaeologists fail to recognize is that analogy is, in itself, no more precarious or dangerous than any other inductive procedure. Of course, any translation from form to meaning *can* be dangerous—there is no direct and simple way to be sure that such a link is logically "true."

To guard against incorrect interpretations arrived at through ethnoarchaeological analogy, and to negate the effects of "time distance" in such an exercise, it might be wise to view ethnographic analogy as more than just formal translation. Under the definition proposed here, analogy would comprise two parallel chains of reasoning, two parallel explanations. Imagine a two-sided equation, one side being occupied by behavior observed among a modern primitive group, and the other by observations taken from the archaeological record. If they are to be comparable at all, these two "scenes" must possess more than a superficial formal similarity. They can only be compared validly in a processual way, and this is only possible if it can be argued that the processes in operation on both sides of the equation are similar or in some way bear upon another. First, it must be shown that certain processes are operative or determinant in the living case; these processes are then applied to the archaeological case. Of course, the sequence can be reversed—processes leading to the accumulation of the archaeological record can be applied to observed human behavior, as well (see, for instance, Reid, Schiffer and Rathje 1975). When treated in this way, analogy can be recognized for what it is: a productive idea-generating device which points the way to a more complete understanding of the processes which shape past and present human behavior.

A year-long regional archaeological, ethnological, and ecological survey of the Central District of Botswana carried out in 1975–76 provided an opportunity to test the practicality of such an approach. The primary foci of this fieldwork were Bushmen (Basarwa), over 25,000 of whom still live a more-or-less hunting and gathering way of life there, and the Middle and Late Stone Age archaeology of Botswana's Central Basin (see figure 2.1). The Kalahari Bushmen have been studied extensively in the past, usually by anthropologists con-

Figure 2.1. Botswana, Central District (study area shaded).

centrating on specific local groups; this has resulted in a number of seemingly conflicting statements concerning Bushman group structure and composition, subsistence, and mobility. Through a larger-scale, large-area survey, it was hoped that such differences in ethnographic reporting might be reconciled under a more general, if less specifically detailed, framework. This was also a rationale behind the study of Middle and Late Stone Age archaeological remains in the area: these sites represent a valuable addition to the hunter-gatherer data base which may have been deposited under conditions greatly different from those which beset hunter-gatherer groups today. Ethnoarchaeology was to serve as a link between the material records, past and present, and the general behavioral patterns which we hoped would connect the two.

Basarwa Ethnoarchaeology: Observations on the Nature of Toolkits and the Archaeological Record

The initial impetus to my own reconsideration of the form that ethnoarchaeological reasoning might best take was provided by observations of butchering of both wild and domestic animals by Central District Bushmen. The butchering of animals is an area well explored by archaeologists, and thus it was reasoned that the recording of such operations would allow the ready comparison between the Bushmen I was studying and other Bushmen, as well as more widely scattered hunter-gatherer groups.[1] During this period of the fieldwork, which can only be briefly outlined here, I also considered other types of information which might be gathered during butchering—one of which involved butchering tools, their use, and their discard.

Ethnographically documented toolkits and the remains found in the archaeological record are, of course, not the same thing. The metal knives and axes used by Botswana Bushmen today differ in many ways—for instance, their economic value, their effectiveness and longevity, and perhaps even the cultural or symbolic value placed upon them by their owners—from the stone implements of earlier hunter-gatherers in the same region. Nonetheless, certain aspects of their use and discard or loss must be the same. Contemplation of this idea provided an illustration of the most efficient use of ethnoarchaeology: as an idea-generating process. One interesting observation which I made early in my butchering documentation was that, at certain junctures, the butchers would set down one tool and pick up another, alternating primarily between the use of a knife (usually a folding pocketknife) and an ax. On a surprising number of occasions the disused implement was lost in the deep Kalahari sand; its owner would search long and hard for the missing tool, and several times never did recover it. Since everything found in the archaeological record is either discarded purposely or lost, it seemed that this type of behavior might be important to the understanding of past technological remains. Each juncture at which a Bushman misplaced an implement represented a point at which a tool could potentially be lost— and while lost metal pocketknives, purchased with rare currency at distant stores, were sought with great diligence, more easily reproducible stone tools may not have been.

Some 100 instances of butchering were observed with attention to the frequency with which knives and axes were set down and picked up, at which point in the butchering sequence these actions occurred, and the contexts in which tools were misplaced or lost. My hope was to arrive at a small number of generalizations about tool loss—and hence the frequency with which tools might enter the archaeological record. The results of these observations transcend the point which I would like to make in this paper, and will be discussed in later publications; what *is* important is that, when viewed in the specific context of my acquaintances and friends cutting up animals to be eaten at a curing dance, or to be taken to their mother-in-law, or to serve as the feast at the wedding of their daughter, "generalizations" were very difficult to arrive at. Variables in the number of times implements were placed on the ground (and either found or lost) included the intended dispensation of meat from the carcass, whether the butchering took place in camp or in the bush, how many people participated in the actual cutting, how many "helpers" (usually adolescent males) were present, how many tools were in the possession of the butchers, elapsed time of butchering, the size of the animal, and whether operations took place in light or darkness.

Clearly, many of the specific aspects of each situation were far more important than the "toolkit" present in determining the probability of tool loss and thus the potential appearance of the archaeological record. What is more, the great bulk of these specific circumstances probably cannot be determined from the archaeological

record, and this fact prevents any sort of simple formal translation between the present as observed by the ethnologist and the past as
revealed by discarded or lost remains. Attempts at direct formal comparison of the toolkits of living peoples and archaeological assemblages may be "dangerous" indeed.

Artifact Assemblages and the Concept of Types

Unfortunately, direct and simple formal translations are traditional in
archaeology, for they form the basis of much of the science today—
and archaeologists are particularly prone to attempts in such directions. Since its beginnings, the discipline has favored a methodology
which works from artifacts and their form to inferences based on
these observations; its starting point is the grouping of stone tools, assemblages and sites into types, much in the manner of biological
classification. Although it has been contended that American archaeologists of the 1950s and 1960s hotly debated—and resolved—the
question of the reality or arbitrariness of types (Ford 1954), there
never seems to have been any doubt that types existed, that the attributes on which they were founded were inherent in some way, and
that the divination of types was the road to archaeological success.
Whether one argues that culture is a device which categorizes human
experience, and that the archaeologist can only attempt to closely approximate original categories (Ford 1954), that "classes are characterized by one or more attributes which indicate a custom to which
the artisan conformed" (Rouse 1960:313), or that real types form the
basis of cultural behavior but can only be discovered by the use of
statistical techniques or factor analysis (Spaulding 1953; Glover
1969), the direction of reasoning is the same. The division of artifacts
into types begets information about past cultures.

This methodology, adhered to by almost all archaeologists confronted with stone tool assemblages, presents a set of problems that
has caused many to virtually abandon the analysis of stone artifacts in
favor of faunal remains, settlement patterns, and the like. If stone
tool analysis consists of classifying tools and assemblages into types,
followed by the examination of formal deviation from an average or
norm, then the results are preordained not only to "reveal" but to
define culture and what it does. The theoretical implications of such

an approach have been labeled "normative theory" (Binford 1965), and are based upon an ideational or psychological view of human behavior. All human actions and products are seen to be the results of ideas shared by members of a culture; discontinuities in archaeological data indicate deviations from the ideal norm and may be due to "drift" in time, the ineptitude of stoneworkers or the inappropriateness of their materials, separation in time or space, or the introduction of new ideas from other cultural sources. A systemic view of culture, culture viewed as man's "extrasomatic means of adaptation" (after White 1959), might be a more productive approach; and while there are few archaeologists today who would argue with this, there seem to be even fewer who have applied it in their work with stone tools. The author has found virtually no published examples of lithic analysis which do not proceed from artifact measurement and the scaling of measures against percentages of the total assemblage to the contemplation of why some of the tools differ from the averages, or why two assemblages are different in percentage composition.

There are other problems which prevent a direct and simple comparison between traditionally handled archaeological data and observations of Kalahari Bushmen. A purely methodological problem arising from a dependence on percentage composition of stone tool assemblages in the explanation of human behavior involves the "sampling paradox," the inability to know the degree to which any sample accurately represents the population from which it was drawn. If it is important to the archaeologist to know, say, the percentage of retouched blades from one site to the next, how can he be sure that his sample adequately informs him of the correct percentages of these tool types? The answer is simple: he cannot, for one can never be sure if he has a representative or total sample. An approach which is independent of reliance on the proportional composition of an assemblage would be free of such problems.

Finally, even short-term ethnographic observations seem to indicate that archaeologists have adopted a view of technological systems which is far too simple. Any assemblage consists of tools and materials left behind, discarded or lost, at a site by past people; if the tools were manufactured, used, and then discarded in a single place, then their composition might in fact reflect activities at that spot. This is apparently not the case with all human technological behavior, however; in some situations there is a payoff involved in manufacturing tools with certain activities in mind and carrying or curating these implements for use at other times and locations. The peculiarly human characteristic of being able to plan for future times and distant events may be responsible for much of the patterning seen in the archaeological record since the beginning of the Middle Stone Age. The implications of this may be seen in almost any ethnoarchaeological situation today. It was noted in Botswana that Bushmen almost universally carried knives, bows and arrows, and axes, but that these were almost never found in an "archaeological" context; a set of very similar observations was made by Binford (1976) during his work with Nunamiut Eskimos. Primitive technologists need not be the sole source of such ethnoarchaeological observations: a glance around a modern garage, kitchen or workshop will reveal that the most-used, most "important" or popular tool types may be the least frequently found in situations of loss and discard.

Human Mobility and the Measurement of Assemblage Characteristics

If these caveats are taken to heart, and if we agree that perhaps the comparison of percentages of artifact types is not a proper starting point in technological analysis, then what *is* the archaeologist to do with his stone tools? Some of the best ideas about productive directions in technological analysis, it may be argued, become obvious when one proceeds from the starting point of ethnoarchaeology. When the archaeologist makes choices about just what variables might be measurable in lithic assemblages on the basis of their comparability with variables also visible in the behavior of living hunter-gatherers, ethnoarchaeology becomes doubly productive.

A vivid example of this is provided by one of the areas of concentration of my archaeological and ethnographic fieldwork in the Kalahari: human mobility. "Mobility" is an increasingly popular and useful concept in anthropology, and figures in many current explanations of culture and population change, invention, and adaptation among both past and present groups. When ethnographic data are consulted, however, mobility appears to be a complicated concept, and difficult to define in operational terms. In moving around, people change their locations for different purposes, in differing group compositions, and for varying lengths of time. An attempt at defining some of the dimensions of this variation through the study of modern Bushman movements has revealed marked differences in seasonality, group composition, and task orientation across even our limited study area; these observations are presently being tabulated and mapped. A preliminary conclusion, however, is clear: most of the activities of Bushmen can be discussed in terms of the mobility contexts within which they occur. Mobility is a useful theoretical concept which can provide an ethnoarchaeological bridge between today's Bushman and the past inhabitants of the Kalahari.

How do various kinds of mobility relate to stone tool assemblages in an adaptive way, and what can stone tools tell the archaeologist (and the cultural anthropologist as well) about human mobility? The samples discussed here were collected in the course of a regional archaeological survey of the central sandveld and Makgadikgadi Pans area of Botswana; most of these occur in a surface context, and most are undatable except through formal comparison with sealed deposits occurring outside Botswana. These are problems that may be characteristic of the great majority of archaeological situations in the world, and it is not only desirable in the present case, but necessary on the whole, that means be developed to deal with such data. The Middle and Late Stone Age materials found in Botswana have been related to Umguzi or Rhodesian Magosian, Bambata or Rhodesian Stillbay (Cooke 1967), Stillbay (Cooke and Patterson 1960), and Wilton (Malan 1950) industries or "culture types." These analyses, however, reveal little about mobility in behavioral terms.

There is no obvious set of rules or principles by which to relate mobility to tools, and I will make use of a set of bridging assumptions for this purpose. These concepts are of the sort discussed elsewhere as "middle range theory" (Ebert, Hitchcock, and Taylor 1974); very simply, they deal with the dynamic implications of static differences in observable data. In this paper, only two of these assumptions will be discussed. These have been derived in the course of ethnological fieldwork, and can be seen to hold true for much human tool-using behavior not only by hunter-gatherers but in more complex societies as well. They are general principles of the use of implements by *Homo sapiens,* perhaps applicable in all places and at all times, and can be "tested" in an observational way in most homes and garages today.

1. Tools manufactured with the object of being carried about are expected to be smaller than tools intended to be used in one place.

2. Tools intended for multiple episodes of use are expected to be the result of a greater input of energy during manufacture and maintenance than tools used once and then discarded.

These assumptions deal with variations in measurable tool form as they relate to tool mobility, the tasks for which tools were intended, and the periodicity of tool use. They link cultural dynamics with the static archaeological record in an expectable way.

Concepts like these are easily related to the form of tools that comprise the Botswana archaeological assemblages, as well as the tools used by people there today. A simple tool size index is provided by the product of an artifact's length, width, and thickness—an index familiar from past lithic analyses. The difference is that here it has a stated and expectable relationship with higher theoretical principles. Similarly, an approximate index of energy expenditure can be compiled by counting the number of flake scars resulting from the removal of flakes during manufacture and maintenance of a tool. Thus any assemblage or group of tools can be represented in these two variable formal dimensions, in turn referable to middle range and ultimately cultural variables.

These measurements could, of course, be listed as percentages of each value apparent in each assemblage or site. This would mask the patterning inherent in the assemblage, however, and would tell us nothing. Instead, since the measures are taken to be in some way representative of a number of middle range variables that may well vary in independent ways, the distribution of measured variables within each group will be compared one with another. For the sake of simplicity, the present illustration of this process will be limited to the two variables listed above: implement size and energy expenditure invested in each tool. For clarity, the range of variation between these two measures will first be represented on a contingency table (figure 2.2). Some of the implications of tools falling within each of the numbered boxes are listed below.

Box 1. Curated, small, specific-use tools, possibly pieces of a mobile tool kit. Used in jobs or tasks in which a specific set of operations is carried out.

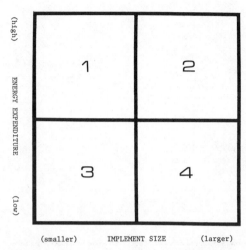

Figure 2.2. Four-box contingency table illustrating the relationship between theoretical linking arguments for points falling in different parts of size/energy graphs (see text for explanation).

Box 2. Specific-use or "specific job" tools probably not transported as far as those in Box 1, but curated. These might also be tools with high symbolic content.

Box 3. Expedient, single-use, immediately discarded tools; a situation of raw material stress may be indicated because of small size.

Box 4. Other things, such as number of working edges, being equal, these should be tools manufactured expediently, used only once, and not transported.

All of the above implications follow directly, in a more-or-less common-sense way, from the bridging assumptions. Any real assemblage can be plotted against the two axes, with the resulting point swarm falling into one or more of these boxes. In practice, using artifacts from the Botswana survey collections, tools found together usually occupy several of the boxes. Examples of two such plots of Botswana Middle Stone Age assemblages are presented in figures 2.3 and 2.4.

Upon contemplation of these distributions in the light of the previous contingency table, several general things become apparent. First, assemblages like those graphed here do not represent a single technological strategy, but are likely to be composed of tools repre-

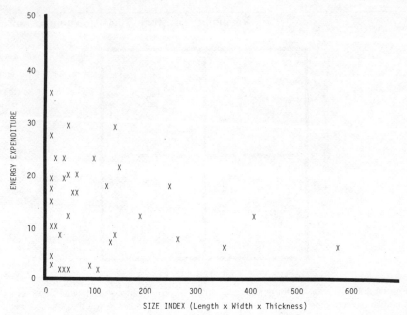

Figure 2.3. Plot of energy-expenditure index against size index for artifacts from Middle Stone Age site KP47, Lake X/au Area, Botswana.

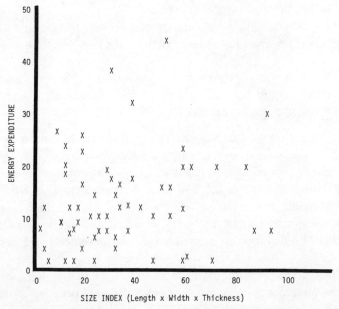

Figure 2.4. Plot of energy-expenditure index against size index for artifacts from Middle Stone Age site KP48, Lake X/au Area, Botswana.

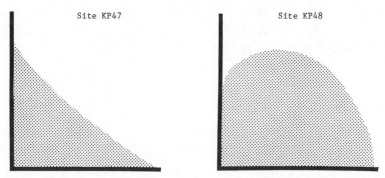

Figure 2.5. Shapes of limits of the point-swarms plotted on implement size/energy expenditure graphs for the two Botswana Middle Stone Age sites graphed in figures 2.3 and 2.4.

senting several strategies. These may have been deposited at one time by a single individual or group, or may be the result of several separate but indistinguishable episodes. The resolution of this problem depends upon a full examination of the fact that human mobility is not necessarily the same thing as tool mobility, and is beyond the scope of this paper. Secondly, this sort of approach to explaining stone tool variability does not depend upon a large sample of tools; the point scatter composed of only a few tools or conceivably only one tool has meaning in these terms.

In a more specific way, such scatter plots can serve as a means of comparing two or more archaeological assemblages and thus deriving ideas about possible differences between the behavior which caused their formation, ideas which can subsequently be tested deductively using other data. For instance, inspection of the point swarms and swarm-shape graphs presented in figure 2.5 suggests that, at site KP47, the largest energy expenditure is invested in small tools; this is not the case at site KP48 where "medium-sized" tools—those roughly at the center of the size range—are invested with the highest energy input. If one assumes that at least one reason for size variation in tools is mobility, and that smaller tools are more easily carried than larger ones, then it follows that, at KP47, greater energy is being invested in the most mobile tools; tasks for which high mobility is required must be predictable to a large degree, since tools with the highest energy input would probably be most highly curated and maintained. The pattern at KP48 is somewhat different, with energy being expended primarily in medium-sized and *not* the smallest implements. Perhaps the most mobile tasks for which tools were maintained at this site were not as predictable as tasks carried out in a more sedentary context.

Conclusion

The author has found the approach outlined here productive not only in explaining or reconstructing specific mobility types and tasks from collections of tools, but useful in an inferential way in deriving new ideas about additional middle range variables that might be explored and measurements that could be meaningful. Some of the issues presently being considered in the course of ongoing analysis of the Botswana materials are material type and quality, varying situations of manufacture and discard, the differences between single and multicomponent assemblages, and the appearance of different tool-carrying strategies such as carrying "blanks" versus cores for future fabrication into tools. It is also interesting to ponder whether the sort of analysis presented here might help determine just what some other archaeologists were measuring when they divided southern African tool assemblages into types.

In concluding, it must be emphasized that the formulations presented here are largely intuitive, and that they will require rigorous testing before they in any sense constitute laws or rules of interpretation. These analyses are presently being related to information derived from a study of present and past site placement, ecological and climatological relationships in the sandveld and Lake Makgadikgadi areas of Botswana in an attempt at such testing.

Although the linking assumptions and specific conclusions presented here must for these reasons be taken as inconclusive at present, there are a number of methodological conclusions that can be drawn from their application. First, an approach to the explanation of variability in stone tool assemblages such as that discussed here relieves the archaeologist of some of the sample-size and accuracy problems that plague the application of normative approaches; small, sporadically occupied sites can be comprehended in this way just as readily as sealed stratified deposits. Second, artifact-oriented analyses aimed at the definition of modal types, whether these be artifact classes, structural poses, or "cultures," have little to offer the anthropological archaeologist. Finally, and perhaps most importantly, the above exercise suggests that ethnoarchaeology, approached with the proper theoretical orientations and goals, holds ever-increasing promise for linking our understanding of past peoples with those of the present in a general and useful way.

Notes

1. Details of Basarwa butchering practices, and other aspects of the 1975–76 research which are not discussed here, will be treated in future publications.

References Cited

Binford, Lewis R.
   1965. "Archaeological Systematics and the Study of Culture Processes." *American Antiquity* 31:203–10.
   1976. "Forty-Seven Trips: A Case Study in the Character of Some Formation Processes of the Archaeological Record." In Edwin S. Hall, Jr., ed., *Contributions To Anthropology: The Interior Peoples of Northern Alaska,* pp. 299–351. National Museum of Man Mercury Series. Archaeological Survey of Canada, Paper 49. Ottawa: National Museums of Canada.
Chang, K. C.
   1967. *Rethinking Archaeology.* Random House Studies in Anthropology. New York: Random House.
Cooke, C. K.
   1967. "A Preliminary Report on the Stone Age of the Nata River, Botswana." *Arnoldia* (Rhodesia) 2(40):1–10.
Cooke, C. K. and Mary L. Patterson
   1960. "Stone Age Sites: Lake Dow Area." *South African Archaeological Bulletin* 15(59):119–22.
David, Nicholas
   1971. "The Fulani Compound and the Archaeologist." *World Archaeology* 3:111–31.
Ebert, James I., Robert K. Hitchcock, and Richard L. Taylor
   1974. "Middle Range Theory in Archaeology." Paper presented at the 39th Annual Meeting of the Society for American Archaeology, Washington, D.C.
Ford, J. A.
   1954. "On the Concept of Types: The Type Revisited." *American Anthropologist* 56:42–57.
Glover, I. C.
   1969. "The Use of Factor Analysis for the Discovery of Artifact Types." *Mankind* 7:36–51.

Gould, Richard A.
    1971. "The Archaeologist as Ethnographer: A Case from the Western Desert of Australia." *World Archaeology* 3:143–77.
    1973. "Australian Archaeology in Ecological and Ethnographic Perspective," Warner Modular Publications. Module 7, pp. 1–33. Andover, Mass.
Griffin, P. Bion
    n.d. "Ethnoarchaeology of the Eubid Agta Hunters, Northern Luzon, Philippines." Research Proposal submitted to the National Science Foundation. Honolulu: University of Hawaii, Department of Anthropology.
Johnson, LeRoy, Jr.
    1972. "Problems in 'Avant-garde' Archaeology." *American Anthropologist* 74:366–77.
Malan, F.
    1950. "A Wilton Site at Kai Kai, Bechuanaland Protectorate." *South African Archaeological Bulletin* 5(20):140–42.
Reid, J. Jefferson, Michael B. Schiffer, and William L. Rathje
    1975. "Behavioral Archaeology: Four Strategies." *American Anthropologist* 77:864–69.
Rouse, Irving
    1960. "The Classification of Artifacts in Archaeology." *American Antiquity* 25(3):315–22.
Spaulding, Albert C.
    1953. "Statistical Techniques for the Discovery of Artifact Types." *American Antiquity* 18(4):305–13.
White, J. Peter
    1967. "Ethno-archaeology in New Guinea: Two Examples." *Mankind* 6:409–14.
White, J. Peter and David H. Thomas
    1972. "What Mean These Stones? Ethno-Taxonomic Models and Archaeological Interpretations in the New Guinea Highlands." In David L. Clarke, ed., *Models in Archaeology*, pp. 275–308. London: Methuen.
White, Leslie A.
    1959. *The Evolution of Culture*. New York: McGraw-Hill.
Yellen, John E.
    1974. "The !Kung Settlement Pattern: An Archaeological Perspective." Ph.D. dissertation, Harvard University.

3/The Cognitive Basis of Productivity in a Decorative Art Style: Implications of an Ethnographic Study for Archaeologists' Taxonomies

Margaret Ann Hardin
Department of Anthropology
University of Maine, Orono

Hardin's article describes the major axes of variability in ceramics produced in a contemporary Tarascan community in Mexico, providing data which may be compared with those for Shipibo-Conibo ceramics discussed below by DeBoer and Lathrap. Focusing both on vessels' functions and on decision-making during the manufacturing process, Hardin outlines the major features of the craftsmen's taxonomy, whose categories involve such attributes as vessel shape, size, and surface decoration. The discussion points up significant differences between natives' and archaeologists' approaches to classification, and may be used to develop and refine archaeological approaches to the interpretation of microstylistic variability in ceramics (and perhaps in other artifact classes). While not explicitly addressing the widely discussed question of the feasibility of inferring aspects of social organization from archaeological ceramics,

Presented at the annual meeting of the American Anthropological Association, Washington, D.C. (November 19, 1976), in the symposium "Ethnoarchaeology: Implications of Ethnography for Archaeology." This paper is based on ethnographic fieldwork begun in 1966 under a National Institute of General Medical Science Research Training Grant (National Institute of Mental Health) and continued in 1967 with the support of a Public Health Service Predoctoral Fellowship (5F1-MH-32, 844-02). The vessels illustrated are from a collection of San José pottery made by the author for the Field Museum of Natural History; further study of these materials was supported by a Wenner-Gren museum research fellowship. I would like to thank Susan Hopkins for her drawings and John Alderson for his photographs. Michael Silverstein, Robert Fry, Brian Hesse, and Robson Bonnichsen provided helpful discussion of the problems that arose in the writing of this paper.

Hardin provides valuable empirical data pertaining to the cognitive bases of stylistic variability that indirectly bear on this and related issues.

Speculation about the relationship between the typologies of artifacts created by archaeologists and the cognitive structures [1] that were employed by the artisans who made them is a longstanding theme in the literature of anthropological archaeology (Brew 1946; Spauding 1953; Ford 1954; Rouse 1960; Hill and Evans 1972). A more recent phrasing of the problem compares the formal structure of a traditional archaeological pottery typology with that of a variety of folk taxonomies (Whallon 1972). It suggests that the utility of traditional archaeological types is related to their formal correspondence to ethnographically known taxonomic structures. A sharply contrasting view argues against both the feasibility and utility of discovering in significant detail the cognitive structures underlying the patterning observed in prehistoric artifacts (Eggert 1977).

Questions about the cognitive reality of artifact typology are more appropriately investigated in an ethnographic context, where the full range of native classifications associated with an ongoing tradition of material culture may be examined. Unfortunately the growing field of ethnoarchaeology has shown relatively little interest in the nature of the folk classifications that are associated with material culture. Further, archaeologists working ethnographically have focused their attention on one level of the craftsman's competence. Most ethnoarchaeologists have limited their investigations to problems involving the classification of completed artifacts. The most explicit work has dealt with stone tools, where the focus has been on the relationship between named tool categories and their distinctive attributes (Gould 1971; White and Thomas 1972) and on the correspondence between named categories and artisans' classification behavior (White, Modjeska, and Hipuyu, n.d.). In contrast, the folk classifications associated with traditional ceramics have been little treated by ethnoarchaeologists. Linguistic terms and vessel categories are perfunctorily listed (Pastron 1974) or the kinds of attributes important to the native taxonomy are mentioned in passing (Stanislawski 1974).

Surprisingly little attention has been devoted to the level of the craftsman's competence directly reflected in the form of the completed artifact. Ethnoarchaeologists have not studied how traditional artisans organize their specialized knowledge of their craft. Moreover, the related question of how they use the information codified to produce artifacts remains largely unexplored. A salient exception is Arnold's study of the composition of Maya pastes (1971). An experimental approach is particularly appropriate for the investigation of the cognitive systems underlying artifact production (Bonnichsen and Young n.d.; Young and Bonnichsen n.d.) and provides a valuable supplement to studies conducted in less controlled ethnographic contexts. The relationship between craftsmen's specialized knowledge and their classifications of finished products remains an open question, which requires investigation in an ethnographic context.

This paper seeks to remedy the narrowness of focus that has characterized the ethnoarchaeology of craftsmen's taxonomies. It examines the range of cognitive structures associated with an ongoing pottery making tradition. Both levels of the craftsmen's competence previously distinguished are treated. The account first outlines classificatory schemes associated with the more general level of the craftsman's competence. These schemes provide the categories normally used by potters in identifying and distinguishing between vessels. The paper then discusses the relatively neglected question of how information is classified for use in the manufacturing process. Pottery painting provides an example of this more detailed level of the craftsman's competence. The analysis deals with the ways in which painters working within a traditional decorative style organize design information and then employ these classifications during the painting process. After each level of the potters' competence has been described, the possibility that an archaeologist, given a sufficient range of evidence, might infer the same underlying organization of information, is then assessed. These discussions are offered as general ethnographic analogies in the hope that they will contribute to the effectiveness of archaeologists' studies of patterned variation in material culture and decorative style.[2]

Ethnographic Context

This analysis is based upon field work conducted from November of 1966 through December of 1967 in the small village of San José, located in the state of Michoacán in Mexico. San José's total population was about three hundred people, most of whom were bilingual, speaking both Tarascan and Spanish. The village consisted of about forty households; the majority of these engaged in pottery making. The income from pottery manufacture supplemented that from agriculture. Households varied greatly in the extent to which they engaged in and were economically dependent upon pottery production.

Pottery manufacture in San José was a cottage industry. The craftsmen did not produce pottery simply for their own use but for a number of villages within the area. The well-developed system of craft specialization and local markets that operated in the Tarascan region provided for the distribution of San José's distinctive ceramic products. The extent of craft specialization in the area may be judged from the fact that San José potters did not manufacture all of the vessels that they used in their own homes. They routinely purchased certain kinds of vessels from other pottery manufacturing communities.

The organization of San José pottery manufacture was relatively flexible. Normally, a man and his wife shared in the work, and although each work group might develop its own pattern for pottery production, specific pottery making tasks were not rigidly assigned to men or women. While both men and women painted pottery, not all potters were able to master this aspect of the craft. Pottery painting was considered to be a specialist's domain.

Vessel Classification: Named Categories and Distinctive Attributes

San José potters used terms that indicated ware, shape and size to classify completed vessels. The categories marked by these terms were relatively simple. They reflected only a small portion of potters' knowledge of their craft. These terms occurred frequently in conversations about pottery making. Typical uses of these vessel categories included identifying the characteristic products of a household, stating kiln capacity, and planning pottery production. More systematic information about the application of these terms was obtained from a house-to-house census of pottery making units, their resources, and products. In this context, potters responded by listing vessel types and giving the number of each kind that would be included in a typical kiln load. Frequently several listings were given in order to show how differences in ware, form, and size affected the number of vessels that would fit into a particular kiln.

Three major ware categories were distinguished by San José potters (figure 3.1). The terms used reflected the color of the vessel's most salient surface. Ware category was determined by the color of the glaze or clay seen on the insides of shallow vessel forms and on the outsides of enclosed vessel forms. Each ware was associated with a distinctive function. Ware categories varied in the complexity of their internal variation.

The most common kind of pottery made in the village was the plain red utility ware. These vessels were glazed with a clear glaze although small amounts of green glaze might be used to accent their rims. The name of the ware reflected the red color of the clay itself. When vessels of this ware were intended for their primary function, cooking, they were not glazed on the outside (figure 3.1, left). The dribbles of glaze seen on the redware vessel's outside were not deliberate, nor were they considered to flaw this practical everyday ware. The second ware was the rarely produced blackware. San José potters reserved this glaze for ritual objects, such as the incense burner seen in the center of figure 3.1. Greenware, the third major type, was a decorative ware (figure 3.1, right, and figure 3.2). Potters identified it as the distinctive product of the village.

Greenware displayed the most complex internal organization of the three ware categories. A wide variety of decorative techniques were used. The smooth greenware (figure 3.1, right) was of particular interest because its decorations reflect a productive art style. Intricate designs were painted with white slip on the most visible surfaces of these vessels. The decorated surfaces were then covered with the green glaze for which the ware was named. Other surfaces were treated less elaborately; for example, the inside of the green pitcher was covered with clear glaze (figure 3.1, right). Alternatively, greenware was decorated with textures; in these cases the entire decorative field was uniformly covered with white paint in order to bring out the green color of the glaze. Textures were of essentially two kinds. Some textures were produced by special vessel molds, which have designs cut into their working surfaces, as may be seen on the body of the left vessel in figure 3.2. Other textures were modeled and at-

Figure 3.1. Major San José ware categories. *Left*, redware. *Middle*, blackware. *Right*, greenware of the smooth, painted subcategory.

Figure 3.2. Textured subcategories of San José greenware. *Left*, textures produced by vessel mold. *Right*, hand-modeled texture.

tached by hand, as in the case of the spines seen on the right vessel in figure 3.2. Separate molded decorations, like the leaves seen on the lids of both vessels in figure 3.2, occurred on both kinds of textured greenware as well as on painted greenware.

Potters named seven traditional vessel forms which were widely produced in San José. As may be seen in figure 3.3, the basic vessel form was determined by the mold. While rims, ring bases, handles, and feet were formed from separate pieces of clay, these added portions did not substantially alter the molded form. In these seven cases, the terms used for the finished vessels and the molds that produced them coincided. In contrast, separate shape terms identified the more complex non-utilitarian vessel forms. Both simple molded forms and hand molded constituents were used to construct these composite vessels. For example, the incense burner seen in the center of figure 3.1 was based on a small casserole mold. Its lacy rim was constructed from hand molded coils, while its base was made in a more specialized mold. In addition, San José potters recognized and named the range of vessel forms that some of them manufactured for a wider market, even though these nontraditional forms were not used in the village.

While terms of form appeared to be based on function, they were actually shape terms. A given form, produced in appropriate size and ware, might be typically and normally used for the function indicated by its name. The same form could also be made in another size and ware and have an entirely different use. For example, the vessel shown in figure 3.4 was called a *comal*. Large redware vessels of this form were used to cook tortillas; however, the primary use of this somewhat smaller, elaborately painted, green glazed *comal* was decorative. Typically, vessels of this kind were placed conspicuously on kitchen shelves. They were reserved for serving special occasion foods and might be used to carry these foods to another household.

San José vessels were classified with respect to size as well as form. With the exception of cups and bowls, the seven traditional form classes were crosscut by size categories. In two cases, those of the *olla* and the casserole, the result was a series of form-size names. Although similar in its structure, the San José system was less elaborate than those described in detail for other villages in the Tarascan region (Foster 1948; Posas 1949). While there was obviously some variation from mold to mold, as well as from household to house-

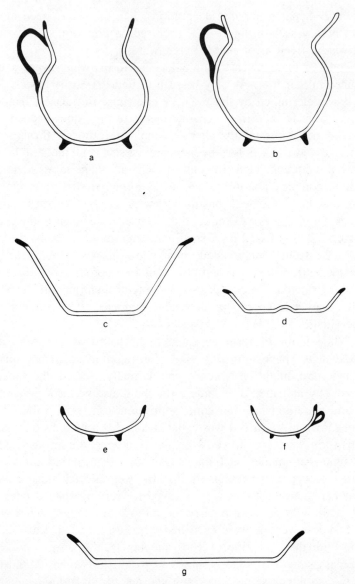

Figure 3.3. Simple vessel forms widely distributed in San José: (a) *olla;* (b) pitcher; (c) casserole; (d) *jicara;* (e) bowl; (f) cup; (g) *comal.*

Figure 3.4. Painted greenware *comal*.

hold, potters quite correctly considered these categories to be standardized; that is, the named size-form categories indicated specific volumes.

Implications of Potters' Vessel Classifications for Archaeologists

It seems plausible that an archaeological analysis of a representative range of San José ceramics would yield a scheme of vessel classification that approximated the three ware categories used by painters. Both extensive excavation and a large sample of the ceramic inventory would be essential. Because the black pottery was manufactured in small quantities and occurred in a relatively narrow, function-specific context, this major named ware category might go unnoticed in a small archaeological sample.

A tentative classification of vessels by glaze color would be supported by associated attributes. Black glaze would occur on a small number of complex vessel forms. Neither white paint nor surface textures would occur on vessels with this glaze. Further, green glaze would be associated with two ways of producing elaborate embellishments of the vessels' most salient surfaces. Finally, the most salient surface of the red utility ware vessels would be typically unglazed. Because most redware vessels were used directly on the fire, glaze was used only on their insides. The obvious covariation of stylistic attributes in San José ceramics suggests a sorting of vessels that parallels the native classification into wares. While the archaeologist would not be able to demonstrate that potters phrased this classification in terms of color alone, this would not diminish the cognitive validity of the classification itself or its analytical value.

The crosscutting categories of vessel form and size associated with redware and greenware would be easily isolated. In both wares the range of vessels produced displays obvious discontinuities along these dimensions. Because it is volume that is standardized, measurements of vessel capacity would yield the most clear cut patterning. Whether the archaeologist working with these ceramics would be likely to investigate the possibility of standardization remains an open question. Two lines of evidence lead in this direction. First, San José pottery manufacture is a specialized peasant craft. Because its products are intended for a wider regional market, they can be expected to display standard forms and sizes, which have standard values. Second, the fact that San José vessels are mold-produced facilitates standardization. Because the same molds remain in use over long periods of time, gradual shifts in vessel form and size cannot occur with the same ease as they might in other technologies. Recognition of the implications of the technology as well as the economic context in which it is employed could play a useful role in the development of schemes of vessel classification.

Specialists' Knowledge: How Painters Talk about Design

San José potters organized their knowledge of pottery making in terms of a number of distinct cognitive structures. Classifications associated with this specialists' knowledge codified information needed for vessel production. Terminology used in technical discussions of the craft also reflected this level of the potters' competence. While specialists' knowledge provided the basis for vessel classification, these two levels of the craftsmen's competence were distinct.

Painters' knowledge of design provides an example. Painted design played a minor role in the classification of San José ceramics into wares. The simple presence or absence of painted decoration was one of the defining characteristics of the smooth subcategory of green-glazed ware. While the designs themselves were intricately painted, the patterned variation they exhibited played no role in the usual classifications of completed vessels.

Pottery painters shared a number of often repeated and partially standard ways of talking about pottery design. The view of the cognitive basis of painted design presented in this paper was derived from the analysis of their verbalizations about graphic style and painting process. These statements were particularly rich in information because the Tarascan language has a number of grammatical features that facilitate the description of form and spatial relations. It was painters, rather than consumers or other potters, who most freely offered information about this aspect of the craft. They were the best able to discuss the system within which they worked.

Painters readily provided information about the designs painted on completed vessels. While responses to painted decoration were easily elicited, they also occurred normally in technical discussions. Three kinds of information were given about single vessels. These were a vessel encoding sequence, a vessel decoding sequence, and an aesthetic evaluation of the vessel.

The vessel encoding sequence summarized the order of operations that should have produced the painted designs on the completed vessel (figure 3.5). The ideal sequence began with the subdivision of the decorative field with pairs of lines (figure 3.5a–d). It described in turn the placing of configurations in each area (figure 3.5e–h) and ended with the outlining of the mouth and handle with thick bands of paint (figure 3.5i,j). Encoding sequences emphasized the order in which operations were performed, the locations of painted elements, and painting actions. The configuration actually painted in a particular area was of secondary importance.

A vessel decoding sequence consisted of a list of the designs painted on the vessel (figure 3.6). The order of the decoding sequence, from top to bottom, was arbitrary. It bore no relation to the encoding sequence for the same vessel (figure 3.5). Only design configurations, the complex arrangements of elements placed within each bounded area, were mentioned. Boundary marking elements were ig-

Figure 3.5. Vessel encoding sequence, showing the order in which painted arrangements would be discussed.

Figure 3.6. Vessel decoding sequence, showing the order in which design configurations would be described.

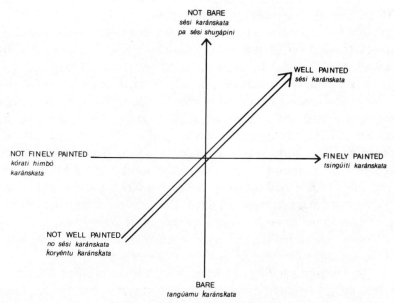

Figure 3.7. Aesthetic framework showing one general dimension (well painted/not well painted) and two specific dimensions (finely painted/not finely painted; bare/not bare).

nored. Aesthetic evaluations of vessels were phrased in terms of a small set of terms and set phrases that had specific meanings in the painting context. As may be seen in figure 3.7, these terms and phrases marked one general dimension (well painted/not well painted) and two specific dimensions (finely painted/not finely painted, bare/not bare). Figure 3.8 shows how painters varied in the extent to which they met these aesthetic criteria. The vessels shown on the left and in the middle are by a painter who was considered to paint very well. The vessel on the left provides an example of her best work. Sometimes portions of her vessels are left too bare of design; for example, on the shoulder of the middle vessel coveredness was sacrificed for fineness. In contrast, the painter whose work is shown on the right in figure 3.8 produced less well painted vessels that sacrificed fineness for coveredness.

Analysis of the internal organization of painters' responses to whole vessels suggested further avenues for investigating painters' organization of information about design. Figure 3.9 summarizes the process of inquiry, which has been treated in detail elsewhere (Hardin 1977a). Five more structured questioning strategies were developed.

Three strategies employed formal questionnaires, which required painters to respond to selected sets of vessels. The three questionnaires focused on design names, aesthetic rankings, and the classification of painted decoration. Triad tests, which required that painters group two of three similarly painted vessels, provided a vehicle for investigating design classification. The fourth strategy required painters to indicate on a blank vessel the location of the named subdivisions of the vessels's surface. The fifth body of evidence was provided by one very talented young person who painted sets of designs out of context, using the white slip on black paper. The value of the triad tests and the design sets was enhanced by the commentary that accompanied them. Painters' three responses to single vessels together with information gained from the five questioning strategies constituted the verbal evidence for the following statements about the cognitive basis of painters' competence.

In San José painting, the basic procedure for creating decoration rested upon two interrelated but distinct systems. The first of these systems was analytic. It divided the surface of the vessel to be dec-

Figure 3.8. Vessels illustrating aesthetic criteria, showing from left to right: a well-painted vessel, a vessel which is not sufficiently covered, a vessel which is not finely painted.

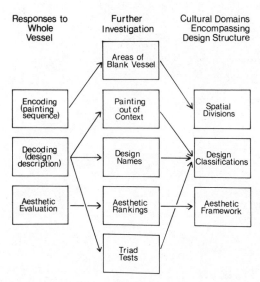

Figure 3.9. The relationship between painters' verbalizations about design and the underlying design structure.

orated into a set of spatial divisions, some of which might be further subdivided. The basis of the analytic system lay in the divisions of the unpainted vessel surface (figure 3.10a–j). The greatly elaborated patterning of painted boundaries suggested that a more complex hierarchical organization was imposed upon the subdivisions of the vessel's surface during the painting process (figure 3.10k–s). The second system was synthetic. It provided for the construction of an array of designs from smaller elements. Designs produced by the synthetic system were painted within the spatial divisions defined by the analytic system.

Designs painted out of context provided important insights into the organization of the synthetic component (figures 3.11–3.13). First, painters organized information about design in terms of configurations, which were arrangements of sufficient complexity to fill a spatial division. This was indicated in the design sets by the pairs of lines, which, like those that mark boundaries on vessels, were used to separate configurations. Painters were quite capable of analyzing configurations into their constituents; for example, the two outline elements that appear in the lower left of figure 3.13 were painted in response to an inquiry about the difference between the "tower" con-

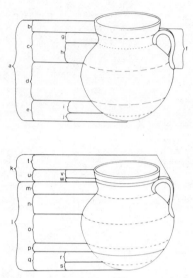

Figure 3.10. Comparison of the named divisions of the unpainted vessel and the divisions imposed by painted boundaries: *a–j*, named vessel parts showing boundaries of divisions (——) and subdivisions (—————); *l–t*, spatial divisions defined by required (——) and optional (–·–·–·) painted boundaries.

figuration (figure 3.12) and the "mountain" configuration (figure 3.13). Second, painters placed these configurations in paradigmatic sets; that is, configuration classes were internally organized into categories defined by the intersection of crosscutting dimensions. All of the members of a class were constructed around the same arrangement of basic elements. The five design sets shown in figures 3.11–3.13 represented such classes. It should be understood that the painter's intent was not to reproduce each member of a particular class but to show the ethnographer what constituted a class and to specify the dimensions along which its members might vary. Painters' classification of configurations is quite shallow; that is, there was no explicitly stated higher level taxonomy of paradigmatic sets.

Painters also called upon the aesthetic framework (figure 3.7) while painting vessels. It provided ways of making decisions about graphic style not sufficiently covered by other aspects of design structure. In a sense, aesthetic values provided criteria for judging both the cognitive and technical skill with which a painter decorated a particular vessel.

Figure 3.11. Design sets called "eyes" (*left*) and "little shells" (*right*).

Figure 3.12. Design set called "towers."

Figure 3.13. Design sets called "mountains" (*left*) and "hooks" (*right*).

The Painting Process: How Painters Apply Their Knowledge of Design

Painters did not set out to paint a vessel with an image of its completed decoration clearly in mind. Rather, each decoration was the result of a problem-solving process that continued throughout the painting sequence. Both artists' verbalizations and their painting behavior showed that they approach the painting of a vessel as a series of increasingly refined problems. This process is summarized in figure 3.14.

The decorative field defined on the blank vessel constituted the initial problem, which the painter further refined by marking the required horizontal subdivisions. These in turn pose a series of separate problems. This interpretation was supported not only by the separation of design and space in the standard verbalizations about painting and by painters' ability to produce designs out of context but also by painting procedure itself. The sequence of production was frequently broken at this point. Further, this was the only point at which it was permissible for one painter to take up another's work and finish it. For example, both of the vessels shown in figure 3.15 were begun by the painter who completed the vessel on the right. The

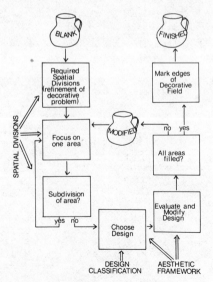

Figure 3.14. Diagram showing how the painting strategy used for a particular vessel is produced and how painters use their knowledge of design during this process.

vessel on the left was finished by her husband, who paints with a somewhat heavier hand; thus, the lines used in crosshatching are heavier than the paired lines used for the horizontal boundary markers, which is the opposite of the normal pattern. In considering each marked area, the painter had two options. The area might be further subdivided or it might be filled with a design.

Two kinds of information went into the selection of an appropriate design. The painter called upon an array of configurations, arranged in a long series of paradigmatic sets. Aesthetic values provided additional criteria for deciding what configurations were appropriate for a particular area. These decisions seemed to occur in two ways. First, a painter might consider a design before it was painted and accept it or reject it on the basis of its imagined aesthetic effect. Second, a painter might modify an already painted design to correct aesthetic deficiencies. For example, the top portion of the flower on the vessel in figure 3.16 was added so that the area would not be left bare of design. At times designs were deliberately varied to test alternative solutions. Both the central band and the lower shoulder band of the vessel seen in figure 3.17 provide ex-

Figure 3.15. Two vessels showing the effect of multiple authorship. The vessel on the left was begun by the author of the vessel on the right but finished by her husband. Consequently, on the left vessel, the paired horizontal boundary markers are too fine for the rest of the design.

Figure 3.16. Vessel showing modification of flower design to satisfy aesthetic criterion of not leaving spatial division too bare.

Figure 3.17. Vessel showing experimental variation of designs on lower shoulder and in central band.

amples of this practice. Fortunately, although it was technically possible to "erase" painted designs by scraping off the white paint with a sharp knife, even the most proficient of San José painters did not bother.

Implications of the Organization of Specialists' Knowledge for Archaeologists' Classifications

The probability that an archaeologist working with a sufficiently large sample of painted pottery from San José would achieve some understanding of the cognitive basis of productivity and variability in painted decoration would depend upon the assumptions with which his study was begun. Phrasing the problem in terms of defining types of painted vessel decoration that approximated the painter's own would involve the archaeologist in a tangential and artificial exercise. San José painters have no comprehensive classification of design configurations. Similarly, within the category of smooth painted greenware, vessels are not classified by their painted decorations.

The limits placed on classification by design are best demonstrated by painters' responses to triad tests. Vessels were considered members of the same class when the designs painted in their central bands, the most salient subdivision of the decorative field, came from the same paradigmatic class. In the first triad (figure 3.18), painters grouped the left and middle vessels but considered the right vessel to belong to a different class. Other attributes of the painted design, such as the patterning of spatial divisions on the vessel, did not override this principle of classification; thus, in the second triad (figure 3.19), the left and middle vessels were placed in one class while the right vessel was excluded. When a triad did not contain two vessels which satisfied this narrow criterion of similarity, painters simply refused to respond to the question, as in the case of the third triad (figure 3.20). Decisions were not made on the basis of higher level criteria such as the organization of space or broader categories of design configurations based on shared elements or patterns of symmetry.

The assumption that painters codify their specialized knowledge of their craft in a set of painted vessel types could prove detrimental to archaeologists' attempts to produce useful classifications of pottery

Figure 3.18. First triad test. The left and middle vessels were grouped together while the right vessel was placed in another class.

Figure 3.19. Second triad test. The left and middle vessels were grouped together despite the pattern of spatial division shared by the left and right vessels.

Figure 3.20. Third triad test. Painters would not place any pair of these vessels together on the basis of their painted designs.

design. The structured sets of information painters used involved a number of independent and fine-grained distinctions. The reflections of all of these could be seen in the patterns of variability exhibited in the work of different painters. Some of these resulted in differences of kind, such as design content, while others resulted in variation along a continuous dimension, such as distance between lines in crosshatching. The two specific dimensions of aesthetic evaluation provided a particularly instructive example of the latter pattern. Because these aesthetic values provided continuous dimensions (finely painted/not finely painted, bare/not bare) along which a painter might succeed to varying degrees, differences in their application were best compared by providing a metric measure. For example, while the two painters whose work is shown in figure 3.8 shared the same aesthetic framework, they placed different emphases on the two specific dimensions. Sets of vessels produced by the two painters were readily compared by scoring each vessel on a scale of zero to one along each specific dimension and graphing the results. The vessel scores graphed in figure 3.21 were obtained by scoring each spatial division as either meeting (a score of one) or failing (a score of zero) the criteria of fineness and coveredness. The vessel's scores were then computed by averaging the scores from its various spatial divisions. While the comparison graphed in figure 3.21 represented the direct application of the aesthetic values, similar results would be obtained from measures of vessel decoration itself (for example, percentage of area covered with design for bareness and line width for fineness).

The lesson to be learned is that the obvious clustering of two sets of vessels, rather different in appearance from each other, might be erroneously taken as evidence for subtypes of painted vessels (figure 3.21). The pattern is, however, epiphenomenal. It does not represent painters' shared classifications of vessels on the basis of their decorations, but rather the conjunction of two painters' different ranking of the same aesthetic values with other features of their individual painting styles.

Summary and Conclusions

In summary it is suggested that in studying the cognitive basis of form in decorated ceramics it is useful to distinguish two levels of

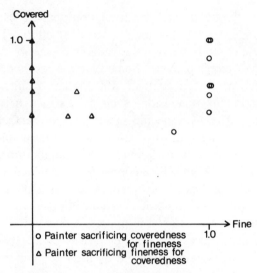

Figure 3.21. Graphic comparison of the work of two painters in terms of scores derived from the two specific dimensions of aesthetic evaluation.

craftsmen's competence. At the more general level, potters use rather simple and easily understood classifications to categorize whole vessels according to ware, shape and size. Painted design provided an example of the level of specialists' knowledge. Painters used structurally distinct kinds of classifications, having various formal shapes during the vessel painting process. They did not classify vessels in terms of the resultant painted designs. The painting of a vessel was treated as an ongoing problem-solving process. If San José painters did have mental images of the vessels they painted, these were not fully formed until the decoration itself was completed.

The Tarascan case has several implications for the study of variation within a single stylistic system, such as might be associated with a community or several related communities. On the one hand, notions of vessel decoration type are not appropriate. It would not be useful to develop a comprehensive set of taxonomically or paradigmatically organized categories in an attempt to approximate artisans' knowledge of design. On the other hand, the archaeologist working with variation within a stylistic system may choose attributes that measure substylistic differences in a number of ways that reflect the cognitive basis of design. It is hoped that the account presented will suggest refinements in this selection strategy. The examples given show that the patterns of variation exhibited by Tarascan painted designs reflect both the organization of specialists' knowledge of design and the patterning of interaction between artisans. Effective interpretation of this structure of variation requires a detailed knowledge of the painters' organization of information about design.

Notes

1. The term cognitive structure, as it is used in this paper, refers both to artisans' conceptual units or categories whether or not these are explicitly marked by a particular word or phrase, and to the ways in which artisans related these units to each other by organizing them in terms of larger classifications.

2. This more specific level of the craftsman's competence, and in particular that aspect that deals with painted description, also has implications for the uses to which archaeologists put their taxonomies in reconstructing social structure (Hill 1970; Longacre 1970; Whallon 1968). From an ethnographic point of view the problems involved are complex and would involve a lengthy digression from the central theme of this paper. For these reasons the interested reader is referred to earlier work of the author (1970, 1977a, 1977b).

References Cited

Arnold, Dean
  1971. "Ethnomineralogy of Ticul, Yucatan Potters: Etics and Emics." *American Antiquity* 36:20–40.
Bonnichsen, Robson and David E. Young
  n.d. "Cognitive Archaeology." Manuscript.
Brew, John O.
  1946. "The Use and Abuse of Taxonomy." In *The Archaeology of Alkalai Ridge, Southeastern Utah,* pp. 44–66. Papers of the Peabody Museum of American Archaeology and Ethnology, Harvard University, no. 21. Cambridge: Harvard University Press.
Eggert, Manfred K.H.
  1977. "Prehistoric Archaeology and the Problem of Ethno-Cognition." *Anthropos* 72:242–55.
Ford, James A.
  1954. "The Type Concept Revisited." *American Antiquity* 56:42–63.
Foster, George M., assisted by Gabriel Ospina
  1948. *Empire's Children: The People of Tzintzuntzan.* Smithsonian Institution, Institute of Social Anthropology Publication No. 6. Mexico, D.F.: Imprenta Nuevo Mundo.

Gould, Richard A.
1971. "The Archaeologist as Ethnographer: A Case From the Western Desert of Australia." *World Archaeology* 3:143–77.

Hardin (Friedrich), Margaret Ann
1970. "Design Structure and Social Interaction: Archaeological Implications of an Ethnographic Analysis." *American Antiquity* 35:332–43.
1977a. "Structure and Creativity: Family Style in Tarascan Greenware Painting." Ph.D. dissertation, University of Chicago.
1977b. "Individual Style in San José Pottery Painting: The Role of Deliberate Choice." In James N. Hill and Joel Gunn, eds., *The Individual in Prehistory: Studies of Variability in Style in Prehistoric Technology*, pp. 109–36. New York: Academic Press.

Hill, James N.
1970. *Broken K Pueblo: Prehistoric Social Organization in the American Southwest*. Anthropological Papers of the University of Arizona, no. 17. Tucson: University of Arizona Press.

Hill, James N. and Robert K. Evans
1972. "A Model for Classification and Typology." In David L. Clarke, ed., *Models in Archaeology*, pp. 231–73. London: Methuen.

Longacre, William A.
1970. *Archaeology as Anthropology: A Case Study*. Anthropological Papers of the University of Arizona, no. 18. Tucson: University of Arizona Press.

Pastron, A.G.
1974. "Preliminary Ethnoarchaeological Investigations Among the Tarahumara." In Christopher B. Donnan and C. William Clewlow, Jr., eds., *Ethnoarchaeology*, Monograph 4, pp. 93–114. Los Angeles: University California, Institute of Archaeology.

Posas, Richardo
1949. "La Alfaria de Patamban." *Anales del Instituto Nacional de Antropología e Historia* 3:115–46.

Rouse, Irving
1960. "The Classification of Artifacts in Archaeology." *American Antiquity* 25:313–32.

Spaulding, Albert
1953. "Statistical Techniques for the Discovery of Artifact Types." *American Antiquity* 18:305–13.

Stanislawski, Michael B.
1974. "The Relationships of Ethnoarchaeology, Traditional and Systems Archaeology." In Christopher B. Donnan and C. William Clewlow, Jr., eds., *Ethnoarchaeology*, Monograph 4, 15–26. Los Angeles: University of California, Institute of Archaeology.

Whallon, Robert, Jr.
1968. "Investigations of Late Prehistoric Social Organization in New York State." In Sally R. Binford and Lewis R. Binford, eds., *New Perspectives in Archeology*, pp. 223–44. Chicago: Aldine.
1972. "A New Approach to Pottery Typology." *American Antiquity* 37:13–33.

White, J. Peter, Nicholas Modjeska, and Irari Hipuyu
n.d. "Group Definitions and Mental Templates: An Ethnographic Experiment."
In R. V. S. Wright, ed., *Stone Tools as Cultural Markers: Change, Evolution,
Complexity.* Canberra, Australia: Institute for Aboriginal Studies. (In press)
White, J. Peter and D. H. Thomas
1972. "What Mean These Stones? Ethnotaxonomic Models and Archaeological
Interpretations in the New Guinea Highlands." In David L. Clarke, *Models in
Archaeology,* pp. 275–308. London: Methuen.
Young, David E. and Robson Bonnichsen
n.d. "A Cognitive Approach for the Study of Material Culture." Manuscript.

4 / The Making and Breaking
of Shipibo-Conibo Ceramics

Warren R. DeBoer
Department of Anthropology
Queens College,
City University of New York

Donald W. Lathrap
Department of Anthropology
University of Illinois, Urbana

DeBoer and Lathrap discuss the ceramic industry of the Shipibo-Conibo of eastern Peru, documenting the passage of objects from their context in a contemporary behavioral system to their incorporation into the archaeological record. They describe the procurement of raw materials, vessel manufacture, and distribution within households, the primary functions and secondary uses of vessels, and patterns of ceramic discard. While not primarily concerned with classification, the authors, like Hardin, provide useful information about a native taxonomy (particularly as it relates to vessel function), and about variations among potters. In focusing on variations in vessel use and longevity, and on the processes which transform ceramic objects into archaeological artifacts, the article contributes to a growing literature illuminating formation processes of the archaeological record, and has implications for the formulation of archaeological sampling design.

This report is part of the long term research program into the culture history of the Upper Amazon launched by Donald Lathrap in 1956. Our investigations of Shipibo-Conibo ethnography have been generously supported by numerous agencies including the Fulbright-Hays Commission, the National Science Foundation, and the Research Foundation of the City University of New York. Particular gratitude is due our Shipibo-Conibo hosts whose hospitality, cooperation, and patience made fieldwork an enjoyable as well as informative experience.

The archaeologist is forever estranged by time. The past cultural behavior, which he seeks to understand, he will never see. In lieu of a time machine, the very possibility of understanding depends on the fact that cultural behavior has material by-products and on the premise that the archaeological record of these by-products is patterned in ways which permit inferences about the patterned behavior which produced it. This premise, however, can be rephrased as a question: what is the nature of the relationship between cultural behavior and its archaeological representation? This question has perhaps not received the systematic attention it deserves, given its basic epistemological status in archaeology (Ascher 1961, 1962, 1968; Chang 1967; David and Hennig 1972; Schiffer 1972, 1975).

In practice, many of our attempts at understanding the past are short-circuited through a comparison of unlike phenomena. We compare ethnographic observations of contemporary behavior with archaeological observations on the remnant by-products of past behavior. If our goal is the understanding of cultural behavior in the past, such a comparison harbors the assumption that a relatively obvious isomorphism exists between behavior and its derived archaeological representation. If such isomorphism can be shown not to apply to a majority of cases, then the archaeologist is left in either of two peculiar situations. Either he becomes a practitioner of an over-extended uniformitarianism in which past cultural behavior is "read" from our knowledge of present cultural behavior, or he must eschew his commitment to understanding behavior altogether and engage in a kind of "artifact physics" in which the form and distribution of behavioral by-products are measured in a behavioral vacuum. This is the familiar quandary of choosing between a significant pursuit based on faulty method or one which is methodologically sound but trivial in purpose.

In the context of this dilemma, the importance of studying the archaeological record of contemporary communities is evident. Since both behavior and its archeological record are observable, it is possible to specify the relationship between the two rather than to assume that the nexus is one of isomorphism or "fossilization." Such specification lays the groundwork for a comparison of similarly conceived units: the archaeological records of the present and of the past as transformations of the respective behavioral systems which produced them.

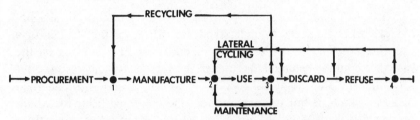

Figure 4.1. A flow chart for the passage of artifacts through a cultural system. Numbered nodes indicate points where storage (temporal displacement) or transport (spatial displacement) may take place. Modified from Schiffer (1972: fig. 1).

In the present paper, we provide a brief and selective sketch of the ceramic industry of the Shipibo-Conibo Indians of the Peruvian Amazon. Our intent is to specify some of the relationships between behavior and the formal and distributional patterns manifest in a particular class of behavioral by-products. For this purpose, we have found it useful to organize our observations according to the general model which Schiffer (1972) has developed for the flow of artifacts through cultural systems. Schiffer's model, a modified version of which is diagrammed in figure 4.1, plots the passage of artifacts from their context in a behavioral system to their context in the archaeological record in terms of several sequent stages: the procurement of raw materials; manufacture which converts raw materials into cultural form; use and reuse of the artifact; and finally discard to form the refuse of the archaeological record. First, however, we must briefly introduce the Shipibo-Conibo and their ceramics.

The Shipibo-Conibo and Their Ceramics

The Shipibo-Conibo Indians inhabit the tropical forests flanking the Ucayali River, a large southern tributary of the Amazon which flows northward along the eastern base of the Peruvian Andes (figure 4.2). The Shipibo occupy the Central Ucayali north of the Pachitea River; their close linguistic and cultural neighbors, the Conibo, are found primarily on the Upper Ucayali, south of the Pachitea. Settlements are generally situated on the levees bordering the Ucayali mainstream or on the bluffs of *terra firma* at the edge of the flood plain, locations which guarantee access to the fertile agricultural lands and to the abundant aquatic and riparian fauna of the flood plain. Major tributaries such as the Pisqui and Tamaya are also occupied. Subsistence staples are plantains and bananas, manioc, maize, and fish. Settlements vary greatly in size. About 1,000 Shipibo reside in San Francisco de Yarinacocha, a town located only two hours from the Peruvian city of Pucallpa. More common are intermediate-sized communities such as Panaillo with about 100 inhabitants (Bergman 1974:26) and Shahuaya with a population of 55 (Bodley 1967:12). Small communities, exemplified by Iparia and Sonochenea on the Upper Ucayali, are composed of two or three matrilocal households, each occupied by a sister with her husband and children. Similar units of a few adjacent households occupied by a core of related women and their families are frequently maintained in the larger settlements. The total Shipibo-Conibo population is estimated to be about 15,000 (Faust 1973).

The Shipibo-Conibo produce a distinctive ceramic style which can be traced back to archaeological antecedents. Numerous and specific features relate the style to the Cumancaya ceramic tradition which was well established on the Ucayali by the late first millennium A.D. (Lathrap 1970a; Raymond, DeBoer, and Roe 1975). Despite the increasing availability of metal and plastic containers and a growing tourist market for Indian crafts, this ceramic tradition remains intact to a remarkable extent. Most Shipibo-Conibo women are potters, and most pottery is produced for use within the potter's household.

The Shipibo-Conibo potter distinguishes two basic classes of ceramic ware: cooking ware or, more accurately, ware which is used over a fire, and non-cooking ware (figure 4.3). Cooking ware includes two distinct vessel forms: *ollas*, or cooking pots (*kënti*),[1] and a bottomless vessel (*mapú ëite*) used as a kiln for firing painted pottery. *Ollas* come in three sizes, each designed for a different use. Large *ollas* (*kënti ani*) are most commonly used in brewing alcoholic beverages, particularly manioc beer which is consumed in large quantities. The medium-sized *olla* (*kënti anitama*) is the standard vessel for cooking the daily meals which usually consist of boiled fish and plantains or manioc. The small *olla* (*kënti vacu*) is especially designed for the heating of medicines for arthritis and other ailments.

Non-cooking ware includes four vessel forms: jars (*chomo*), beer mugs (*kënpo*), food bowls (*këncha*), and a form called *shrania*. Jars are trimodal in size. The large jar is the customary container for serv-

Figure 4.2. The central and upper Ucayali basin showing location of archaeological sites of the Cumancaya tradition, modern Shipibo-Conibo settlements discussed in the text, and the sources of certain ceramic supplies. Base map based upon Operational Navigation Charts (ONC-M25 and ONC-N25).

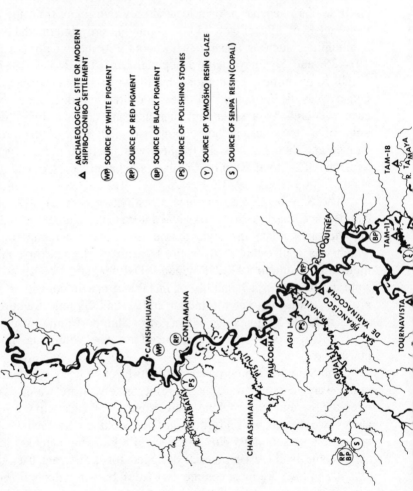

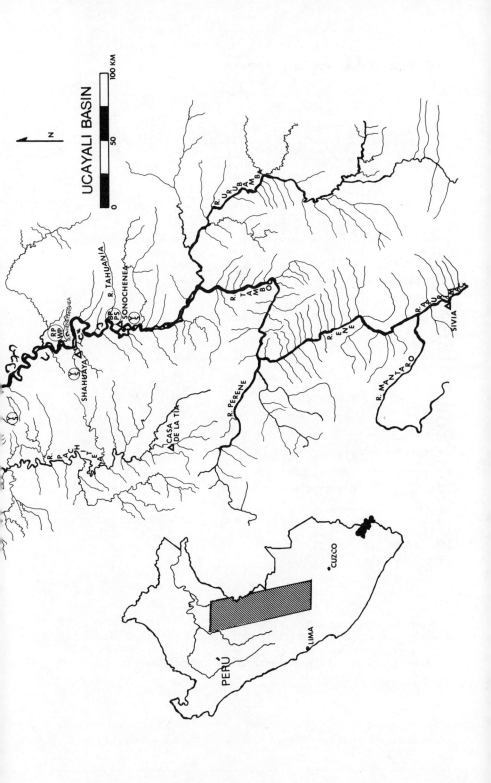

	VESSEL FORM		CLAY BLACK	WHITE	RED	TEMPER SHERD	CARAIPÉ	BOTTOM FLAT	CONCAVE	RATTLE	NONE	BASE			BODY		
C O O K I N G	OLLA	UPPER			X	XX	X										
								X						X	X		
		LOWER	X			X	XX										
	MAPU ËITE		X			X	XX			X		X					
N O N - C O O K I N G	JAR		X	X		XX	X	O	O				S,M	M,L	X	O	
	SHRANIA		X	X		XX	X	X					X				X
	BEER MUG		X	X		XX	X	O	O	O			X			O	
	FOOD BOWL											X					
			X	X		XX	X	X					X		X		
													X				X

Figure 4.3. A paradigmatic classification of the Shipibo-Conibo ceramic style modified from Lathrap (1970b). The following key is used: *X*, features which are most commonly present; *O*, frequently employed options; *S*, on small vessel; *M*, on medium vessel; *L*, on large vessel; *W*, over white slip; *B*, option on base.

NECK		RIM		SURFACE TREATMENT								SIZE		
				EXTERIOR				INTERIOR						
		/	⌐	RESIN GLAZE	TEXTURING	WHITE SLIP	RED SLIP	RESIN GLAZE	COPAL RESIN	PAINT/NATURAL	SMUDGING	SMALL	MEDIUM	LARGE
X		X		X							O			
		X		X										
S	X	X		X	X	B		X						
X		X		X	X	B	X							
.		X		X	X	B	X							
		O	O	W	O	O			O	O				
		X		W	O	O			O	O				
		X		W	O	O			O	O				

ing beer and during frequent fiestas is used in much the same way as our punchbowl. The medium sized jar is primarily a water-carrying and storage vessel. The small size serves as a canteen used in carrying beverages while traveling on the river. Like *ollas* and jars, beer mugs come in three sizes: a large, "communal" mug used during fiestas when it is passed from person to person; a medium-sized mug used in the daily consumption of beer; and a small mug which is carried on trips, often inverted over a small jar. The third category of non-cooking ware is the food bowl. During a meal, food is served in these bowls, several persons usually finger-dipping their portion from a common bowl. The adult male or males usually eat from one bowl, while women and children sit separately and eat from a second bowl. The final vessel category is the *shrania,* a vessel which, although rare today, has a variety of traditional uses, including use as a serving vessel in transferring beer from a large jar to beer mugs.[2]

Procurement

In producing her distinctive ceramics, the Shipibo-Conibo potter exploits a variety of raw materials distributed along several hundred kilometers of the Ucayali (Lathrap 1973; DeBoer 1975; Myers 1976). Table 4.1 lists the sources of the major raw materials marshaled by several potters in seven settlements. The location of many of these sources is plotted in figure 4.2. The alluvial clays utilized in ceramic manufacture are usually obtained locally—within a few kilometers of the potter's village. At the clay bed, the clay is hand-cleaned of large-sized vegetal and stone inclusions and is packed into loaves the size of volleyballs. The clay is transported back to the village and stored in this form. Most potters distinguish three clays, each having specific uses in ceramic manufacture: a black clay (*huiso mapú*) rich in organic matter; a white kaolin clay (*ošo mapú*); and a red clay (*oshin mapú*).

In addition to three basic clays, the Shipibo-Conibo potter employs two major tempering materials (not listed in table 4.1). One consists of the charred and ground silica-containing bark of certain trees (*Licania* spp.), called *mui* by the Shipibo-Conibo and commonly known as *caraipé* (Carneiro 1974). *Caraipé* trees, although sporadically distributed, are generally available within one-day's round trip of the potter's settlement. They tend to occur inland, away from the river. The bark strips are brought back to the village in a carrying basket. The unmodified bark may be stored as is, or immediately processed to usable form. The processing involves charring, pulverizing the charred bark beneath a stone rocker pestle, and sifting through a loose-weave cloth. The resultant temper is customarily stored in an old pot until needed.

The second major temper consists of ground potsherds (*këngkëshr*). Sherd temper represents a recycling of modern, broken pottery or, when available, of archaeological ceramics. The latter are generally preferred—the ancient ceramics are said to be softer and easier to pulverize—and the presence of an archaeological midden is one factor governing settlement location. The modern settlements of San Francisco de Yarinacocha, Iparia, and Shahuaya all rest upon sherd-bearing archaeological deposits. Sherd temper is produced in three stages: the sherds are first broken into small fragments through pounding with a hammerstone, itself an imported item; the pulverized sherds are then finely ground between a trough-shaped log mortar, generally fashioned from the wood of the *capiruna* tree (*Collicophyllum spruceanum*), and a rocker pestle; and the resultant granular temper may then be sifted through a loose-weave cloth. Like *caraipé*, sherd temper is often stored in an old pot.

A third variety of temper, of minor importance and of recent use, consists of the wood ashes of the *shana* tree. *Shana poto,* as this temper is called, is regarded as an inferior surrogate for *caraipé* and is used primarily in the manufacture of tourist wares.

In contrast to clays and tempers which are used in large quantities and which are generally procured locally, other ceramic supplies are often obtained from great distances. Three major mineral pigments furnish the slips and paints used in ceramic decoration: a white kaolin pigment (*maoösh*); an ocher which fires red (*mashinti*); and a black manganese pigment (*itanhuana*). Of these, the white pigment is most limited in its distribution, found only near Canshahuaya on the Lower Ucayali and on the Henepanshea, an eastern tributary of the Upper Ucayali (figure 4.2).[3] The Canshahuaya deposit is described as a lens of white clay intercalated between layers of brownish-red clay (Guizado and Girard 1966:268). In recent years, according to Spahni

Table 4.1 Sources of Ceramic Supplies Used by Several Shipibo-Conibo Potters

Locality	Clay			Pigment			Resin		Polishing Stone	Cumulative Distance to All Materials (Km)
	white	red	black	white	red	black	yomošho	sënpa		
San Francisco Potter 1	Cashibo-caño (1)	Cashibo-caño (1)	Yarina-cocha (1)	Henepan-shea (280)	Utoqui-nea (10)	Alto Pisqui (280)	Imaría-cocha (125)	Imaría-cocha (125)	Aguaitía (65)	888
San Francisco Potters 2–3	Cashibo-caño (1)	Cashibo-caño (1)	Yarina-cocha (1)	Cansha-huaya (240)	Utoqui-nea (10)	Tamaya (100)	Imaría-cocha (125)	Imaría-cocha (125)	Aguaitía (65)	668
San Francisco Potters 4–5	Cashibo-caño (1)	Cashibo-caño (1)	Yarina-cocha (1)	Cansha-huaya (240)	Utoqui-nea (10)	Tamaya (100)	Imaría-cocha (125)	Imaría-cocha (125)	Aguaitía (65)	668
San Francisco Potter 6	Cashibo-caño (1)	Cashibo-caño (1)	Yarina-cocha (1)	Cansha-huaya (240)	Contamana (180)	Tamaya (100)	Imaría-cocha (125)	Imaría-cocha (125)	?	773 +
San Francisco Potter 8	Cashibo-caño (1)	Cashibo-caño (1)	Yarina-cocha (1)	Henepan-shea (280)	?	Alto Pisqui (280)	Imaría-cocha (125)	Imaría-cocha (125)	Aguaitía (65)	878 +
San Francisco Potter 10	Cashibo-caño (1)	Cashibo-caño (1)	Tamaya (100)	Henepan-shea (280)	Henepan-shea (280)	Alto Pisqui (280)	?	?	Tahuanía (360)	1302 +
San Francisco Potter 11	?	?	?	Cansha-huaya (240)	Alto Pisqui (280)	Alto Pisqui (280)	?	?	?	—

									Total
San Francisco Potter 12	?	Cashibo-caño (1)	Yarina-cocha (1)	Cansha-huaya (240)	Utoqui-nea (10)	?	?	?	?	—
San Francisco Potter 13	?	?	Pacacha (180)	Cansha-huaya (240)	?	?	?	?	?	—
San Francisco Potter 14	?	?	Pacacha (180)	Cansha-huaya (240)	Contamana (180)	Alto Pisqui (280)	Imaría cocha (125)	?	?	—
San Francisco Potter 15	Cashibo-caño (1)	Cashibo-caño (1)	Yarina-cocha (1)	?	?	?	Imaría-cocha (125)	?	?	—
Iparia Potter 16	Sharara (10)	not used	Pacacha (30)	Henepan-shea (70)	Henepan-shea (70)	Urubamba (260+)	Alto Iparia (10)	Alto Iparia (10)	Tahuanía (150)	610+
Sonochenea Potter 17	Haticha (5)	Haticha (5)	not used	Henepan-shea (85)	Henepan-shea (85)	Tahuanía (5)	Haticha (5)	Haticha (5)	Tahuanía (5)	200
Shahuaya Potter 18	Cumaria (25)	Aruya (5)	Aruya (5)	Henepan-shea (15)	Henepan-shea (15)	Urubamba (175+)	Aruya (5)	Aruya (5)	Tahuanía (65)	315+
Panaillo Potter 19	Callaria (5)	Callaria (5)	Callaria (5)	Cansha-huaya (200)	Contamana (140)	Tamaya (140)	Imaría-cocha (165)	Imaría-cocha (165)	Tahuanía (400)	1225+
Panaillo Potter 20	Callaria (5)	Callaria (5)	Callaria (5)	Cansha-huaya (200)	Contamana (140)	Alto Pisqui (240)	Imaría-cocha (165)	Imaría-cocha (165)	Aguaitía (25)	950

Table 4.1 (continued)

Locality	Clay			Pigment			Resin		Polishing Stone	Cumulative Distance to All Materials (Km)
	white	red	black	white	red	black	yomošho	sēnpa		
Panaillo Potter 21	Cashibo-caño (40)	Cashibo-caño (40)	Callaria (5)	Cansha-huaya (200)	Alto Pisqui (240)	Alto Pisqui (240)	Imaría-cocha (165)	Imaría-cocha (165)	Cushaba-tay (170)	1265+
Panaillo Potter 22	not used	not used	Callaria (5)	Cansha-huaya (200)	Alto Pisqui (240)	Alto Pisqui (240)	Cushaba-tay (170)	?	Cushaba-tay (170)	1025+
Panaillo Potter 23	Cashibo-caño (40)	Cashibo-caño (40)	Callaria (5)	Cansha-huaya (200)	Alto Pisqui (240)	Alto Pisqui (240)	?	?	Aguaitía (25)	790+
Charashmaná [a]	single clay used; obtained locally (1)			Cansha-huaya ? (180)	Alto Pisqui (100)	Alto Pisqui (100)	?	Alto Pisqui (100)	?	—
Paucocha (Spahni 1966)	?	?	?	Cansha-huaya (145)	Contamana (85)	Alto Pisqui (165)	?	?	?	—
Average distance to material (Km)	10	8	31	201	129	195+	111	103	125	826+

Note: Numbers in parentheses indicate distance in kilometers, generally along rivers, between source and potter's village.
[a]Information provided by Roberta Campos.

(1966:101), this *maoš̈h* deposit has been situated on hacienda property, and a Shipibo or Conibo man will exchange two days of labor for three large balls of pigment.

The red pigment is less restricted in its distribution and comes in two varieties: a yellow limonitic variety (*kana mashinti*) which is found at Contamana and on the Utoquinea and Henepanshea; and a red-colored variety (*shahuán mashinti*), the major source of which is found on the Upper Pisqui. After firing, both varieties yield the conspicuous red of the Shipibo-Conibo ceramic style. The black pigment is most commonly acquired from the Pisqui, although additional sources occur on the Tamaya and Tahuanía. Some Conibo potters on the Upper Ucayali secure this pigment from Piro traders who descend the Ucayali from the Urubamba. Unlike the white and red pigments which are found as clay deposits, *itanhuana* occurs as small chunks exposed in the submerged or damp earth of the banks of tributary rivers. It must be stored in water or wrapped in a moist cloth or it will quickly lose its pigmenting properties.

Yet other raw materials are required in the manufacture of ceramics. Two varieties of resins, *yomoš̈ho* (*Protium* spp.) for lending a glaze-like finish to white-slipped surfaces and *sënpa* (*Hymenaea courbaril*) for waterproofing the interior of liquid-containing vessels, must often be imported. Stone is a rare commodity on the Ucayali, and water-worn pebbles (*rëncati*), preferably of black color, used in the polishing of ceramics, are valued possessions. Such pebbles have a limited occurrence; beaches of the Aguaitía and Tahuanía are the main sources given by our Shipibo-Conibo informants.

The acquisition of the more exotic raw materials utilized in ceramic manufacture is made possible by the Shipibo-Conibo occupancy of the Ucayali mainstream, a riverine highway which facilitates long-distance travel and transport. Both Shipibo and Conibo are great travelers, and Shipibo-Conibo voyagers in the traditional dugout or in the modern motor launch are common sights on the Ucayali. During August of 1971, for instance, our Shipibo hosts in San Francisco de Yarinacocha were frequently visited by friends and relatives from such nearby locales as the Utoquinea River and from the considerably more distant Pisqui, Tamaya, and Shahuaya Rivers. Potters in San Francisco often visit relatives at Imaríacocha on the Tamaya, in part to obtain resins. Such a network of informal visitation is sufficient in itself for circulating many of the raw materials utilized in ceramic manufacture. In addition, men often travel great distances to work in lumbering operations during the rainy season from November to April; ceramic supplies are often obtained during this seasonal employment.

Thus, although elaborate ceramics embodying widely dispersed ingredients are not necessary consequences of the Shipibo-Conibo occupancy of the Ucayali mainstream, they are made possible by such occupancy and underscore the fact that, in addition to good agricultural and fishing lands, the flood plain confers accessibility to an extensive resource zone flanking the Ucayali and its major tributaries.

Manufacture

A detailed study of Shipibo-Conibo ceramic manufacture requires monographic treatment, and only a few observations can be presented here. Potting may take place in the potter's house or in a special shed made for this purpose. Although ceramics are made year round, the dry season from May to October is preferred. Two major factors account for this seasonality: the submergence of clay deposits and the fewer number of clear days suitable for pottery drying during the flood season.

The ratio of clay to temper volume ranges consistently between 2 and 3; however, the ways in which different clays and tempers are mixed depends on the kind of vessel to be made. Non-cooking ware—including jars, beer mugs, food bowls, and *shrania*—is ideally made from a mixture of equal parts of white and red clay tempered with two parts crushed sherd to one part *caraipé*. Cooking ware follows a more complicated recipe. In *ollas,* black clay tempered with two parts *caraipé* to one part crushed sherd is ideally used for the base and body of the vessel, while the neck is made from red clay tempered with reversed proportions of *caraipé* and sherd. These ideal rules or recipes for combining clays and tempers, however, are not always actualized and, in some cases, are not reliable guides to actual potting behavior.

For example, potters of Charashmaná on the Pisqui use only one clay, while only two clays are employed at Sonochenea and Iparia (table 4.1 and figure 4.4). At San Francisco, clay-temper mixtures vary from potter to potter and from occasion to occasion. The clay composition of non-cooking ware is particularly variable. As shown in figure 4.4, only 6 of 24 instances conform to the stated ideal of equal parts of red and white clay; 8 cases represent simplifications of this formula and consist of only red or only white clay; in 7 cases, black clay is substituted for either red or white clay; and in 3 cases, black clay is added to both red and white clays. Although the simplifications and substitutions may reflect the unavailability of pre-scribed materials at the time of manufacture and thus not vitiate the "rule," such an inference could hardly be made on the basis of the pottery alone. For archaeological purposes, clay composition in these vessels could better be considered a polythetic set of red, white, and black clays. In contrast, rules for clay and temper composition in cooking ware are more consistently translated into actual behavior.

Construction is by coiling. Welding of the coils, shaping of the growing vessel, and smoothing of the vessel surface are ac-complished with oval-shaped scrapers (*shapa*) which are cut from calabash rind with a machete and then smoothed on the edges with a rasp-like bony element from the *paiche* fish (*Arapaima gigas*).[4] The construction process is, of course, goal-directed behavior which cul-minates in the construction of a particular vessel. The potter's view of this process is one of a sequential series of choices which is diagrammatically summarized in figure 4.3: choice of a bottom form (*poinke*), base form (*chipón*), body form (*poro*), neck form (*tëshro*), and rim form (*kësha,* or unmodified rim, versus *këshpa,* or everted rim).

Surface finish and decoration vary according to vessel form. Decoration of cooking ware is restricted to such surface manipulative techniques as incision (*shëpamán aca*), punctuation (*chacha*), and finger impressions (*mëquëmán mëia*); interior surfaces may be smudged after firing.[5] Non-cooking ware is painted. The exterior neck and body segments of jars and *shrania* are generally painted in black and red over a white slip; interiors are coated with *sënpa* resin after firing. Beer mugs are treated similarly. The exterior of food bowls is usually painted in white over a red slip; interiors may be smudged or painted directly over the natural buff surface. Food bowls with smudged interiors are used for stews, soups, and other "wet" foods, while those with plain or painted interiors are used for broiled fish, plantains, and other "dry" foods. Occasionally a food bowl may be white-slipped and shaped like a beer mug (a variant appropri-

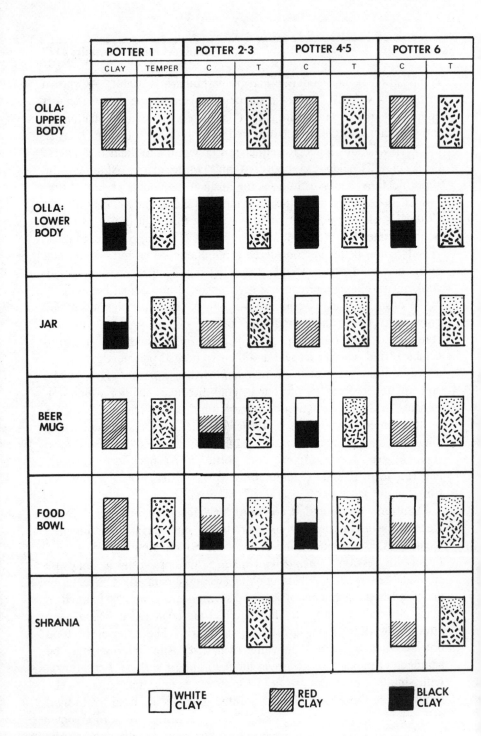

Figure 4.4. Clay and temper composition of ceramic vessels produced by several Shipibo-Conibo potters.

POTTER 7		POTTER 8		POTTER 9		POTTER 15		POTTER 16	
C	T	C	T	C	T	C	T	C	T

 SHERD TEMPER
 CARAIPÉ TEMPER
SHANA POTO

100%
50

ately called *kënpo këncha,* or "beer mug food bowl"), in which case the smudged or painted, resin-free interior, never found on beer mugs, remains the critical distinguishing feature.[6]

Pottery is fired in several different ways. Food bowls, beer mugs, *shrania,* and small-sized jars are fired singly in a *mapú ëite.* The unfired vessel is inverted inside the bottomless *mapú ëite* and covered with wood ash *(chimapú).* The *mapú ëite,* today customarily supported by a metal grill, is then placed over the fire. Small and medium-sized *ollas* are ordinarily fired in a special crib consisting of two parallel logs between which the *olla* or *ollas* are placed and then covered with a pyramid of bark *(otukuru)* or cane *(tohua)* fuel placed over each vessel. Large *ollas* and jars are always fired singly. The vessel, inverted and supported on a tripod of old pots, metal cans, or bricks, is gradually heated over a low fire placed in a small, shallow pit. After this priming fire, the final firing involves completely covering the vessel with a pyramid of bark strips or cane poles, the two preferred fuels. Resins are applied immediately after firing. While the

Table 4.2 Time Invested in the Manufacture of Several Ceramic Vessels

Vessel Form	Began date	Began hour	Completed date	Completed hour	Total Elapsed Time days	hrs.	mins.
A. *Shrania*	9/3	9:02 A.M.	9/10	4:16 P.M.	7	7	14
B. Food bowl	9/8	3:50 P.M.	9/13	4:50 P.M.	5	1	0
C. Medium *olla*	9/9	2:06 P.M.	9/13	12:24 P.M.	3	22	18
D. Small *olla*	9/9	2:06 P.M.	9/13	12:24 P.M.	3	22	18
E. Large jar	9/6	2:45 P.M.	9/13	3:20 P.M.	7	0	35

	A	B	C	D	E
Kneading	(14)	—	—	—	—
Rolling of coils	18	4	9	5	50
Coiling	10	3	14	7	25
Scraping	159	45	82	56	230
Slipping	8	5	0	0	16
Polishing	24	20	14	12	50
Decoration	110	45	16	7	260
Priming fire	189	120	73	73	224
Firing	69	35	35	35	30
Application of resin	5	0	0	0	10
Total (minutes)	592 [a]	277	243	195	895

[a]Excludes kneading time.

vessel is still sufficiently hot to melt resins, a ball of *yomošho* or *sënpa* affixed to the end of a manatee, tapir, or cow rib handle is coated over the appropriate surface.

Although *mapú ëite* may occasionally be used over an ordinary cooking hearth, ceramics are generally fired in special fires near the potter's house or ceramic shed. Several ash concentrations may be found in the vicinity of a Shipibo-Conibo household, each representing a separate firing or set of firings.

The time invested in manufacture varies according to potter and vessel form. Table 4.2 gives the times which one potter invested in the production of five vessels. The process was observed from beginning to end. Drying time is not included. As expected, the greater the surface area of the vessel, the greater the time expended in coiling, scraping, polishing, and painting. Table 4.2 also points out the fact that several vessels are generally made in one potting episode.

Although ceramic manufacture is primarily an individual enterprise, two or more women of one household may occasionally cooperate in certain phases of the process. Women may alternate in the polishing or even in the decoration of a vessel and may work together in the firing of a large *olla* or jar.

Use

Most ceramics are used in the household of their manufacture. Notable exceptions are ceramics made for sale. In a 1971 ceramic census of 18 households, this category comprised 34 of 320 total vessels (table 4.3). Tourists provide the major market for Shipibo-Conibo ceramics.[7] Small and medium-sized jars are also in demand in local non-Indian households where they are used as water-carrying containers. Of the 286 vessels in table 4.3 used by the Shipibo-Conibo themselves, only 3 were imported from outside the community, while 9 were made in different households within the community. Of this latter group, 3 were large jars on loan to a household hosting a fiesta and in need of extra beer-containing vessels. Four were so-called *Pasqua këncha*, a special variety of food bowl made for use in a fiesta held during the Easter holiday. These bowls, made by the

Table 4.3 A Ceramic Census of Several Shipibo-Conibo Households

	Number of Inhabitants				Ollas			Jars	
	Total	Adults	Children	Potters	Large	Medium	Small	Large	Medium
San Francisco House 1	6	2	4	1	– / 1 –				1 / 1 –
San Francisco House 3	7	5	2	1	1 / 1 –	1 / – –		2 / – –	1 / – –
San Francisco House 7	6	3	3	1	3 / 1 –	2 / 2 –	1	1 / – –	1 / – –
San Francisco House 8	4	2	2	1		2 / – –		1	4 / – –
San Francisco House 9	6	2	4	1		2 / – –		1	2 / – –
San Francisco Houses 10–11	7	4	3	2	4 / 2 –	3 / 1 –	1 / 1 –	2 / 2 –	2 2 / 2 2
San Francisco House 12	3	2	1	1	2 / – –	1 / – –		– / 1 –	2 / – –
San Francisco House 13	6	4	2	2	1 / – –	4 / – –	1 / – –		5 / 1 –
San Francisco House 14	8	3	5	2	2 / – –	– / 1 –	1 / – –	2 / – –	3 / – 3
San Francisco House 15	9	4	5	1			1 / – –	2 / – –	– / 1 –
Boca Tamaya	6	2	4	1	2 / – –	3 / – –	1 / – –	1 / – –	1 / – –
Puerto Junio	6	3	3	2	2 / – –		1 / – –		2 / – –
Iparia House 1	3	2	1	1	1 / 1 –	6 / – –	3 / – –	1 / 3 –	2 / 4 –
Iparia House 2	5	5	0	2	1 / – –	1 / – –	1 / – –	1 / – –	5 / 1 –
Iparia House 3	6	3	3	1	– / 1 –	– / 2 –		– / 1 –	
Sonochenea House 1	2	2	0	1	1 / – –	4 / 1 –	2 / – –	1 / – –	4 / – –
Sonochenea House 2	6	2	4	1	1 / – –	2 / 2 –	2 / – –		1 / 1 –
TOTALS	96	50	46	22	21 / 7 –	31 / 9 –	15 / 1 –	15 / 7 –	36 / 11 5

Note: Each cell gives the number of complete (upper) and broken (lower left) vessels used within the household, and the number made for sale (lower right).

Jars (cont.)		Beer Mugs		Food Bowls		Other		
Small	Toy	Large	Regular & small	Regular	Toy	Mapú éite	Shrania	TOTALS
1			1	2				5
–	–		–	1	–			3 –
1			1	2				9
–	–		–	–	–			1 –
1		1	2	4				16
–	–		–	1	–			4 –
	1		1	6				15
–	–		1	2	2			3 2
				4	1			10
–	–			–	–			– –
1			2	3	2	2	1	23
–	–		1	1	7	–	–	10 9
		1	2	4				12
–	–		–	1	–			1 1
2		1	2	4		3		23
–	–		–	–	–	1	–	2 –
1			2	6				17
–	–		–	–	12			1 15
			3	2		1		9
1	1		–	–		–		2 1
								8
								– –
2						1		8
–	–					–		– –
	1			3	1	–		18
–				–	–	1		9 –
2			2	5				18
–	6		–	1	–			2 6
2			1	7	1			11
1	–		–	–	–			5 –
				3		1		16
				1	–	–		2 –
1			3	7	1	1		19
–	–		–	1	–	–		4 –
14	2	3	22	62	6	9	1	237
1 6			4 2	7 21	1 –	1 –		49 34

women of the host household, are given as gifts to women from other households who have helped in the preparation of food and beer consumed during the fiesta.

When not in use, vessels are ordinarily stored on racks suspended from rafters or on special outdoor racks. Heavy vessels such as large jars and *ollas* commonly stand on the packed dirt floor of the kitchen—a structure which is separate from the house—or they may be kept beneath the elevated floor of the house.

The census data tabulated in table 4.3 do not suggest any correlation between the size or composition of a household and the number of ceramic vessels. One factor which probably obscures any such correlation is the differential replacement of ceramic vessels by aluminum pots and enameled bowls. Metal containers are now present in almost all households; however, we do not have information on their frequency. A second factor is that the frequency of ceramic vessels is not directly governed by immediate household needs. In the Conibo village of Iparia, for example, fully half of the complete vessels were stored in the rafters as future replacements for broken vessels or as "special occasion" ware immediately available for serving guests. Traditional etiquette requires that each household have one or more newly made beer mugs on hand. When a visitor first arrives at a house, he is served beer in one of these vessels. If the mug does not give the appearance of being freshly made, this is an insult to the guest and is a reflection on the propriety of the hostess. Other factors apply in individual cases. Accomplished potters generally produce more pottery than less talented potters. The ceramic production of women with suckling infants is generally less than that of potters free of children or with older, less demanding children. Household vessel counts thus reflect a number of variables other than the number of household occupants.[8]

As noted earlier, each Shipibo-Conibo vessel form is associated with a different stated use, a fact which is evident in our appellations "food bowl," "beer mug," etc. In a majority of cases, this set of ideal functions is a reasonable indicator of actual usage; however, it does not encompass the numerous subsidiary and secondary uses to which vessels can be put. Figure 4.1 diagrams the major ways in which vessels may be modified in order to prolong or alter use. Maintenance refers to repairs or other modifications which permit continued use in the same set of activities. Lateral cycling refers to the

Table 4.4 Observed Use of Shipibo-Conibo Ceramic Vessels

	Food			Ceramic supplies				Containers — Other								Containers — Empty		Misc.					
	solid food	beer	water	clay	temper	pig-ments	resins	acces-sories	cotton	medi-cine	dyes	clothes	water for ducks	live turtles	shell	domes-tic use	made for sale	pot support	chicken roost	comal	mapú ëite	saved for temper	Total
Ollas																							
Large complete	1			2				1				1			1	14							20
Large broken				1	1																4	4	10
Medium complete	4		1	3				2			2					18			2	1			33
Medium broken																		1			2	5	8
Small complete	1			3				5	1	1						5							16
Small broken							1											1					2
Jars																							
Large complete	2	6		1												10							19
Large broken	1												1									4	6
Medium complete	1		9	2				3	1		1					18	3	1					39
Medium broken				1										1								7	9
Small complete	3					1										10	6						20
Small broken																		1				1	2
Beer Mugs																							
All sizes complete		1						2						1		22	2						28
All sizes broken				1		1										2							4
Food Bowls																							
All sizes complete	3			1		4		2						1		56	21						88
All sizes broken																10						1	11

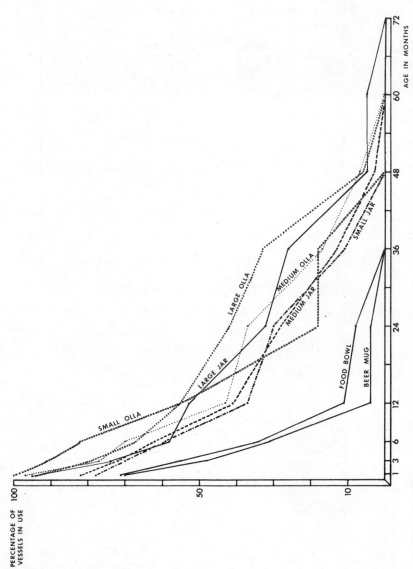

Figure 4.5. "Survivorship" curves for major Shipibo-Conibo vessel forms. The curves are generally consonant with results obtained from a census of nearly 2,000 Shipibo-Conibo vessels which one of us made in the 1960s. One difference in the earlier census is the presence of large jars and *ollas* well over a decade in age.

reuse of vessels in new sets of activities. Recycling is a special instance of lateral cycling in which potsherds become ingredients for
the manufacture of new ceramic vessels.

There are two major techniques for repairing damaged vessels;
both are employed in the repair of cracks in the vessel rim. In one,
the vessel wall on either side of the crack is perforated and twine or,
when available, metal wire, is run through the perforations and tied
to bind the break. In the second, a resin glue is used to seal the crack.
Vessels are cleaned by rinsing with water. *Ollas* may be scoured with
sand.

Table 4.4 summarizes the various uses to which 315 vessels
were put at the time of observation.[9] Any vessel may serve as a general purpose container. As expected, medium jars commonly contain
water obtained either from a nearby river or lake or, more rarely,
from a recent rain. Large jars often contain beer. A host of other container functions, however, is not obviously related to the primary or
stated vessel function. Other examples of lateral cycling include the
use of *ollas* or jars as pot supports, the use of large *olla* sherds as
comales,[10] the conversion of large or medium *ollas* into chicken
roosts, and the refashioning of medium *ollas* with broken bottoms
into *mapú ëite.*

As noted earlier, either ancient or modern potsherds are
frequently recycled as sherd temper. Jars and *ollas* are the two modern forms selected for such recycling (table 4.4).

Discard and Refuse

The procurement and manufacture activities embodied in ceramics
represent a considerable investment of time and energy, and ceramic
vessels are ordinarily kept in use or "curated" until damaged beyond
repair.[11] Figure 4.5 graphically illustrates the duration in use of the
major Shipibo-Conibo vessel forms. In table 4.5, these data are
rephrased in terms of the median age, frequency in use, and projected
frequency in the archaeological record for each vessel form. The longevity data pattern in interesting ways. Food bowls and beer mugs
have a rapid turnover rate, a fact which reflects their frequent use,
their portability, and their thin-walled construction and consequent
fragility. Large jars and *ollas* are used less frequently, are moved less

Table 4.5 Median Age, Frequency in Use (N_0), and Projected Frequency in an Archaeological Midden

Vessel Form	N_0	Percent	Median Age in Years	N_{100}	Percent	$K =$ Percent N^0 / Percent N_{100}
Large *olla*	33	12.5	1.38	1,196	4.6	2.72
Medium *olla*	30	11.4	.88	1,704	6.6	1.73
Small *olla*	11	4.1	1.13	487	1.9	2.16
Large jar	19	7.2	1.13	841	3.2	2.25
Medium jar	39	14.8	.78	2,500	9.8	1.51
Small jar	27	10.3	.71	1,901	7.4	1.39
Beer mug	23	8.7	.24	4,792	18.7	.47
Food bowl	73	27.8	.31	11,774	46.1	.60
Mapú ëite	6	2.2	1.00	300	1.1	2.00
Shrania	1	.3	—	—	—	—
Totals	262	99.3		25,495	99.4	

Source: The table incorporates and increases the sample of vessels reported by DeBoer (1974).

Note: N_{100} represents 100 years of deposition of major Shipibo-Conibo vessel forms.

often, have thicker vessel walls, and are correspondingly longer lived. Infrequently used vessels such as small *ollas* and *mapú ëite* have comparatively long life spans. An assessment of the relative importance of these various factors in vessel breakage and discard would require detailed life history information on many vessels.[12]

Most ceramics are manufactured, used, broken, and discarded within the household, an area which is defined by a cleared plaza which is kept meticulously free of vegetation and which includes a minimum of two structures, a house and a kitchen. The plaza is cleaned on a daily basis by sweeping with a broom made of palm leaves and by raking with a wooden implement shaped like a common garden hoe. Kitchen refuse, broken pottery, and other debris resulting from daily activities are cleared centrifugally away from the household and accumulate immediately beyond the perimeter of the clearing. In isolated households, the effect over time is a doughnut-shaped midden. When several households share a common plaza, the effect is a scalloped midden surrounding the entire plaza. Topographic variations may modify this pattern. Much of San Francisco de Yarinacocha, for instance, straddles a bluff over which refuse may be swept. Ravines which cut into the bluff also serve as dumps.[13] If a ceramic vessel is dropped or otherwise broken in the area of the household, the resultant sherds are likely to be swept or raked to a site of secondary refuse within a few days. In some cases, however, weather may alter this fate. During or after heavy rains, small sherds, when stepped on, may become firmly embedded in the plaza surface. Since the daily sweeping lowers the plaza surface over time, these sherds, as well as any archaeological sherds which may be present, commonly protrude from the ground.

The Shipibo-Conibo furnish a specific example of an expectable general pattern: within a sedentary community, primary refuse, where sites of use and discard coincide, is probably ephemeral, and midden accumulates exactly where behavior is minimal (Schiffer 1972:162). For example, at Iparia, where a thriving ceramic industry exists, test pits placed immediately next to a house yielded only 3 modern sherds (DeBoer 1972–74:97). In contrast, secondary refuse at San Francisco de Yarinacocha is laden with sherds and over a period of about fifty years has accumulated to depths varying between 7.5 and 15 centimeters (Lathrap 1962:144–45). Exceptions to the impermanence and archaeological invisibility of primary refuse are primarily confined to activities which take place outside of the household area. For example, sherds resulting from the accidental breakage of water-carrying jars are frequently strewn along the trail which connects every household to a nearby river or lake.

In order to examine discard patterns further, it is useful to consider a particular example in greater detail. Figure 4.6 maps the surface distribution of selected categories of refuse, including potsherds, around houses 9 and 10 at San Francisco de Yarinacocha. In figure 4.7, a schematic rendition of the same area is given which plots the surface density of potsherds. Although these plots of refuse are not necessarily typical, they do reveal certain processes of refuse accumulation which operate in all Shipibo-Conibo settlements. Note that the house areas and plaza are virtually barren of refuse; that refuse which does occur (e.g., the fish bones centering at O17) was derived from activities which took place immediately before the preparation of the map and which had not yet been cleared. As expected, secondary refuse accumulates among the trees which mark the western border of the plaza and along the fence which marks the eastern border. Sherd counts in these border areas represent minimal frequen-

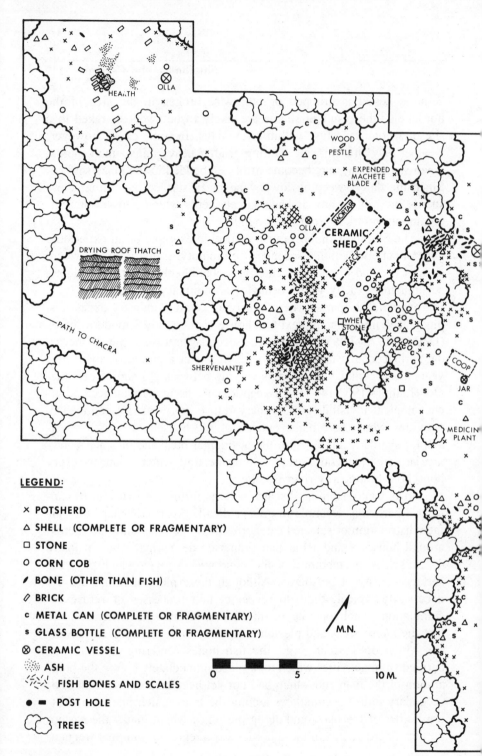

LEGEND:

× POTSHERD

△ SHELL (COMPLETE OR FRAGMENTARY)

□ STONE

○ CORN COB

✔ BONE (OTHER THAN FISH)

⌀ BRICK

c METAL CAN (COMPLETE OR FRAGMENTARY)

s GLASS BOTTLE (COMPLETE OR FRAGMENTARY)

⊗ CERAMIC VESSEL

ASH

FISH BONES AND SCALES

● ▬ POST HOLE

TREES

Figure 4.6. Surface distribution and selected categories of refuse around houses 9 and 10, San Francisco de Yarinacocha.

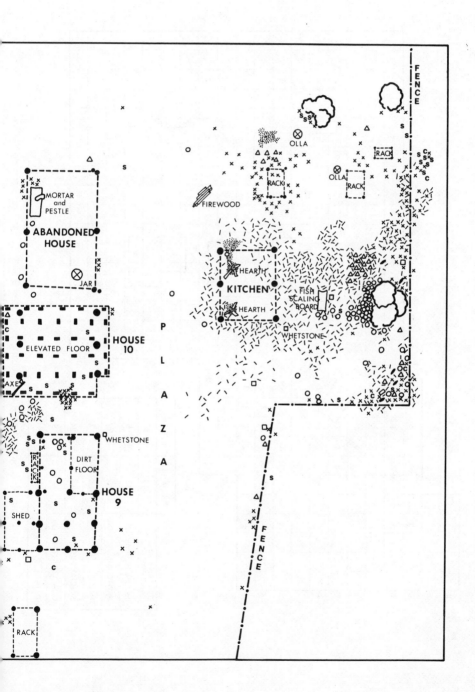

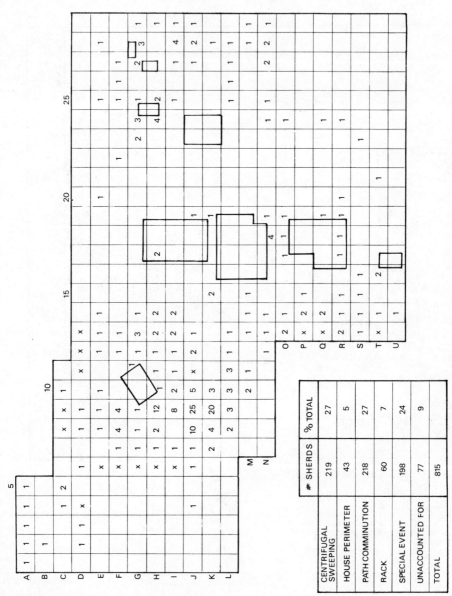

Figure 4.7. Surface density of potsherds, houses 9 and 10, San Francisco de Yarina-cocha. X indicates presence at indeterminate density.

cies since weedy growth and piles of manioc scrapings and banana peels which also accumulate in these areas tend to obscure small-sized items such as potsherds.

Other distributional phenomena are also evident in figures 4.6 and 4.7. A common accident involves the falling of vessels from outdoor storage racks which consequently tend to be "hot spots" where sherds are periodically produced (U17, G24, G27). Rain falling on the eaves produces a shallow trench in which sherds may accumulate (H17, J19, N18). Sherds which occur along the path leading from the houses to the ceramic shed tend to be smaller in size than sherds in secondary refuse resulting from centrifugal sweeping (figure 4.8). This latter fact is readily attributable to sherd comminution by people walking along the path.[14] The dense cluster of sherds at J9 resulted from the recent accidental breaking of a large jar and is coded under "special event" in figure 4.7.

One other feature in figure 4.6 deserves comment. The northernmost house was abandoned when several roof supports snapped during a powerful windstorm. The occupants built House 10 immediately to the south. In this case, of course, there was no problem in moving all household furniture and utensils to the new home. The old

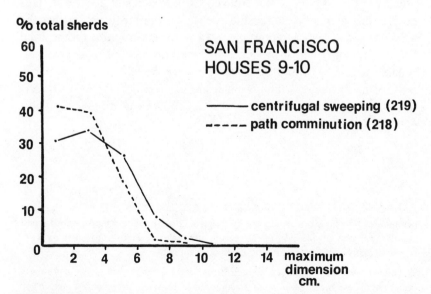

Figure 4.8. Maximum dimensions in centimeters of potsherds in two depositional contexts.

structure, although dilapidated, continued to be used as a work area by the members of House 10. In other cases, when greater distances separate the abandoned and new residences, we might expect a greater amount of material to be left behind.[15]

Summary

As Walter Taylor (1948:145) emphasized thirty years ago, all archaeological inferences are ultimately dependent on three kinds of data: (1) the frequency, (2) formal properties, and (3) spatial distribution of behavioral by-products. We have tried to provide these data for the Shipibo-Conibo ceramic industry. Our discussion has focused on the procurement of widely dispersed raw materials, ceramic manufacture which welds these raw materials into finished form, the use of ceramics in both primary and secondary contexts, and the refuse-forming behavior which acts as ultimate editor of the archaeological record. It is the latter stage of refuse formation which has been neglected in the otherwise splendid and archaeologically useful studies of traditional ceramic crafts available in the general anthropological literature (e.g., Guthe 1925; Bunzel 1929; Fontana et al. 1962). This neglect has perhaps fostered the occasional optimistic claim that the archaeological record represents a "fossilized structure of the total cultural system" which produced it (Binford 1964:425). A more reasonable appraisal would be that the archaeological record primarily reflects that behavior which produces refuse. A curious fact about refuse is that while archaeologists obsessively seek to discover it, most people, including the Shipibo-Conibo, seek to get rid of it.

Notes

1. Here and in the following discussion, the Shipibo-Conibo term is introduced in parentheses. We have decided to use the English term throughout the subsequent text and in the figures for the sake of the reader, although the English term is not always a precise equivalent for the Shipibo-Conibo meaning.

2. Other vessel forms, not represented in our 1971 ceramic census, were formerly important. These include phallic and zoomorphic beer mugs designed for suspension from a fishing pole type apparatus in order to withdraw beer from large jars (Tessmann 1928: table 58). These individual beer mugs were used in fiesta situations by

children under twelve years of age and by the elderly of the grandparental generation. The Shipibo-Conibo rationale for lumping these alternate generations is that the
young and old would drool into the communal mugs used by the rest of the community.

3. An inferior grade of white pigment which is not represented in the sample of potters discussed in this report is said to occur at Imaríacocha (Lathrap 1973:172).

4. Shells and edge-ground sherds used as pottery scrapers are also reported (Farabee
1915:94; Greg Roberts, personal communication).

5. In former times, when the girls' puberty ceremony was still in full swing, the
large *olla* used in cooking the pig served at this ceremony was painted. Ordinarily,
ollas are never painted, and this practice can be reasonably regarded as a sacred
reversal of normal decorative grammar.

6. Resined surfaces have been noted on archaeological ceramics of the Cumancaya
tradition (DeBoer 1972:36; Roe 1973:99) but are not commonly preserved. Pigments
have a greater archaeological visibility. Red slipped and painted vessels and faceted
lumps of ocher commonly occur in the middens of archaeological sites on the
Ucayali (e.g., Roe 1973:96). A black pigment resembling *itanhuana* has also been
recovered (DeBoer 1972:18–19). The white pigment *maoïh* utilized by the Shipibo-
Conibo is extremely fugitive, and the archaeological representation of this pigment is
undoubtedly deflated from its frequency in use (Myers 1970:80–81).

7. Lathrap (1970c) has pointed out that the pottery that the Shipibo produce for
tourists is readily distinguishable from the ceramics made for their own use.

8. In traditional Shipibo-Conibo culture, a major institution affecting ceramic
frequencies was the girls' puberty ceremony. As recently as 1955, as much as half of
ceramic production and breakage was directly associated with these ceremonies and
with the entertainment of distant friends and relatives which they necessitated. All
pottery used on these occasions had to be brand new. The number of vessels in the
households of host families immediately prior to the ceremonies may have been ten
or twenty times the amount normally present. Most of the beer mugs and food bowls
would customarily get broken during the three-day fiesta, especially during the
drunken brawls which culminated a successful fiesta. This pottery got smashed with
the same spirit that champagne glasses were smashed by Englishmen on particularly
meaningful occasions. By 1971, the time at which the observations upon which this
report is based were collected, the puberty ceremony was largely memory culture.

9. Table 4.4 includes information on all vessels for which use was observed. This
sample is not entirely coincident with the ceramics tabulated in the census given in
table 4.3.

10. This use was reported a half century ago by Tessmann (1928:146).

11. An exception occurs in the case of burials where traditionally the ceramics used
by the deceased were smashed. The traditional burial mode of primary or secondary
interment inside a large *olla* or jar placed beneath the house floor has been abandoned. Today the cadaver is placed in a wood coffin or sealed canoe and buried in a
special cemetery area (DeBoer 1972:65–68).

12. The Shipibo-Conibo also produce several ceramic artifacts other than vessels. One of these, the *shërvenante,* is a solid object, rectangular or oval in shape, which is inserted in the vulva of a young girl after she has undergone the clitoridectomy which is part of the traditional puberty ceremony. The *shërvenante* is made for the ceremony and discarded in village midden (see figure 4.6, J6) after a short period of use by the girl. This artifact affords an exception to the suggested generalization that ritual-associated items have a longer life span than non-ritual items (Schiffer 1972:163).

13. The filling of ravines is not a casual matter. The development of these three or four foot deep gullies is extremely rapid, given the amount of run-off from the cleared plaza. Unless this erosion is checked, the plaza area would be totally dissected within a year or two. The logs, large sherds, and other debris dumped into these gullies serve to stabilize sediments and to retard further erosion.

14. For other attempts to correlate degree of sherd comminution with intensity of human activity see Meggers and Evans (1957:247–48) and Grebinger (1971:48).

15. More information on what remains in abandoned Shipibo-Conibo houses should be forthcoming from current investigations by Peter Roe and his students at the University of Delaware.

References Cited

Ascher, Robert
  1961. "Analogy in Archaeological Interpretation." *Southwestern Journal of Anthropology* 17:317–25.
  1962. "Ethnography for Archeology: A Case from the Seri Indians. *Ethnology* 1:360–69.
  1968. "Time's Arrow and the Archaeology of a Contemporary Community." In K. C. Chang, ed., *Settlement Archaeology,* pp. 43–52. Palo Alto: National Press Books.
Bergman, Roland
  1974. "Shipibo Subsistence in the Upper Amazon Rainforest." Ph.D. dissertation, University of Wisconsin.
Binford, Lewis R.
  1964. "A Consideration of Archaeological Research Design." *American Antiquity* 29(4):425–41.
Bodley, John H.
  1967. "Development of an Intertribal Mission Station in the Peruvian Amazon." Master's thesis, University of Oregon.
Bunzel, Ruth L.
  1929. *The Pueblo Potter: A Study of Creative Imagination in Primitive Art.* New York: Columbia University Press.
Carneiro, Robert L.
  1974. "'Cariapé': An Instance of the Standardization of Error in Archaeology." *Journal of the Steward Anthropological Society* 6(1):71–75.

Chang, K. C.
1967. "Major Aspects of the Interrelationship of Archaeology and Ethnology."
Current Anthropology 8(3):227–34.

David, Nicholas and Hilke Hennig
1972. "The Ethnography of Pottery: A Fulani Case Seen in Archaeological
Perspective," pp. 1–29. McCaleb Module in Anthropology 21. Reading, Mass.:
Addison-Wesley.

DeBoer, Warren R.
1972. "Archaeological Explorations on the Upper Ucayali River, Peru." Ph.D.
dissertation, University of California, Berkeley.
1972–74. "Binó Style Ceramics from Iparia." *Ñawpa Pacha* 10–12:91–108.
Berkeley: Institute of Andean Studies.
1974. "Ceramic Longevity and Archaeological Interpretation: An Example from
the Upper Ucayali, Peru." *American Antiquity* 39(2):335–43.
1975. "Aspects of Trade and Transport on the Ucayali River, Easter Peru."
Paper presented at the Conference on Anthropological Research in Amazonia,
May 1975, Sky's Edge, Pennsylvania.

Farabee, William C.
1915. "Conebo Pottery." *Museum Journal* 6:94–99. Philadelphia: University of
Pennsylvania.

Faust, Norma W.
1973. "Lecciones para el aprendizaje del idioma Shipibo-Conibo." Instituto
Lingüistico de Verano, Documento de Trabajo 1. Pucallpa, Perú.

Fontana, Bernard L., William J. Robinson, Charles W. Cormack, and Ernest E.
Leavitt, Jr.
1962. *Papago Indian Pottery*. Seattle: University of Washington Press.

Grebinger, Paul
1971. "The Potrero Creek Site: Activity Structure." *Kiva* 37(1):30–52.

Guizado, Jorge and Dino Girard
1966. "Reconocimiento por calizas en la región de Orellana-Cushabatay."
Comisión Carta Geologica Nacional (Servicio de Geología y Mineria) Boletín
13:259–72. Lima.

Guthe, Carl E.
1925. *Pueblo Pottery Making*. Andover: Phillips Academy, Department of Archaeology.

Lathrap, Donald W.
1962. "Yarinacocha: Stratigraphic Excavations in the Peruvian Montana."
Ph.D. dissertation, Harvard University.
1970a. *The Upper Amazon*. New York: Praeger.
1970b. "A Formal Analysis of Shipibo-Conibo Pottery and its Implications for
Studies of Panoan Prehistory." Paper presented at the 35th Annual Meeting of
the Society for American Archaeology, Mexico City.
1970c. "Shipibo Tourist Pottery." Paper presented at the 69th Annual Meeting
of the American Anthropological Association, San Diego.
1973. "The Antiquity and Importance of Long-distance Trade Relationships in
the Moist Tropics of Pre-Columbian South America." *World Archaeology*
5(2):170–86.

Meggers, Betty J. and Clifford Evans
    1957. "Archeological Investigations at the Mouth of the Amazon." Washington, D.C.: Bureau of American Ethnology Bulletin 167.
Myers, Thomas P.
    1970. "The Late Prehistoric Period at Yarinacocha, Peru." Ph.D. dissertation, University of Illinois.
    1976. "Isolation and Ceramic Change: A Case from the Ucayali River, Peru." *World Archaeology* 7(3):333–51.
Raymond, J. Scott, Warren R. DeBoer, and Peter G. Roe
    1975. "Cumancaya: A Peruvian Ceramic Tradition." University of Calgary, Department of Archaeology, Occasional Papers, no. 2.
Roe, Peter G.
    1973. "Cumancaya: Archaeological Excavations and Ethnographic Analogy in the Peruvian Montana." Ph.D. dissertation, University of Illinois.
Schiffer, Michael B.
    1972. "Archaeological Context and Systemic Context." *American Antiquity* 37(2):156–65.
    1975. "Archaeology as Behavioral Science." *American Anthropologist* 77(4):836–48.
Spahni, Jean-Christian
    1966. *La Cerámica Popular en el Perú*. Lima: Peruano Suiza.
Taylor, Walter W.
    1948. *A Study of Archeology*. Washington, D.C.: American Anthropological Association, Memoir 69.
Tessmann, Günter
    1928. *Menschen ohne Gott*. Stuttgart: Strecker und Schröder.

5/An Archaeological View of a Contemporary Kurdish Village: Domestic Architecture, Household Size, and Wealth

Carol Kramer
Department of Anthropology
Lehman College,
City University of New York

Utilizing data on residential architecture in a contemporary village in central western Iran, Kramer attempts to pinpoint some of the causal relationships between variation in architectural features, household size and composition, and economic rank. She suggests that while both economic variation and aspects of household size and composition might be inferred from the archaeologically retrievable architectural remains of this village, different classes of data may be required to reconstruct each of these aspects of village organization. The architectural and demographic data presented by Kramer may be compared with those discussed by Jacobs and Sumner, and with those for Hasanābād outlined by Watson. The article bears on the analysis of excavated early village architecture in Southwest Asia as well as on the more general issue of architectural variability.

A shorter version of this paper was presented at the seventy-fifth annual meeting of the American Anthropological Association (November 1976, in Washington, D.C.). The research on which the article is based was supported by the National Science Foundation (NSF SOC-75-08507). Implementation of the field research was greatly facilitated by Mr. Mahmud Khaliqi and Dr. Firuz Bagherzadeh of the Ministry of Culture and Arts of the Imperial Government of Iran; to them and their colleagues I owe a debt of gratitude. Constructive comments on earlier drafts of this article were made by colleagues who bear no responsibility for flaws in this version; I thank Janet Chernela, Sheila Dauer, Ann Farber, Laura K. Gordon, Lee Horne, Gregory A. Johnson, Philip Kohl, Steve Kowalewski, Karen Oppenheim Mason, William Mason, Nan Rothschild, Leni Silverstein, Brian Spooner, Elizabeth Stone, Mary Voigt, Patty Jo Watson, and Harvey Weiss. Figures 5.2, 5.3, and 5.4 were prepared by Claus Breede, for whose assistance and expertise I am grateful; figure 5.1 was prepared by Susan Gallucci. Judith Berman provided valuable assistance in the initial stages of data analysis. The village name is pseudonymous.

The Zagros Mountains of Iraq and Iran have been the focus of extensive archaeological investigation, which has yielded a rich and varied body of data. For at least eight millennia, the region has supported sedentary village-dwelling populations subsisting on cultivated plants and domesticated animals. Much archaeological data has been retrieved from mounds, the accumulated remains of ancient nucleated settlements. Building on the general assumption that aspects of cultural behavior have material correlates which are patterned and observable in the archaeological record, this paper explores some specific ways in which variations in household population and wealth are reflected in contemporary Zagros village architecture. The data discussed here indicate that variations in ethnographically documented domestic architecture are related both to variations in household population size and to economic status, and suggest that an archaeologist excavating the remains of such architecture could reliably infer aspects of these relationships.

Data were obtained during the summer of 1975 in a small Kurdish village referred to here as Shāhābād. The village was selected because in many respects it can be considered "traditional," partly, perhaps, a function of its distance from contemporary roads and urban centers. Further, it is located in an area in which recent archaeological work has provided considerable evidence of village life as far back as about 7000 B.C. (Braidwood, Howe, and Reed 1961; Hamlin 1974; Levine and McDonald 1977; Meldgaard, Mortensen, and Thrane 1964; Mortensen 1974; Smith 1972, 1975; Young and Levine 1974). The available ethnographic literature for this region, however, only weakly illuminates the numerous contemporary parallels to archaeological data (see Barth [1953] and Leach [1940] for descriptions of Zagros Kurdish villages). Recent studies by archaeologists (Hole 1975, and this volume; Watson 1966, 1978, and 1979) have been designed to diminish discrepancies between the archaeological and ethnographic coverage of the Zagros area. It is hoped that the following discussion will similarly contribute to filling some of the gaps in our knowledge of Zagros village architecture noted twenty years ago by Braidwood and Reed (1957:26). The following pages briefly describe some salient features of Shāhābād's architecture. Some relationships between architectural features and aspects of the village population and variations in economic status are then discussed.

Shāhābād Village: Setting and Architecture

Shāhābād lies at about 1,650 meters above sea level, approximately midway between the provincial capitals Kermānshāh and Hamadān in western Iran (see figure 5.1). As in much of the Zagros area, the village economy is based on mixed farming of crops which are both rain-fed and irrigated. The principal crop is wheat; barley, alfalfa,

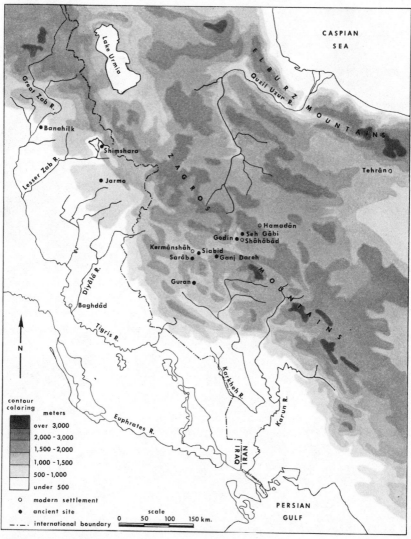

Figure 5.1. Shāhābād and other Zagros settlements.

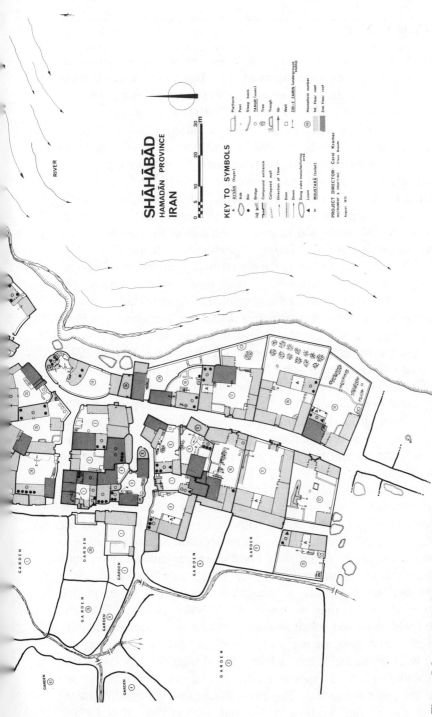

Figure 5.2. Shahābād Village, Iran (1:250).

clover, lentils, beans, and chickpeas are major subsidiary crops, all planted in an alternate-year fallow cycle.[1] The major animal domesticates are sheep and goat; cows and donkeys are less numerous, and there are but two horses in the village. The presence of animals in a compound is reflected architecturally by a variety of troughs, pens, stables, coops, and hives, as well as underground stables in some houses. Harvested plants are kept in gunny sacks, storage bins of packed mud (*chīneh*), and special rooms earmarked for the storage of food and fodder. The major domesticates, which have been heavily utilized in this area for more than 7,000 years, would thus be represented in the archaeological remains of Shāhābād not only by bones, seeds, and pollen, but by a variety of architectural features.

Shāhābād's population is supported by approximately 300 hectares of arable land,[2] which in most years produces little surplus. The village itself covers an area of approximately three hectares, extending along one side of a river which is dry during two months of most summers (see figure 5.2). The village threshing floor lies across the river, and the cemetery extends beyond its north end. During 1975, Shāhābād's three hectares were occupied by 418 people in 67 house compounds.[3] Compound residents numbered from 1 to 15, with a mean house population of 6.2. There is a stated and apparent preference for both virilocal residence and extended families; each nuclear family sleeps in a separate room, around either a hearth or an oven, but coresiding nuclear families jointly participate in food preparation and consumption.

Architecture in Shāhābād is predominantly residential. There are a few "shops" in the village, as well as an architecturally unique government school and a public bath which has not functioned for several years.[4] The village possesses no specialized religious rooms, structures, or areas. Shāhābād's houses are constructed of various combinations of *chīneh* and sun-dried brick; only one room in the village, and small portions of the school, are built of the expensive baked brick which must be imported. Wooden beams and twigs, capped with mud and rolled annually, are the most common roofing materials; most roofs are flat, and even those which are vaults of unbaked brick terminate in flat surfaces. Wood is sufficiently costly that when major structural renovations are carried out, house beams are saved for some future use. The environment and the building materials in this region combine to facilitate preservation of walls and

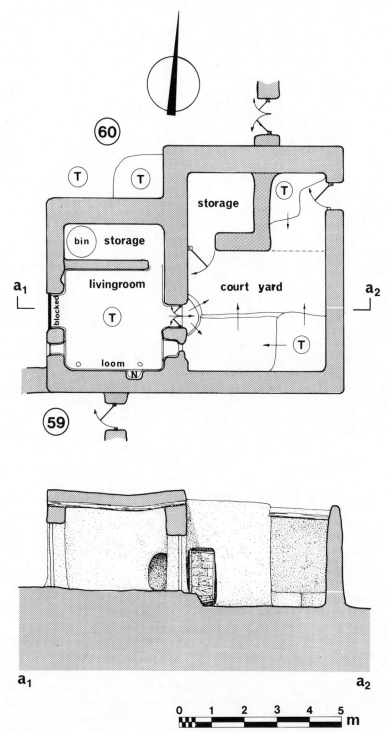

Figure 5.3. Household 61, one of the smallest houses in Shāhābād (1:50).

Table 5.1 Sizes of Architectural Areas, Shāhābād

Architectural Area	All Compounds				Landed Compounds				Landless Compounds			
		Area (sq. m.)				Area (sq. m.)				Area (sq. m.)		
	N	$\bar{X}$	Median	S.D.	N	$\bar{X}$	Median	S.D.	N	$\bar{X}$	Median	S.D.
Total compound [a]	67	252.5	194.0	199.7	33	307.4	251.0	244.6	34	199.0	160.5	130.3
Courtyard [a]	67	103.3	74.0	112.2	33	118.3	86.0	130.8	34	88.8	64.5	92.2
Kitchen [b]	74	18.0	16.0	8.8	40	19.8	17.5	10.4	34	15.9	15.5	5.7
Living Room	90	22.4	21.5	7.9	50	20.9	20.0	8.1	40	24.2	24.5	7.2
Storeroom	137	21.6	19.0	13.0	79	23.9	21.0	27.7	58	18.6	17.5	11.2
Stable [c]	33	24.0	25.0	12.0	17	27.1	27.0	12.3	16	21.3	21.0	11.8

Note: All figures are based on the village plan (figure 5.2; 1:250) and include wall thickness.
[a] The larger village compounds are included here and excluded in other samples.
[b] Figures include kitchens used as "living rooms."
[c] Figures include stables used seasonally or intermittently as "storerooms."

roofs; theoretically, the archaeological remnants of Shāhābād would include a representative range of building materials as well as the architectural features described below.

Each of Shāhābād's 67 house compounds consists of several rooms and an unroofed courtyard enclosed by a high *chīneh* wall. It is this perimeter wall that defines the area referred to here as "compound area." Except for those old rooms which were formerly towers and are currently used as kitchens or for storage, village rooms are rectilinear (see Whiting and Ayres 1968), although compound walls need not be. The smallest village house covers an area of 42 square meters; the largest, at 1,358 square meters, is more than 30 times that size. Mean compound area for all houses is 253 square meters; the median is 194.

Both the smallest village houses (see figure 5.3, for example) and the single house occupied by one person are subdivided into at least three discrete areas. One room is the locus for such human activities as cooking, eating, entertaining, and sleeping; it is referred to as *khāneh*, glossed here as "living room." A second room is used for storage (of twigs, fodder, occasional sacks of grain and legumes, and dung cakes, the chief fuel source). The third essential area is the unroofed courtyard, in which many activities are carried out and in which such non-portable *chīneh* features as animal pens, troughs, beehives, chicken coops, latrines, and warm-weather ovens, and wells, are often located. In addition, most houses possess kitchens (*āshpazkhāneh*) which are morphologically and spatially distinct from their living rooms. Many houses also have stables at ground floor level, and some have additional stables in the form of subterranean tunnels (*zīr-e zamīn*s). Some pertinent metric data are summarized in table 5.1.

Each of these domestic areas typically has distinctive built-in features, such as troughs, hearths, ovens, and storage bins. Ovens are the diagnostic attributes of kitchens; these are unbaked clay features sunk into the floor. Because they are approximately one meter deep, ovens are always located on ground floor level. The kitchen is also the preferred location of the household's loom, if it has one, and of its storage bins. Vertical looms would be identifiable archaeologically by two small shallow holes in the floor. Storage bins are footed *chīneh* structures up to two meters in height; because of their weight, bins are not installed in second-story rooms. Hearths are peculiar to living rooms; these features are invisible beneath carpets during warm months, but are the focus of family activity during the winter. The hearth is a shallow, circular, clay-lined pit sealed with a clay plug when not in use, and heated by a portable brazier when functioning. At such times, a low table-like wooden frame is set over the hearth, supporting tablecloths and quilts and allowing eaters and sleepers to sit and sleep around the hearth, warming their feet. In contrast with ovens, such hearths, found throughout the Zagros (see Mokri 1961) and elsewhere in Southwest Asia, are often situated in second-story rooms, and as such have been found at an archaeological site near Shāhābād (Hamlin 1974; Levine and Hamlin 1974).

The floor of each area within a house compound is peculiar to that kind of area and therefore diagnostic of its primary function. For example, living room floors are carefully smoothed, usually plastered, and often whitewashed; kitchen floors are rarely whitewashed, and storeroom floors are only very roughly plastered with chaff-tempered mud. Stable floors are not finished, and are covered with a treacherous but most diagnostic combination of animal dung and decomposing fodder. Villagers say that kitchen, living room, and foyer (ayvān) floors should be resurfaced annually. However, families without fields may not be able to resurface their floors this often because they have too little, or none, of the chaff considered necessary for proper resurfacing; thus even frequency and quality of floor refinishing may reflect variations in economic status.

Approximately half of Shāhābād's houses are two-story structures. As in the house illustrated in figure 5.4, the second story would be reflected archaeologically in the stairway leading up from the courtyard and in the secondary walling added to widen the original wall and to support the heavy living room built several years later than the ground floor portion of the compound. Such a second-story room is often added so that a newly married son can continue to reside with his parents; if such a room is added for a single resident nuclear family, the former ground floor kitchen, or living room, may be converted to a stable, its oven or hearth filled in, and its walls made to support a brick vault beneath the second story. Second-story rooms are considered desirable because they catch cooling breezes during summer months.

The village's open areas, alleys, and "commons" beyond and between house blocks, total approximately one-third of the village area. Like house courtyards, village "commons" and alleys could be archaeologically identified as unroofed by the very nature of their surfaces; these are uneven, pitted, and marked by damp patches and channels of varying width and depth, as well as by ash deposits and the raw materials and ongoing excavations peculiar to dung cake manufacturing areas (see figure 5.2). "Outdoor" surfaces are characteristically embedded with potsherds, fragments of discarded ovens, pebbles, rare scraps of animal bone, animal dung, and fragments of textile, plaster, and rubber. Courtyard surfaces are generally substantially cleaner than those of village "commons" and alleys.

To summarize the foregoing: it is quite likely that an excavator of Shāhābād could readily discriminate between roofed and unroofed areas on the basis of floor surfaces. Further, within the category "roofed," it would be feasible to identify stables, storerooms, kitchens, and living rooms. This could be done by evaluating variations in floors, and by recording the presence and associations with floors of such features as bins, ovens, hearths, and troughs. In other words, within those portions of the village defined as having been roofed, a rough but probably fairly accurate breakdown by primary function would not be very difficult. Houses could thus be compared in terms of their overall size, and on the basis of the number and sizes of different kinds of rooms within the compound wall, including second stories. We may now return to the initial question.

How, and to what extent, does Shāhābād's domestic architecture reflect variability in economic status, and/or in the number and distribution of its inhabitants? Do wealthier families reside in larger houses? Or do larger houses reflect more inhabitants regardless of their occupants' economic statuses?

Architectural Variability: Household Population and Wealth

The history and current nature of Iranian land tenure and inheritance laws and practices are far too complex to review here (see Lambton 1953, 1969). It is, however, relevant to this discussion that of the 67 houses in Shāhābād, 33 are headed by landowners, and the heads of 34 are landless. Landowning families have, in most cases, been in Shāhābād for two or more generations. In contrast, many of those

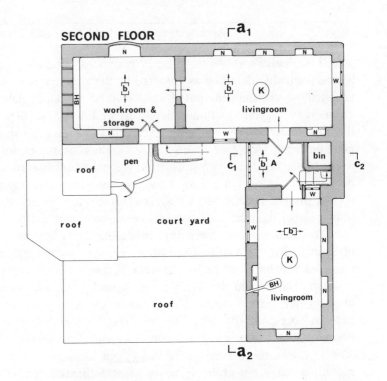

SECOND FLOOR

a₁

N   N   N   N

BH

b

workroom & storage

N

b   K

livingroom

w

bin

c₁   b   A   c₂

roof

pen

roof

court yard

w

-[b]-

K

N

BH

livingroom

N

roof

N

N

N

a₂

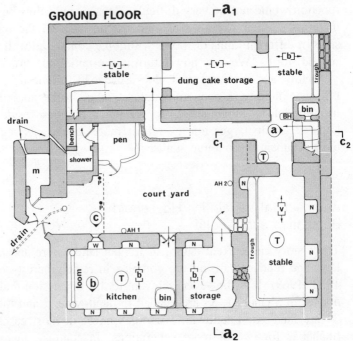

GROUND FLOOR

a₁

-[v]-   -[v]-   -[b]-
stable   dung cake storage   stable

trough

bin

BH

a

drain

bench

pen

shower

c₁

T

m

P

AH 2

N

v

court yard

N

P

c

N

T   stable

drain

AH 1

W   N

N

N

trough

loom

b   T   b

kitchen

bin

b

T

storage

N

N

N

N

c₂

a₂

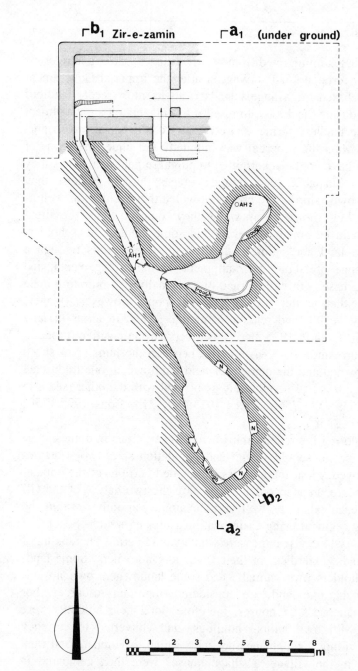

Figure 5.4. Two-story house, Shāhābād (1:50). *A*, foyer; *AH*, air hole leading from underground stable (see *zīr-e-zamīn*, above) to courtyard surface; *b*, ceiling of wooden beams; *BH*, beehive(s); *K*, hearth; *m*, latrine; *N*, niche; *p*, post supporting roofing; *T*, bread oven; *v*, vaulted ceiling; *W*, window.

owning no fields immigrated from nearby villages, settling here originally as sharecroppers but staying on after the Imperial Government of Iran purchased the village's lands from its most recent landlord and began, during the 1960s, to resell it to villagers on an installment basis. These landless former sharecroppers could not afford to purchase land when the program was initiated, and under the terms of land reform have not been permitted to purchase field land since; they remained in Shāhābād (and similar villages) largely because they were given ownership of the houses in which they resided, as well as the right to build houses from which they could no longer be alienated. It should be noted, however, that some landless householders own garden land and animals; they obtain staple crops through a complex range of labor- and equipment-sharing arrangements, and through purchase with cash earned by seasonally out-migrating male kin. Despite their participation in a cash economy, however, villagers still discuss wealth, and relative economic status, in terms of land and animals. Even in 1975 there was a very strong positive (product-moment) correlation ($r = .87$; $p \lessapprox .01$) between the number of sheep and goats owned and the amount of field land owned; one traditional form of wealth is still very closely associated with the other (see also Alberts 1963: 732, 756f.; Bates 1973:189, 213; Irons 1975:175f.; Stirling 1965:225f.).

In exploring the relationships between variations in domestic architecture and household wealth and population size, two strategies were employed. First, the landless and landed portions of the population were segregated, in order to compare the two halves of the village with each other, as well as to examine variability within the landholding segment using traditional measures of wealth. Second, it was necessary to devise a measure which would permit the ranking of all households, regardless of their status as landowners. Some landless householders own animals, and some landowners own no animals; animals, like land, are considered important resources. For each of Shāhābād's 67 houses, therefore, total field holdings were combined with total animal holdings, and converted to currency (riāls), providing a rough measure with which to compare and rank all houses in the village.[5] Village houses were then compared in terms of three metric attributes which could, theoretically, be retrieved archaeologically: total compound area, total roofed area within compound, and dwelling area. The objective was to determine

Table 5.2 Product-moment Correlations (r) between Architectural Areas, Compound Wealth,[a] and Household Size [b]

Architectural Areas (sq. m.)	All Compounds		Landed[c] (n =33)[e]		Landless[d] (n =34)[e]	
	Wealth	Household Size	Wealth	Household Size	Wealth	Household Size
Compound Area	.76	.58	.84 *	.78	.22	−.03
Roofed Area [f]						
within Compound	.54	.70	.53	.84	.49	.24
Dwelling [g] Area	.64	.61	.73	.75	.37	.43

Note: p ≲.01

[a]Total animal and land holdings converted to riāls (65 Iranian riāls = $1.00 U.S.).

[b]All compound residents older than two years were counted.

[c]Mean household size: 6.3 (see note b; when all residents are counted, mean household size = 6.8; median = 6).

[d]Mean household size: 5.1 (see note b; when all residents are counted, mean household size = 5.7; median = 6).

[e]Except where otherwise noted.

[f]Mean area for landless: 111.3 (S.D. = 49); mean area for landed: 194.3 (S.D. = 137.8).

[g]Kitchens and living rooms; n for landed = 29; n for landless = 33; mean area for landless = 50.5 (S.D. = 20); mean area for landed: 60.6 (S.D. = 30.5).

whether variations in these attributes correlate with variations in wealth or in numbers of residents or both. Table 5.2 summarizes some of the correlations discussed below.

Within the landowning group, there is a very strong correlation ($r = .87$; $p ≲.01$) between amount of field land owned and overall compound size. Since they own no land, it is impossible to make a comparative statement for the other half of the population. However, when the riāls measure of wealth is used, clear differences between the two halves of the village emerge (see table 5.2). When the entire village is treated as one sample, the correlation between a household's wealth (expressed as riāls) and the total metric area of its compound is a somewhat deceptively high .76 ($p ≲.01$), reflecting the enormous wealth of the few households in the upper quartile of the village. One explanation for the discrepancy between landed and landless with respect to total compound area is that the ancestors of the landed household heads were the original settlers of Shāhābād, and therefore had first claim to non-arable land. Although villagers may now purchase house sites, land within the village is said to cost as much as field land, and there are few available building sites within the village or at its periphery; nonlandowners who can afford to purchase new building sites are thus limited to relatively small plots. Further, in house building, the perimeter wall is ordinarily the first structure erected, and functions as a boundary marker even before the minimal number of rooms is constructed; it seems plausible that this principle has a long history in Shāhābād. This suggested explanation is supported by data on residential history and mobility collected during 1975, which suggest that the poorer families have a shorter genealogical history in the village; conversely, data on relative compound chronology indicate that Shāhābād's largest compounds are its oldest. Interestingly, these are located upstream of more recent compounds (see figure 5.2).

As table 5.1 indicates, mean size of landowners' compounds is more than 100 square meters larger than that of landless compounds; median size is also substantially larger. In view of this difference, it was necessary to examine roofed area within compounds, to determine whether landowners actually have proportionally more roofed space or whether their compounds' larger sizes simply reflect larger (unroofed) courtyards. The data indicate that whereas considerable differences in overall compound area exist between landed and landless compounds, for total roofed area the differences between the two halves are less. Mean roofed area of the landed exceeds that of landless compounds by about 80 square meters, but there is a much wider range of variation within the landed half (see table 5.2). However, for both halves of the population, total roofed area is moderately rather than strongly correlated with wealth. The slightly stronger correlation for the landed segment ($r = .53$, as compared with a value of .49 for the landless) may reflect the fact that wealthier people can not only better afford wooden beams, but have a somewhat greater need for them in roofing stables and storerooms. This suggestion appears to be supported by the moderate correlations between wealth in riāls and number of storerooms ($r = .51$, $p \lessapprox .01$; $n = 61$) and, in the landed half alone, between amount of field land owned and number of storerooms ($r = .53$, $p \lessapprox .01$; $n = 31$).

In contrast with total compound area and total roofed area, dwelling area (living rooms and kitchens) does not appear to be substantially greater in homes of the landed. Mean total dwelling area in compounds of the landed exceeds—by approximately 10 square meters—mean dwelling area in compounds of the landless half of the village. This difference becomes more interesting when one considers that mean household size for the landed is larger by one person (6.3 compared with 5.1 for landless households). There is no significant relationship between wealth and population density; households with comparatively more wealth (in riāls) do not have more square meters per occupant. Rather, density in dwelling space, regardless of economic status, is between 9 and 10 square meters per person, a figure provocatively close to the 10 square meters per person discussed in cross-cultural studies by Naroll (1962), LeBlanc (1971), and others.[6] However, the figures in table 5.2 show a much stronger correlation between wealth (in riāls) and dwelling area for landed than for landless compounds. This apparently reflects the higher proportion of extended families in the landed segment of the population (18 of the 33 landed are joint or extended families, in contrast with 6 of the 34 landless compounds; 55 percent of landed compounds, and 18 percent of landless, therefore require more than one dwelling room, in accordance with the cultural preference for separate sleeping rooms for each coresiding nuclear family described above). This phenomenon, reflected in the figures for kitchens and living rooms in table 5.1, would also appear to be the reason for the difference in correlations between dwelling area and family size shown in table 5.2; the units reflected in these computations are numbers of compound residents and total metric area of living rooms and kitchens, rather than numbers of such rooms. The greater number of living rooms and kitchens in houses of the landed must also account for the divergence between the two halves of the village in correlations between total roofed area and family size. The foregoing suggests that numbers of such rooms are useful predictors of numbers of nuclear families, while their metric area is a more useful predictor of actual numbers of people (very small children excluded).

Unlike metric area, such built-in features as hearths, ovens, and storage bins do not appear to reliably predict either wealth or numbers of residents. Ovens and particularly hearths provide a rough index of numbers of nuclear families; these can, however, number from 2 to 9 individuals. Thus, while they are useful markers of activities and room functions, built-in architectural features are less useful than metric area in estimating household population size, and even composition, for several reasons. First, compound residents may be at a late stage in the domestic cycle (former occupants, such as married offspring, having departed permanently). That domestic architecture changes with the domestic cycle should not surprise us (see

Goody 1958); the fit, however, is not always perfect. A second reason for features being less useful indicators of a compound's population than metric area is that its present inhabitants may have moved into a compound after its bins or ovens were constructed by an earlier occupant; in fact, there has been considerable residential mobility within Shāhābād.[7] Third, a compound may lack certain features, or possess relatively few of a particular type, because its residents are not skilled in their construction, or because they have insufficient time to replace old ones which have already been removed. Data on ovens, for example, illustrate some of the difficulties inherent in evaluating variations in numbers of built-in features.

The ideal (stated) number of ovens is two, one in the courtyard for warm weather and one indoors for cooler months. Variation around this ideal is, however, considerable; some compounds possess only one oven (indoors), while others have two or more indoors and/or outdoors. Not all need be in use in a given year, however. One could argue that the critical variable determining the number of ovens per compound is not the number of coresident families, since women share the work of food preparation, but rather a household's wealth (measured by the extent to which it can afford to fuel more than one oven on any given day), or the number of dishes normally prepared simultaneously, or both. These would be more relevant considerations than the number of people expected to partake of a given meal, since because of a cultural preference for stews, variations in number of diners are generally accommodated simply by using cooking vessels of varying size. Further, as layout and circulation within the compound change during the course of its history, so too does the degree to which an oven's location is convenient (or inconvenient) with respect to smoke dispersal. For these reasons, residents of a compound with four ovens may actually use only one of them throughout the year. Unused ovens may be enlarged and converted to (rare) barley storage pits, filled in, or left standing, to serve in temporary wool, bread, or fruit storage.

Summary and Conclusions

Several points raised parenthetically in the foregoing discussion cannot be developed at length here but may be briefly reiterated because of their broader implications. First, while the utility and limitations of analogical reasoning are legitimate theoretical and methodological concerns (cf. Ascher 1961; Binford 1967, 1968, 1972; Freeman 1968, among others), it is suggested that the Shāhābād data are relevant to certain classes of archaeological materials from the Zagros region for periods in which we have evidence suggesting the existence of variations in socio-economic rank. Using traditional measures of wealth, this paper focuses on variation in economic status as it is reflected in metric attributes of residential architecture. Building materials, coded and ranked separately from the metric and frequency data utilized here, should provide a useful independent test of the economic variation inferred from such measures. Passing reference has been made, for example, to roofing beams, baked and sun-dried brick, and frequency of floor resurfacings; variations in windows and whitewash are only two of several additional variables which should, in future, prove useful in discriminating and quantifying variations in economic status (cf. Flannery 1976:16, 19). Variations in construction materials in Shāhābād appear to generally reflect variations in economic status as they do in Hasanābād, another contemporary Zagros village (Watson 1966, 1978, and 1979).

An additional point which may be noted here is that excavators often seem to assume that the archaeological materials that they uncover adequately reflect some "average" state of the population responsible for these remnants. Ascher (1961) has questioned the validity of this implicit and normative assumption, which he refers to as the "Pompeii Premise," particularly as it applies to portable objects. The Shāhābād architectural data discussed here similarly suggest that families' changing needs are reflected in frequent architectural changes. Because residential architecture is so closely bound to the needs, nature, and number of inhabitants, it is suggested that archaeologists and social anthropologists alike further explore the relationships between architecture and the domestic cycle.

Each of these points relates to another issue: the degree to which archaeological sampling strategies and tactics traditionally used in Southwest Asia are appropriate means of pinpointing architectural (and other) variability. Specific observations based on the Shāhābād data may not automatically be extended beyond this village; just as variability exists between settlements of different sizes within a regional hierarchy, so too does it exist between settlements of the same size. Indeed, additional empirical data are sorely needed. However, while no claim is made that Shāhābād represents all Zagros villages, a review of the limited available comparative data suggests that Shāhābād is neither "unusual" nor particularly complexly stratified. Like most Zagros villages, its houses are clustered rather than dispersed. Small, scattered, randomly-placed trenches in the site which Shāhābād will become would not necessarily provide a representative sample of the range of household or village activities, nor even permit us to reconstruct ranges of variation in compound size. Even using 5 by 5 meter trenches, for example, it might be difficult to estimate the size and layout of even the smallest village house, a mere 42 square meters in area. The threshing floor and cemetery would not be part of the Shāhābād mound site, and would therefore not be reflected in the kinds of excavations most frequently conducted in Southwest Asia. The Shāhābād data, viewed in the light of recent literature on sampling design (e.g., Mueller 1975; Redman 1974; Winter 1976) underscore the importance of carefully designing sampling procedures in accordance with research objectives and with appropriate empirical data.

To conclude: the Shāhābād data described here show that domestic architecture is related to aspects of population and wealth in interesting and complex ways.[8] They suggest that in investigating relationships between these variables, one should distinguish roofed from unroofed areas, and then attempt finer distinctions between different kinds of roofed area. Residential space reflects variation in both compound population and economic status; the degree to which either can be extrapolated from the architectural data depends on which variables are measured and compared.

If one is interested in determining the number of coresiding married couples, the number of dwelling rooms is a useful if not flawless source of information. If, on the other hand, one wishes to estimate the number of people, metric area of dwelling space (i.e., living rooms and kitchens) proves a more reliable indicator, averaging approximately 9.75 square meters per person. However, dwelling area does not seem to provide a useful way of discriminating between more or less wealthy compounds, whereas the total metric area of a compound does. In Shāhābād, as in the minds of most anthropologists, richer people live in bigger houses, with the wealthiest occupying the largest—a point generally either assumed (see Tax 1953:189) or disregarded (e.g., Divale 1977; Ember 1973).

In Shāhābād, presence or absence of second-story areas bears no clear relationship to the number of resident nuclear families, or to numbers of people; two-story dwellings are therefore apparently not relevant to population estimation. Built-in features such as bins, hearths, and ovens, while not reflecting variations in wealth in either their building materials or numbers in a compound, do reflect in a rough way the number of coresiding nuclear families, rather than numbers of individuals, within compounds. Perhaps most importantly, such features, recorded in conjunction with formal attributes of floors, provide a reliable basis for inferring primary functions of rooms. And the identification of areas of different types, combined with metric data, provide, at least in Shāhābād, a key source of information concerning some aspects of demographic and economic variation.

Notes

1. The seasonal cycle and food resources of Shāhābād are discussed in greater detail elsewhere (Kramer, n.d.); the reader is also referred to Lambton (1953:362, 366ff.), and to Barth (1953) and Leach (1940) for accounts of closely similar systems of land use.

2. The published village gazetteer and census indicate a sustaining area of approximately 200 hectares in the immediate vicinity of Shāhābād. Data collected during 1975 suggest, however, that these census figures should be viewed as minimal, since villagers own land which "belongs" to (i.e., is in the *mulk* of) other villages. Thus, in the case of Shāhābād, approximately three-quarters of its field lands are in its immediate environs; an additional one-quarter owned by its inhabitants actually "belongs" to neighboring villages. An additional problem is raised by the unit of land measure: the *juft* (cf. Lambton 1953:4f., 244; 1969:7f.). In Shāhābād, as elsewhere in Iran, *juft* refers both to a team of oxen (meaning, literally, "team" or "pair," and hence the plow team) and, by extension, to the area that can be worked by such a team in a given year. Since a village's holdings vary in quality, and since there is variation between villages' holdings, the work and performance of a plow team vary both within and between villages' holdings in *juft*, for which there is therefore no uniform metric value across Iran. Analysis of the available data, however, strongly suggests that the mean metric value of a Shāhābād *juft* is approximately 7 hectares. In any case, the figures 200 hectares (the village's immediate sustaining area) and 300 hectares (the approximate total sustaining area, computed on the basis of the total holdings in *juft* of Shāhābād's villagers) should be of interest to archaeologists engaged in research focusing on surface surveys, who should note that villages may utilize (and own) field lands not in the area immediately surrounding the village.

3. The house numbers on figure 5.2 range from 1 to 83 because they reflect a list of households (khānevādeh) provided by a major informant. Members of two or more khānevādeh, however, frequently reside together in a single compound. Because it is the architectural data that will be preserved in archaeological form, the 67 compounds rather than the 83 khānevādeh are the units of analysis here; in any event, joint households appear in all cases to pool resources while coresiding.

4. The village "shops" (dokkān) are entered from the alleys (as well as from the houses to which they are attached, in two cases). These are single rooms, totaling five within the village, which stock small quantities of dry goods and could be identified by the presence of niches or shelves or both, platforms, and the absence of other built-in features. Most of the goods required by the residents of Shāhābād are provided not by the village's "shops" (which function largely on the basis of barter, rather than cash exchanges) but by itinerant merchants, and obtained by inhabitants in frequent trips to the nearest towns. This pattern is in contrast with larger neighboring villages, some of which in 1975 had meat "shops." The school is constructed partly of baked brick and, like the bathhouse, is unlike residential structures in layout; neither is included in the 3 hectare figure given for the village's area.

5. Computations for animal holdings exclude fowl (for which good figures could not be obtained, in part because their numbers fluctuate frequently), cats, and dogs (which are not bought, sold, or fed, and hence have no significant economic value). Holdings in gardens (as opposed to field land) are likewise excluded, since reliable metric data are not available for all garden holdings. However, there is a strong association between the ownership of field land and the ownership of gardens: ($\chi^2 = 27.7$, $p \leq .01$). Measures of wealth are treated more extensively in Kramer, n.d. It should be noted that when holdings in land and animals are converted to riāls, compounds' wealth range from 0 riāls (6 compounds, or 9 percent of the sample) to more than 5 million riāls (1 compound, or 1 percent); the mean is 209,296 riāls, the median 100,250.

6. See table 5.2; mean dwelling area divided by mean number of residents (over two years of age) produces the figures 9.9 for the landless sample, and 9.6 for the landed. A second way to compute these figures is to sum, separately, densities for the landed and landless (density = dwelling area divided by number of residents more than two years of age) and divide by sample number; the figures here are 10.9 square meters (mean) for the landed ($n = 29$; median = 10.3 square meters) and 11.5 square meters for the landless ($n = 33$; median = 9.2 square meters). For reasons beyond my control, the two largest compounds in Shāhābād could not be included in the "landed" sample; for this measure, therefore, it is possible that the mean number of square meters per person for landed compounds actually differs slightly from the figures given above.

7. It could be argued that mobility within the village, which includes exchange and sale of houses, occurs at least in part because people periodically "fit" their residential space to their needs in accordance with fluctuations in the domestic cycle. Exchange and sale of houses occur among both landed and landless segments of this village, and are discussed in another publication (Kramer n.d.).

8. Several of the points discussed in this paper have recently been raised in a review of archaeological data from Tollán, Mexico (Healan 1977).

References Cited

Alberts, Robert C.
1963. "Social Structure and Culture Change in an Iranian Village." Ph.D. dissertation, University of Wisconsin.
Ascher, Robert
1961. "Analogy in Archaeological Interpretation." *Southwestern Journal of Anthropology* 17:317–25.
Barth, Fredrik
1953. *Principles of Social Organization in Southern Kurdistan.* Oslo: Universitets Etnografiske Museum, Bulletin 7.
Bates, Daniel G.
1973. *Nomads and Farmers: A Study of the Yörük of Southeastern Turkey.* Museum of Anthropology, Anthropological Papers, no. 52. Ann Arbor: University of Michigan.
Binford, Lewis
1967. "Smudge Pits and Hide Smoking: The Use of Analogy in Archaeological Reasoning." *American Antiquity* 32:1–12.
1968. "Methodological Considerations of the Archaeological Use of Ethnographic Data." In Richard Lee and Irven DeVore, eds., *Man the Hunter,* pp. 268–73. Chicago: Aldine.
1972. "Archaeological Reasoning and Smudge Pits—Revisited." In *An Archaeological Perspective,* pp. 52–58. New York: Seminar Press.
Braidwood, Robert J. and Charles A. Reed
1957. "The Achievement and Early Consequences of Food-Production: A Consideration of the Archaeological and Natural-Historical Evidence." *Cold-Spring Harbor Symposia on Quantitative Biology* 22:19–31.
Braidwood, Robert J., Bruce Howe, and Charles Reed
1961. "The Iranian Prehistoric Project." *Science* 133:2008–10.
Divale, William T.
1977. "Living Floor Area and Marital Residence: A Replication." *Behavior Science Research* 2:109–15.
Ember, Melvin
1973. "An Archaeological Indicator of Matrilocal Versus Patrilocal Residence." *American Antiquity* 38:177–82.
Flannery, Kent V.
1976. "The Early Mesoamerican House." In Kent V. Flannery, ed., *The Early Mesoamerican Village,* pp. 16–24. New York: Academic Press.
Freeman, Leslie G., Jr.
1968. "A Theoretical Framework for Interpreting Archeological Materials." In Sally R. Binford and Lewis Binford, eds., *New Perspectives in Archeology,* pp. 262–67. Chicago: Aldine.

Goody, Jack, ed.
1958. *The Developmental Cycle in Domestic Groups*. Cambridge Papers in Social Anthropology 1. New York: Cambridge University Press; reprinted 1971.

Hamlin, Carol Kramer
1974. "Seh Gabi, 1973." *Archaeology* 27:274–7*.

Healan, Dan M.
1977. "Architectural Implications of Daily Life in Ancient Tollán, Hidalgo, Mexico." *World Archaeology* 9:140–56.

Hole, Frank
1975. "Ethnoarcheology of Nomadic Pastoralism: A Case Study." Paper prepared for School of American Research Seminar on Ethnoarcheology, November 17–21, Sante Fe.

Iran, Government of. Plan Organization
1970. *Village Gazetteer*, Vol. 22: *Hamadan and Ilam Farmandarikols, General Governate*. Tehran: Iranian Statistical Centre.

Irons, William
1975. *The Yomut Turkmen: A Study of Social Organization Among a Central Asian Turkic-Speaking Population*. Museum of Anthropology, Anthropological Papers, no. 58. Ann Arbor: University of Michigan.

Kramer, Carol
n.d. "Ethnoarchaeology in a Kurdish Village."

Lambton, Ann K.S.
1953. *Landlord and Peasant in Persia*. Oxford: Oxford University Press; reprinted 1969.
1969. *The Persian Land Reform, 1962–1966*. Oxford: The Clarendon Press.

Leach, Edmund R.
1940. *Social and Economic Organization of the Rowanduz Kurds*. London School of Economics, Monograph on Social Anthropology, no. 3. London: Percy Lund, Humphries.

LeBlanc, Steven
1971. "An Addition to Naroll's Suggested Floor Area and Settlement Population Relationship." *American Antiquity* 36:210–11.

Levine, Louis D. and Carol Kramer Hamlin
1974. "The Godin Project: Seh Gabi." *Iran* 12:211–13.

Levine, Louis D. and Mary McDonald
1977. "The Neolithic and Chalcolithic Periods in the Mahidasht." *Iran* 15:39–50.

Meldgaard, Jørgen, Peder Mortensen, and Henrik Thrane
1964. "Excavations at Tepe Guran, Luristan." *Acta Archaeologica* 34:97–133.

Mokri, Mohammad
1961. "Le Foyer Kurde." *Ethnographie* 55:79–95.

Mortensen, Peder
1974. "A Survey of Prehistoric Settlements in Northern Luristan." *Acta Archaeologica* 45:1–47.

Mueller, James W., ed.
1975. *Sampling in Archaeology*. Tucson: University of Arizona Press.

Naroll, Raoul
   1962. "Floor Area and Settlement Population." *American Antiquity* 27:587–88.
Redman, Charles L.
   1974. *Archaeological Sampling Strategies*. Reading, Mass.: Addison-Wesley
   Modules in Anthropology, no. 55.
Smith, P. E. L.
   1972. "Ganj Dareh Tepe." *Iran* 10:165–68.
   1975. "Ganj Dareh Tepe." *Iran* 13:178–80.
Stirling, Paul
   1965. *Turkish Village*. New York: Wiley.
Tax, Sol
   1953. *Penny Capitalism: A Guatemalan Indian Economy*. New York: Octagon
   Books; reprinted 1972.
Watson, Patty Jo
   1966. "Clues to Iranian Prehistory in Modern Village Life." *Expedition*
   8:9–19.
   1978. "Architectural Differentiation in Some Near Eastern Communities, Prehistoric and Contemporary." In Charles Redman, Mary Jane Berman, Edward
   V. Curtin, William T. Langhorne, Jr., Nina Versaggi, and Jeffery C. Wanser,
   eds., *Social Archeology: Beyond Subsistence and Dating*, pp. 131–58. New
   York: Academic Press.
   1979. *Archaeological Ethnography in Western Iran*. Viking Fund Publications
   in Anthropology, no. 57. Tucson: University of Arizona Press.
Winter, Marcus C.
   1976. "Excavating a Shallow Community by Random Sampling Quadrats." In
   Kent V. Flannery, ed., *The Early Mesoamerican Village*, pp. 62–67. New
   York: Academic Press.
Whiting, John W. M. and Barbara Ayres
   1968. "Inferences from the Shape of Dwellings." In K. C. Chang, ed., *Settlement Archaeology*, pp. 117–33. Palo Alto: National Press Books.
Young, T. Cuyler, Jr. and Louis D. Levine
   1974. *Excavations of the Godin Project: Second Progress Report*. Royal On-
   tario Museum Art and Archaeology Occasional Paper 26. Toronto.

6/Estimating Population by Analogy: An Example

William M. Sumner
Department of Anthropology
Ohio State University

Drawing on recent census and cartographic data for Fars province in southwest Iran, Sumner examines the relationships between contemporary settlement populations and areas, suggesting a range of figures which should be useful in estimating population sizes of archaeological sites. He applies his findings based on contemporary demographic data in an effort to estimate the population size of a partially excavated prehistoric village in Fars. Sumner's discussion of possible sources of variability in population density within the region today provides an interesting backdrop to Jacobs' discussion of a contemporary Fars village; it also points up the complexity of variables employed in archaeological population estimates based on site size, and suggests approaches to further research and the possible refinement of such estimates.

The idea that a positive correlation exists between population and settlement area has often been the basis for ancient population estimates. Generally, a factor representing average density of population within ethnographically known settlements is used to estimate population from the area of archaeological sites. An effort is usually made to assure that the ethnographic example represents a settlement type similar to the type expected in the archaeological case under analysis. The purpose of this paper is to present some new information on modern village population densities in Fars Province, Iran, and to provide an

This paper is a revised version of material originally included in a dissertation presented to the University of Pennsylvania. The original research was partly financed by a dissertation year fellowship awarded by the Council of the Graduate School of Arts and Sciences at the University of Pennsylvania.

example of how these data might be used to estimate prehistoric population in the same region.

Modern Population Density

The few studies available for modern Middle Eastern villages suggest an average population density ranging between 100 and 200 people per settlement hectare. The density factor used to estimate ancient Middle Eastern population has usually been within this range (Russell 1958:59–68, 146; Adams 1965:123, 124; Adams and Nissen 1972:29; Johnson 1973:66; and Hole, Flannery, and Neely 1969:370).

Recently, a new dam and irrigation system has been constructed in the Kur River Valley. During the early stages of this project, a map was prepared (scale 1:5,000) from aerial photographs taken in October 1965 and March 1966. Enumeration for the second national census of Iran was conducted in November 1966. It was possible to identify 110 villages listed in the census (Iran 1970) on the Dorudzan Authority map.

Some results of a comparison between village population and area are presented in table 6.1. The total population of the 110 villages was 34,376 and the total area was 233.5 hectares. Marv Dasht town is not included in this total. Apparently, the census definition of Marv Dasht includes 12 villages located around the town, some as much as 8 kilometers away, which are not listed separately in the census. If this is the case, then Marv Dasht, including the satellite villages, has a population of 25,498, an area of 223 hectares and a density of 114 per hectare.

The correlation (Pearson's *r*) between population and village area is 0.76 and is significant at the 0.01 level. This correlation is not high enough to give a very satisfactory prediction of population from the area in individual cases. It does seem to be sufficiently strong to allow useful predictions for groups of villages. It may also be possible to identify factors which cause deviation from the norm. Such factors are intrinsically interesting and an understanding of them will be of value in the analysis of prehistoric settlement patterns.

Before reviewing the possible causes of unusually high or low density, it is useful to consider some possible causes of error in the data presented above. The difference in dates of the aerial photographs and of the census enumeration has certainly introduced an error in the data. It seems unlikely that such error would be much more than the annual population growth rate, which in Iran is about 2.5 percent. Even an error of 3 percent in population would not change the results significantly.

A number of small settlements were not named on the map and could not be identified in the census. An inspection of the census reveals that small dependent settlements were counted separately.

Table 6.1 Mean Population, Area, and Density

Villages	N	Mean Population	Mean Village Area (ha.)	Mean Density (people/ha.)
Total	110	313	2.1	147
Large (400 or more)	20	760	4.9	155
Small (less than 100)	18	60	0.9	70
High density (250 people/ha. or more)	17	381	1.3	293
Low density (less than 100 people/ha.)	21	215	3.2	66

Therefore, it is unlikely that the population, and hence the density, of the larger villages in our collection is inflated by including these small settlements. However, there is clearly a bias against very small settlements in the data presented. Thus, the mean values shown for population and settlement area in table 6.1 are somewhat too high. Mean density is probably also overstated since there is a tendency for small villages to have lower densities.

It is assumed that the Dorudzan map is accurate, but it is possible that errors were introduced when village area was measured on the map. More than half the villages in the sample are square or rectangular in plan and are surrounded by a wall. The area of these villages was easy to measure. About forty percent of the villages are irregular in plan but densely built up. The boundaries of these villages were relatively easy to establish and accurate area measurements were not too difficult. The remaining villages (about five percent) consist of scattered buildings separated by considerable open space. Drawing boundaries for these villages was a more or less arbitrary process and the low density calculated for them is not strictly comparable to the calculations for other types of villages.

Keeping in mind these possible sources of error in the data, let us consider various factors that might account for the wide range of densities observed. Most of the comments to follow are basically speculative since data are not at hand to test their validity.

One of the principal reasons for estimating the population of prehistoric settlements is to provide data for the recognition and analysis of settlement size hierarchies. It is generally assumed that settlement size hierarchies are also functional hierarchies. If this is true, then we would expect to find less space in large villages and towns devoted to habitation and more space devoted to administrative, commercial, industrial, religious, and other public functions. We might also predict that the range of living space per person would be much greater in towns, reflecting the greater range in status. Unless the habitation area of a town is very densely occupied, the general density should be lower in towns than in villages.

The only large town in the Kur River Basin is Marv Dasht, which has a population density of 114, considerably lower than the average (147). The town is built around a sugar beet factory which takes up considerable space; there are also many stores, workshops, some administrative buildings, and a public park. Thus, Marv Dasht conforms to the expectation outlined above. However, only 3 large villages are among the places with a density of less than 100 per hectare. Furthermore, as seen in table 6.1, there is a definite tendency for big villages to be more crowded and small villages to be considerably less crowded than average.

The data suggest an interesting possibility. Differences in settlement density due to functionally specialized space may not be great within levels of a settlement hierarchy, but may be significant between levels.

The length of occupation in a village or the cycle of village growth may be related to population density variation. It has been noted that the most common type of village in the valley is enclosed within walls defining a regular rectangular plan. It may be supposed that density will increase within walled villages until crowding outweighs the perceived advantage of living within the walls. At such a time, houses will be built outside the walls. Quite a few villages have houses outside the walls and in a number of cases an original walled plan has been completely obscured by the addition of many buildings. Unfortunately, we can reach no conclusion on this matter in the absence of data on the age of villages.

There can be no doubt that cultural preference plays a large role in determining the plan and layout of villages, which in turn affects the density of occupation. In this case, it is known that a number of the low density villages, composed of scattered houses, are inhabited by recently settled pastoral nomads. It is probable that most of the very low density villages are of this type.

Tolerance to crowding is itself sure to be variable. Any factor which inhibits expansion of a village or the emigration of part of a village population would result in higher densities. The present data provide striking confirmation of this idea. Seventeen of the villages on the Dorudzan map were within the area to be flooded by the new dam. The mean density of these villages is 237 including 6 of the 7 villages with a density of over 300 per hectare. Apparently, building activity ceased when it became known that these villages would soon be destroyed. People who might have emigrated probably did not leave in anticipation of government compensation for the loss of their homes or in the hope of finding employment on the dam construction.

In summary, it has been shown that there is a useful positive correlation between population and settlement area. A number of explanations of settlement density variation have been discussed and it is suggested that an understanding of the causes of settlement density variation will facilitate the interpretation of archaeological data.

Tall-i Bakun: A Population Estimate

It is agreed that reasoning by ethnographic analogy produces the best results when the ethnographic and archaeological examples are known to be similar in a number of ways. In this case, the ethnographic and archaeological examples are in the same river valley and exhibit a number of technological similarities including important elements of the subsistence system, architecture, and settlement patterns. All analogies should be evaluated using independent data from the archaeological record.

In the case presented here, a number of limiting values derived from ethnographic data will be used in an attempt to estimate the population of a prehistoric village. These values include population density within villages as discussed above, as well as more general considerations, such as the range of household size in the Middle East and number of square meters of roofed area per person. Tall-i Bakun A is a small site (about 2 hectares) near Persepolis in the Kur River Valley, which was occupied during the early fourth millennium B.C. Excavations at the site revealed four architectural levels inhabited by people praticing a mixed agriculture (Langsdorff and McCown 1942; Egami and Masuda 1962). The size and number of settlements in the valley, the vigorous ceramic style, and evidence of trade all suggest a period of considerable prosperity.

The most extensively excavated unit (level III) is less than 1,000 square meters in area and represents about one-twentieth of the site. On the basis of inter-connecting rooms, the excavators identified twelve houses in level III. One of these, an incompletely excavated room, is not counted as a separate house and two other partly excavated rooms are not included in the present analysis. Thus, not counting incompletely excavated units, there are eleven houses with one to seven rooms each. In most houses, one room was used for storage and the rest showed signs of domestic activity. The houses constitute a single complex of adjoining structures and there is evidence for open space to the west and southwest. The roofed area of the 44-room complex was about 480 square meters.

The implications of four population estimates for the exposed area of level III are presented in table 6.2. For example, if the population of 20 is correct (line 1, column A), then all of the implications listed in column A must follow. Each set of implications will be discussed in turn.

Mean household size (line 1a) serves to establish a minimum and maximum population estimate. The characteristics of the houses suggest that we are dealing with a nuclear or extended household type rather than a compound household type (Flannery 1972). During the last two census periods, the smallest mean rural household size reported for an Iranian province was 4.2 people (the 1956 census in Khorasan). This figure is for a population undergoing rapid growth (approximately 2.5 percent per year). The minimum mean family size required to maintain a stable population in the most advanced modern countries is just over two people (Wrigley 1969:17). Russell

Table 6.2 Tall-i Bakun A, Level III: Population Estimates

	A	B	C	D
1. Population estimates, excavated houses only	20	40	60	80
Implications:				
a. mean household size	1.8	3.6	5.5	7.3
b. mean roofed floor area per person (square meters)	18	9	6	4.5
2. Settlement density of whole site (people per hectare)				
a. assumed ratio of unoccupied to occupied space 1:1	200	400	600	800
b. assumed ratio 2:1	133	266	400	533
c. assumed ratio 3:1	100	200	300	400

(1958:53) has argued for an estimated average nuclear household size of 3.5 in ancient populations. It seems clear that any population estimate which implies a mean nuclear household size of less than 2 is likely to be an underestimate for prehistoric times.

Modern demographic data would suggest that large household size is associated with high rates of population growth. In Iran, which has an annual population growth rate of 2.5 percent, the largest mean household size recently reported for a province census was 5.9 people (in Ilam, in 1966). It might be expected that large household size would also have been associated with rapid population growth in the past. In general, however, a very low rate of growth is expected to have prevailed in prehistoric times (Cowgill 1975; Carneiro and Hilse 1966). Even the most extreme interpretation of the number and size of settlements in Bakun times would not support an estimate of growth in excess of 0.5 percent per year. Thus, estimates of prehistoric populations implying very large households must be viewed with caution unless it can be shown that households included a number of nuclear families or supernumerary members.

There is considerable cross-cultural evidence for an average of approximately 10 square meters of living floor area per person (LeBlanc 1971; Naroll 1962). This figure agrees well with the amount of roofed dwelling area reported in an Iranian village (Kramer, this volume). Any part of a dwelling used for other functions could cause at least an apparent increase in the amount of floor space available per person and deviations above ten square meters may be common.

Deviation below 10 square meters is less likely. A minimum of about 2 square meters is required just for sleeping. In the absence of other evidence for extreme crowding, we may expect at least 5 square meters per person. The presence of multiple stories would complicate archaeological estimates of floor area available. In the case of Bakun, there is no evidence of second stories and they are unlikely to have been present. Thus, the floor areas listed in columns A and B (table 6.2) fall within an acceptable range but columns C and D imply a smaller floor area than expected.

At this point, the analysis must be expanded to cover the whole area of Tall-i Bakun. This is necessary to account for the possibility that the excavated area was more densely occupied than the rest of the site. Open areas, alleys, and abandoned houses are to be expected in any village. Part 2 of table 6.2 presents the implications of three estimates of the amount of open or uninhabited space in the Bakun village.

The three assumptions regarding the ratio of open or uninhabited to occupied space generate estimates of overall population density within the village. The estimates range from a low of 100 per hectare (column A, assumption 2c) to a maximum of 800 per hectare (column D, assumption 2a). The data presented in the first section of this paper provide a useful means of evaluating these estimates.

There is reason to doubt the estimates in column A on the basis of the implied family size, and in column D on the basis of both family size and square meters per person. Therefore, attention will be focused on columns B and C. In column B, the densities implied by assumptions 2b and 2c are well within the modern range. Assumption 2a produces a high density value, just within the modern range. All of the implied densities in column C are high; the density for assumption 2a is well outside the modern range.

Thus, if Bakun was one of a group of settlements with a density pattern similar to modern villages in the same region, it would have been above average in density and the whole site would have contained two to three times as much open or uninhabited space as occupied space. The total population of the site would probably have been between 400 and 530 (column B, assumptions 2a and 2b).

There is some evidence to suggest that mean village density was higher in Bakun times than in modern times. Large flocks of sheep and goats as well as some donkeys and cattle are maintained by modern farmers in the valley. These animals are sheltered within the villages, usually in courtyards or compounds associated with each house. Thus, the mean density of modern villages, 147 people per hectare, is in part due to space reserved for animals. The excavated area of Bakun shows no space for animals. Seventy percent of the animal bones excavated at Tall-i Gap (Egami and Sono 1962), another Bakun period site in the valley, were of non-domestic species. Thus, herding may have been less important in Bakun times and less space in the village may have been reserved for animals. If this is true, Bakun may have been about average in density or, if it was a particularly densely occupied village, its population could have been as high as 800 people (assumption 2a).

This example suggests that caution should be exercised in using any factor to convert site area to estimate population. It also shows that explicit statement and consideration of a set of alternate assumptions is a useful approach to the study of prehistoric settlements.

Comment

This paper raises a number of questions which can only be answered by further work in ethnoarchaeology. We need to know more about the size and spatial organization of households and how these factors relate to production, population growth, or other variables measurable in the archaeological record. We must also investigate the causes and types of settlement agglomeration as well as the factors which set limits on tolerable population densities within settlements. The functional and density characteristics of settlement hierarchies also need further investigation. If there are significant differences in population density between levels in a settlement hierarchy, related to functionally specialized space, then we have a new approach to the study of archaeological site hierarchies.

The archaeological example using the excavated site of Tall-i Bakun demonstrates two important points. First, it shows that the use of several variables simultaneously, in this case household size, floor area, and density, will provide a useful measure of the range of possibilities in any set of data. The second point, related to the first, is that we should use all the data available. It is no longer sufficient to simply apply a single ethnoarchaeological estimator, such as 200 people per settlement hectare. Where archaeological data are available we must use them to check the implications of the ethnographic analogies involved. This is certainly not a new idea, but I hope the example given will suggest some new ways of evaluating the validity of ethnographic analogies.

References Cited

Adams, Robert McC.
   1965. *Land Behind Baghdad*. Chicago: University of Chicago Press.
Adams, Robert McC. and Hans J. Nissen
   1972. *The Uruk Countryside: The Natural Setting of Urban Societies*. Chicago: University of Chicago Press.
Carneiro, Robert L. and Daisy F. Hilse
   1966. "On Determining the Probable Rate of Population Growth during the Neolithic." *American Anthropologist* 68:177–81.
Cowgill, George L.
   1975. "On Causes and Consequences of Ancient and Modern Population Changes." *American Anthropologist 77:505–25*.
Egami, Namio and Seiichi Masuda
   1962. *Marv-Dasht I. The Excavations at Tall-i-Bakun, 1956*. Tokyo: University of Tokyo, Institute for Oriental Culture.
Egami, Namio and Toshihiko Sono
   1962. *Marv-Dasht II. The Excavations at Tall-i-Gap, 1959*. Tokyo: University of Tokyo, Institute for Oriental Culture.
Flannery, Kent V.
   1972. "The Origins of the Village as a Settlement Type in Mesoamerica and the Near East: A Comparative Study." In P. J. Ucko, R. Tringham, and G. W. Dimbleby, eds., *Man, Settlement and Urbanism*, pp. 409–25. London: Duckworth.
Hole, Frank, Kent V. Flannery, and James A. Neely
   1969. *Prehistory and Human Ecology of the Deh Luran Plain: An Early Village Sequence from Khuzistan, Iran*. Museum of Anthropology, Memoir No. 1. Ann Arbor: University of Michigan.
Iran, Government of. Plan Organization
   1970. *Village Gazetteer*, Vol. 23: *Fars Ostan*. Tehran: Iranian Statistical Centre.
Johnson, Gregory Alan
   1973. *Local Exchange and Early State Development in Southwestern Iran*. Museum of Anthropology, Anthropological Papers, No. 51. Ann Arbor: University of Michigan.
Langsdorff, Alexander and Donald McCown
   1942. *Tall-i Bakun A. Season of 1932*. Oriental Institute Publications 54. Chicago: University of Chicago Press.

LeBlanc, Steven
> 1971. "An Addition to Naroll's Suggested Floor Area and Settlement Population Relationship." *American Antiquity* 36:210–12.

Naroll, Raoul
> 1962. "Floor Area and Settlement Population." *American Antiquity* 27:587–89.

Russell, J.C.
> 1958. *Late Ancient and Medieval Population. Transactions, American Philosophical Society* n.s. 48(3). Philadelphia.

Wrigley, E.A.
> 1969. *Population and History.* World University Library. London: Weidenfeld and Nicolson.

7/ Tell-i Nun: Archaeological Implications of a Village in Transition

Linda Jacobs
Department of Anthropology
University of Oregon

In her description of an expanding contemporary village in Fars Province, Iran, Jacobs outlines the relationships between differing architectural characteristics of the older and more recent portions of the village and concomitant variation in household composition and population density. Like Sumner, Jacobs is interested in the refinement of approaches to archaeological population estimates; while she focuses primarily on village architecture, her figures for the two portions of this settlement have clear implications for estimates based on unexcavated survey data as well as on excavated structures. Jacobs' contribution points up the difficulty of controlling for short-term chronological change, underscores the need for both selective microstratigraphic excavation and reevaluation of sampling procedures, and suggests some ways in which additional data sets might be used to check population estimates derived initially from excavated architecture.

A census conducted in Tell-i Nun[1], a small village in Fars province in southwestern Iran, provides some data that may be germane to a discussion of ethnographic bases for interpreting archaeological remains. Specifically, attempts to estimate population of archaeological settlements have been hampered by the lack of ethnographic data directly related to the problem. Population estimates have been based

The work described here was carried out in conjunction with an archaeological field project which defined the focus for the collection of the data presented. I would like to thank William Sumner, John Alden, and Carol Kramer for making helpful suggestions and comments on earlier versions of this paper. Any flaws, of course, are my responsibility alone. The graphs were prepared by Allen Cox.

on a variety of criteria, including size of the settlement as a whole (Sumner 1972, and this volume), number of square meters of floor area (see Naroll 1962), and the number of square meters of roofed (as opposed to unroofed) area. These estimates may be effective in a comparative approach; if consistent criteria are used across several sites or across several residences, a meaningful idea of the relationship among them may be acquired. However, it is clear that more ethnographic data are needed in order to make absolute estimates more convincing. Although I doubt whether *any* absolute figure from ethnographic data can be used with complete confidence in archaeological contexts, certainly data which have been collected in a place closely resembling a given archaeological settlement in size, subsistence base, and location can be quite useful. It was to this end that I conducted a rather informal census of the village of Tell-i Nun.[2]

Tell-i Nun is located in one of the high valleys of the Zagros Mountains at about 1,300 meters above sea level. Primary subsistence of the village is based on farming, and crops are dependent on *qanāt* irrigation in the low-lying areas and rainfall in the higher areas. There is a very minor dependence on herding, but the families who own herds also farm. Although two absentee landlords own a substantial portion of the arable land near the village, most of the heads of families own a small amount of arable land (one or two hectares per family) on which sugar beets (a cash crop), sesame, wheat, barley, and garden vegetables are planted in a yearly cycle.[3] Sugar beets have recently replaced other cash crops (such as cotton), and most families devote at least one hectare to them, but since the total amount of land owned by each family does not usually exceed two hectares, the rest of the land is planted in subsistence crops.

The village itself is fairly typical of villages throughout the area in its size, methods of construction, and general layout. It is particularly interesting, however, and raises some interesting problems for the estimation of archaeological population figures, because it consists of two distinct parts: an older, walled area, built on the edge of a large mound (*tell*), and a newer "suburban" area built off the *tell* to the east (see figure 7.1). The age of the older village is not known, but some of the villagers think the oldest structure (a square defensive tower) was built some two hundred years ago. This estimate accords with information given by one man who is about fifty-five years old and whose house was built by his grandfather on the site of a house

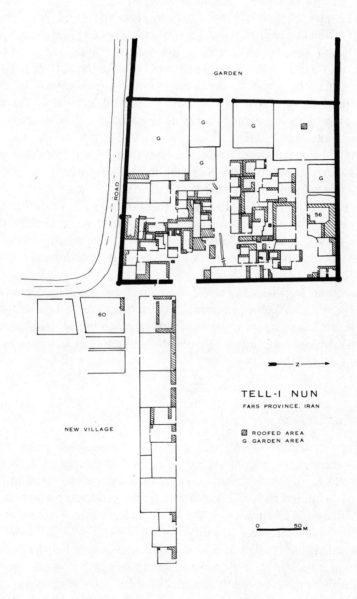

GARDEN

G

G

G

G

G

56

ROAD

Z

TELL-I NUN
FARS PROVINCE. IRAN

ROOFED AREA
G GARDEN AREA

60

NEW VILLAGE

0   50 M

Figure 7.1. Schematic map of Tell-i Nun village, Iran.

built by *his* father. This house is next to the old tower and probably marks the area of earliest settlement in the village.

The new section of the village reflects the rapid population growth of the last twenty years. Expansion of the old village has been limited until now by the extent of the defensive wall; the need for such a wall is no longer felt, so that movement to the outside is now taking place. In addition, the acquisition of farming land by the villagers under the Land Reform bill of 1962 made possible the accumulation of capital, which in turn allowed the villagers to purchase housing plots outside the traditional area. All but two of the plots of land have been purchased from a neighboring village (although the land is much closer to Tell-i Nun than to the other village) at prices ranging from 25 to 50 riāls (about 35¢ to 75¢) per square meter—the higher price reflecting the growing demand of the past year. The size of a piece of land in this area, then, may reflect more directly the wealth of the owner than does the size of a compound in the old village, where inheritance, reconstruction, and abandonment have complicated the picture.

In describing the village of Tell-i Nun, then, and the people living there, I will make a distinction between the older village and the more recent construction and consider the archaeological implications of these two areas for estimating population figures in archaeological contexts.

The Walled Village

A defensive wall of *chīneh* (packed mud) with mud-brick towers surrounds and defines the old village. This wall encompasses 5.7 hectares of land, of which about 1.5 hectares are devoted to gardens or large plots of land with no construction on them. Most of the remaining 4.2 hectares of land within the wall is taken up by the dwellings of 490 people—the great majority of people living in Tell-i Nun. If one considers the walled area alone, one arrives at a figure of 85.9 persons per hectare; and even if one eliminates garden areas (which presumably would be easily distinguishable archaeologically), the population density of the old village is 116 persons per hectare. Both of these figures fall at the lower end of the range of estimates given by Sumner (1972:174). To a visitor, however, the village seems crowded: many people sleep in one room, there are very few empty rooms, and apart from gardens, seemingly very little space. How can one reconcile this impression of crowded conditions with a population density that is apparently somewhat lower than most other places? It is clear that the ways in which space is used in the village are the key; a more detailed description of the old village, then, is in order.

The houses in Tell-i Nun are built of unbaked mud-bricks (a technique which has been in use in the area for at least 7,000 years), which are made in a wooden mold measuring 20 by 20 by 6 centimeters. House walls are generally 2½ to 3 bricks thick (depending on the demands of the owner/builder). The width of a room is limited by the length of wooden roof beams available (a scarce commodity in this area), and for this reason, most of the buildings in the village have rooms no more than 2½ to 3 meters wide. The lengths of rooms, on the other hand, are only limited by preference, space, money, and custom, so that these vary greatly.[4]

The great majority of the houses are built around an unroofed courtyard (figure 7.1), with the houses and/or a wall defining what I call a "house compound." Of the 59 compounds in the old village, 48 are two-story structures, of which the lower story is used for animals, and the upper story for humans. Milking and feeding of the animals are done in the courtyard (most families have some combination of a small number of cattle, sheep, goats, donkeys, and chickens), and fodder, harnesses, and all other appurtenances for animals are kept in the downstairs rooms. These rooms are also used to stable animals in the winter (the heat generated by the animals helps keep the upstairs living rooms warm), and as general storerooms.

Although most of the women in the old village do their washing at the communal water source in the center of the village, some families have their own faucets, which are installed in the courtyards of the compounds. (In the early 1970s, water towers and diesel water pumps were installed by the government in all the villages in the area; these provide the water for these faucets.) Most domestic activity, however, takes place on the roof. The upstairs rooms are generally slightly smaller than the downstairs ones, providing outside space on the roof around the upstairs living rooms for baking, drying greens and grains, washing, basket making, and so on. This is the woman's domain; neighboring houses are connected by their roof-

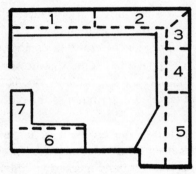

Figure 7.2. Compound 56, Tell-i Nun. Solid lines indicate walls of downstairs areas; dotted lines indicate walls of upstairs areas.

tops so that women can visit each other without ever having to go into the street.

Since virilocality is the ideal postmarital residence rule, many compounds in the old village are inhabited by several families related through the male line. One such compound is shown in figure 7.2; figure 7.3 shows how the men in this compound are related to each other.

The composition of the family unit (that group which inhabits one room) can vary greatly: in the compound in figure 7.2, rooms 4 through 7 are occupied by nuclear families; room 3 is occupied by an unmarried man;[5] room 2 is unoccupied but belongs to the man in room 5; and room 1 belongs to the "patriarch," one of his sons, and that son's family—a total of 28 people.

How typical is the compound shown in figure 7.2? Twenty-one (37.5 percent) of the occupied compounds are owned by extended

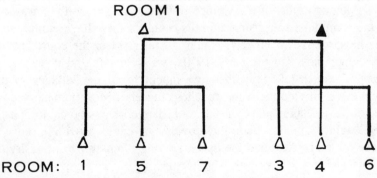

Figure 7.3. Kinship ties among adult males in compound 56.

families such as this one,[6] while 27 (48.2 percent) of the compounds are inhabited by single nuclear families, and 7 (12.5 percent) are inhabited by a nuclear family plus one or two dependent relatives (a widowed parent for example, or an unmarried sister).[7] The single remaining occupied compound is an anomaly: two sisters, their husbands and their families living together.

Although the plan and construction of the compound in figure 7.2 is representative of most compounds in the old village, it is clear from the plan of the village (figure 7.1) that it is larger than most. The mean area of combined roofed and unroofed living space in compounds in the old village is 219.5 square meters (median = 192.5), as opposed to 520 square meters for this compound. The number of inhabitants is greater than any other compound in the old village; mean household size is 8.75 (median = 7) compared to the 28 living in this compound. (Figure 7.4 shows the number of people per household.) It should not surprise anyone that a large family lives in a large house; this is of course what most population estimates are based on—the assumed direct positive correlation between living area and number of inhabitants. When the total number of people per compound is plotted against the total number of square meters of living area (figure 7.5), one can see that there is no simple or obvious relationship between them.

What are some of the factors that influence this relationship? In the first place, the amount of out-migration to Shiraz affects the number of people per household in a somewhat random fashion (see note 7). Since custom precludes members of an overcrowded compound moving into a less-crowded one belonging to an unrelated family, numbers of people per compound do not increase or decrease to take advantage of available space.

Probably more important is that space is circumscribed by the compound walls on the one hand and the village wall on the other. This means that in many cases, despite increases in number of family members, there is simply no room to expand within the walls without encroaching on necessary courtyard space. Since most of the buildings in the old village are already two stories (and since the techniques of construction will not support a third story), building up is out of the question for the majority of villagers. It may be that many of the houses in Tell-i Nun were at one time only one story and were added to as space was needed, but today, even owners of one-story,

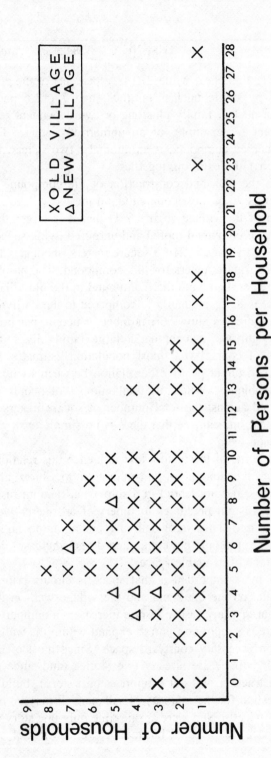

Figure 7.4. Household sizes, Tell-i Nun.

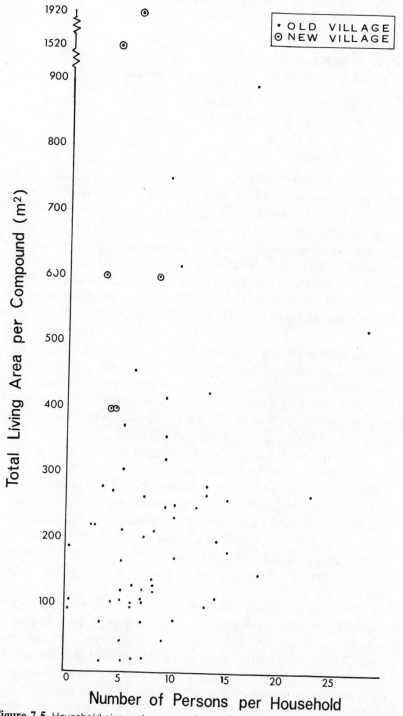

Figure 7.5. Household size and compound area, Tell-i Nun.

newer houses within the walls no longer see this as a solution to overcrowding. They are building new houses outside the village walls.

The New Village

The new village to the east is clearly separated from the older one by the defense wall and towers; it is significant, however, that part of this wall facing the east has been purposely torn down to allow easier communication between the two areas.[8] There are also two roads dividing the areas: one, the main gravel road, and the other, a smaller dirt road which used to be the main road and which is still the only access to a few nearby villages. There is no construction going on on the *tell* itself, since most of the land nearest the village is owned by the landlords or is taken up by the village cemetery.

Although by November of 1976 (when this census was completed), there were only 6 occupied houses in the new area, 16 additional plots of land had been purchased by the Nunis, and now houses on most of these plots are under construction.[9] Some plots are presently being used for gardens until the owners have enough money to build a house, but all of these landowners plan to move to this area eventually. Who are these suburban dwellers?

Although this new area is definitely considered part of Tell-i Nun, one family from another village has purchased a plot of land and is planning to build a house on it during 1977. It is unusual for families to change villages; this family has said that it is moving to Tell-i Nun because the land there is better for farming than the land in their own village. This may be part of a larger process, evident throughout the area, of a gradual shrinking or disappearance of some villages and an enlargement of others—a process often seen in the archaeological record.

The other suburban families (both those who live in the new area now and those who have plans to move) are all Nunis who own or owned residences in the old village. I have no figures on economic status as such, and I have noted above that the size of houses in the old village does not give any clear indication of the wealth of the owners. However, it is significant, I think, that of those men who own markedly bigger compounds in the old village, 3 of the 4 are representatives of the absentee landlords and are thought by the villagers to be quite rich. The 4 compounds which have the smallest actual living area—these are the only houses in the village with no courtyard space—as well as a large number of people per square meter of living area, are occupied by families who are pitied by the other villagers for the meanness of their living conditions. *None* of the inhabitants of these 8 houses—neither those that fall at the upper extreme of size, nor those that are the smallest—has moved or has plans to move out of the village into the new sector. The rich families apparently have all the space they need (their wealth was accumulated long ago while there was still room within the village walls to expand), and the poorest families don't have the capital to buy a house plot.

All of the people moving out fall into a fairly undifferentiated middle economic range (although it seems clear that the smaller houseplots in the new village belong to those families with less accumulated capital). These people give as reasons for leaving the old village the disrepair of their houses, but it seems clear that there are other issues involved—issues which are especially interesting to archaeologists in trying to estimate population figures.

Two of the compounds in the new area are owned by male-related extended families (such as the compound pictured in figure 7.6), but the rest of the occupied houses (4) and *all* of the plots on which houses are planned, are owned by nuclear families or nuclear families with one or two dependents. This is clearly a new trend in household composition. Many of these nuclear families are moving out of what they consider too crowded conditions in extended-family households. One man, when asked what he would do with his house in the old village when his new one was completed, said that he would keep the old house, stable his animals in it, and when his two sons married and had families, they would take over the new house, while the man and his wife would move back into their old house in order to give their sons and families enough space.

This process of family fragmentation, at least as far as the new area of the village is concerned, will probably continue until there is no new land to buy and families are forced to stay together.

Figure 7.6 shows one of the house compounds in the new area. It is owned by an extended family of six: a couple and their unmarried daughter (room 2), their unmarried son (room 1), and a married son and his wife (room 3). Until recently, another son and his wife and children lived in the house (in room 4), but he thought the living situation too crowded and moved with his family to his wife's village, where his wife's father had land and no sons. Room 4 is now unoccupied and is used for storage. The owner of this compound still owns a house in the old village; this house is unoccupied and unused, but he has no plans to sell it.

Although unusual in being occupied by an extended family, the compound in figure 7.6 is typical of other compounds in the new village. The house is one story high with a stairway leading to the roof, but the roof is used little since most domestic activity takes place at ground level near the living rooms. (One of the houses in the new area has one room on the roof where dried greens are stored; this was added on after the house was built and may indicate that the practice mentioned above—that of adding on second-story rooms as needed—is already taking place.) Apart from the lack of a second story, houses in the new sector are still being built according to tradi-

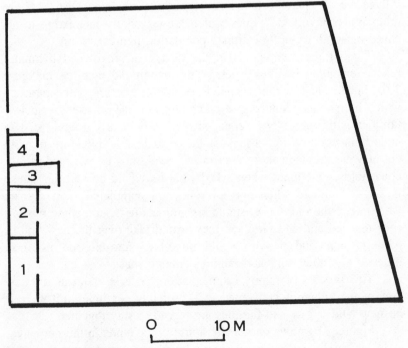

Figure 7.6. Compound 60, Tell-i Nun.

tional ideas: their doors and windows face into the courtyard, they are built of mud-brick (although now stone foundations are being built), and niches take the place of shelves.

Since the houses in this new area are so widely spaced, there is no rooftop communication; instead, a grid of streets has already been planned to allow access to each courtyard.[10]

Two of the 6 occupied compounds have separate outbuildings for the animals; given the amount of space in these compounds (some 1,900 meters in the compound shown in figure 7.6), this shows a new attitude toward the maintenance of animals—a desire to keep them separate from the living quarters. One of the absentee landlords has just had a large stone stable built outside the village walls, and this may have influenced some of the villagers when they were building.

In the new area of Tell-i Nun, in contrast with the older village, the pattern is clearly one of more compound space and smaller households. Although the sample of houses is too small to be valid statistically, it seems useful to note that the mean household size of the newer area is 4.8 (as compared with 8.75 in the older village); whereas the density in the old village is 116 people per hectare, that in the new village is 53.3—less than half. When actual living area is calculated, we find a figure of .03 people per square meter of living space in the walled village decreases to .005 in the new, and the number of persons per square meter of roofed area decreases, less dramatically, from .09 to .03. These dramatic changes portend a new social arrangement evident even now in the new residential compounds, and these changes should be reflected archaeologically.

Implications for Archaeological Interpretation

What are the implications of this "dual" occupation structure—the new and old villages—for interpreting the archaeological record? Clearly, a trench in either of the two areas would give a skewed idea of the living arrangements and number of inhabitants of the village as a whole. A systematic sampling of the site would uncover both types of dwellings, and population estimates based on living area might give one a comparative picture of the two areas. What other kinds of information might be used to supplement population estimates in an attempt to accurately estimate the number of inhabitants of the village as a whole?

First, it is important to realize that if we came upon such a village archaeologically, we would be likely to misinterpret the remains; we might suspect, for example, that the newer, larger compounds belonged to an elite class, although this is certainly not the case. We might also consider the possibility that the two villages were not occupied contemporaneously; the lack of other changes in the material culture would probably be viewed as a reflection of our inability to document micro-chronological changes. It would be difficult to establish their contemporaneity as well, but one must be aware of the fact that although it is certainly possible that the old village may eventually be abandoned, there is a chronological overlap of the two habitation areas—a possibility which should be considered when looking at the archaeological record.

The material culture of Tell-i Nun might give us some corroborating evidence in our attempts to make accurate population estimates. For example, cooking facilities in both the old and new village are usually individual rather than communal; that is, each family unit does its own cooking (with the exception of unmarried dependents who often join another unit for meals). Cooking facilities are generally portable objects such as pots, utensils, and Aladdin heaters on which most women cook (there are one or two traditional women in the village who cook on outdoor hearths). Hearths for baking bread are the only permanent fixture used in cooking. Any redundancy of these tools within compound walls would imply more than one family unit. Indeed, any redundancy of tools normally associated with women's work would imply a multi-family compound, since in Tell-i Nun (and, I suspect, in virilocal societies in general), women's equipment (such as bedding, straw for baskets, pots and pans) is owned by women individually, whereas men's possessions (shovels, animals, farming tools, and so on) are shared within the household.

If one uses this method to determine the number of family units living in a compound, how might one estimate the number of people in a single family unit? One method might be by calculating the number of people served by the rice pots owned by a woman. In Tell-i Nun, every woman has a range of sizes of cooking pots (usually numbering five or six), but the smallest usually accommodates a family unit (those people living in one room).

Non-Residential Structures

The presence of non-residential structures, both within and outside the village walls, presents a problem to the archaeologist trying to estimate population. In survey work, populations are estimated by the number of people per hectare according to the size of the site; yet clearly, non-residential structures can form a substantial part of the hectarage and do not reflect an additional number of people. Some excavation is therefore necessary in order to obtain some idea of the extent of non-residential structures.

In Tell-i Nun, 550 square meters within the old village walls are devoted to non-residential structures: three small stores, each selling essentially the same things (food staples, soap, cigarettes, matches and the like); a privately owned diesel-powered flour mill, which grinds wheat for all but the most traditional families; a public bath, built, paid for, and maintained by the villagers; a new mosque, paid for by contributions from the villagers and landlords; and various small outbuildings for goats, fodder, and storage. All of these "public" buildings are centered around the communal water source, just inside the entrance to the old village.

Outside the walls, a school and a clinic are maintained by the government. The clinic is housed in one of the compounds belonging to a small nuclear family; the school is built on one of the two pieces of land originally owned by the village of Tell-i Nun. It is significant, I think, that those buildings which are considered by the villagers as integral to their lives (e.g., the mosque) are still being built on the small amount of available land within the village walls, whereas buildings dependent on institutions outside the village are built outside its walls.

Conclusions

It is clear from the foregoing that ethnographic data can be valuable both as an aid in interpreting archaeological remains and as a caution. Cultural change which is so evident in the ethnographic record is often difficult to document archaeologically, if only because that change is usually gradual. In the case of Tell-i Nun, the change from the old village to the new seems to be a rapid one (since the construction in the new area all dates from the early 1970s), yet it is still a gradual one, in that the coexistence of the two areas will probably persist at least as long as members of the present parental generation are still living. This coexistence, and hence the real pattern of habitation and population movement, would be difficult to discover archaeologically. In addition, the range of household size is so great, and household composition is so varied, that one would hesitate to use an average figure in archaeological contexts.

On the other hand, this ethnographic information does provide us with a range of possibilities for estimating the number of people per compound, and as more data on population are collected, the applicability of each set of figures will be better understood.

In addition, one can use ethnographic analogy to understand the implications of material remains (such as cooking pots) for population size and therefore come up with a figure which would closely approximate reality in each specific archaeological context. Estimates based on a combination of these kinds of data might indeed merit our confidence.

Notes

1. The village name is fictitious.

2. The census was carried out in the fall of 1976 in a rather informal way and is therefore not as exact as I would now like it to be. The map of the village was drawn by pacing out distances, so that it is schematic. In this way, I measured every courtyard and building, but I did not measure individual rooms in all cases and therefore do not have data on individual room sizes.

   Household compositions were obtained from a member of each household; this information was confirmed in all cases by a non-household member. Very small children, including the newborn, were included in the population count.

   In trying to resolve the problem of whether to count absentees, I decided that for archaeological purposes, absentees were not part of the household; see note 7 below.

3. A future project will involve collecting information on land holdings, herd size, income from farming, and so on.

4. As indicated in note 2, figures for room lengths have not yet been collected.

5. There are only four unmarried (never married) adults in the village. One is a blind man who lives with his mother; one a deaf-mute woman who lives with her brother's family; an unmarried woman of about 28 (who is considered by most to be past marriageable age) who lives with her parents; and the man in the compound pictured in figure 7.2.

6. There are 59 compounds in the old village, of which 56 were occupied during 1976.

7. These numbers do not include families of men who have moved to Shiraz, the nearest big city, to work. These men are considered by the villagers to be Nunis till they die, and so a place is reserved for them in the village. The number of adult males living in Shiraz is 25; since some of them have families, the total number of Nunis in Shiraz is 44. These numbers would significantly decrease the number of nuclear families having their own compound if these families returned to Tell-i Nun. However, despite the fact that their families consider them still part of the household, they themselves all consider themselves permanently settled in Shiraz.

Four men are away doing military service; these men will return and live at home until they are married. For the purposes of this paper, however, I have limited the data to people actually living in the village, since real population is the present concern.

8. Several villagers said that better communication between the old and new villages was the reason for tearing down the wall.

9. The area of the new village now is about two hectares; since its boundaries are totally fluid at the moment, however, the number has little meaning. The density figure given on p. 187 was calculated from the number of people and the amount of square meters they own.

10. The implications of this change for women will be a topic of future study.

References Cited

Naroll, Raoul
    1962. "Floor Area and Settlement Population." *American Antiquity* 27:587–89.
Sumner, William M.
    1972. "Cultural Development in the Kur River Basin, Iran: An Archaeological Analysis of Settlement Patterns." Ph.D. dissertation, University of Pennsylvania.

8/Rediscovering the Past in the Present: Ethnoarchaeology in Luristan, Iran

Frank Hole
Department of Anthropology
Rice University

Pursuing a long-term interest in the transition from foraging to food-producing systems in Southwest Asia, Hole conducted ethnographic research with contemporary nomadic pastoralists in western Iran. The transhumant group with which he worked travels between the Luristan highlands and the Deh Luran plain in Khuzistan, an area whose prehistoric sequence has been investigated by Hole and his colleagues, and for which an unusually bountiful and well-described record of ancient land use practices is available. Here Hole provides a broad overview of his data on contemporary nomadic encampments and pastoralists' material culture, and suggests avenues for future research with such groups. As a means of testing the hypothesis that animal husbandry is as old a subsistence strategy as agriculture, Hole excavated a prehistoric nomadic pastoralists' campsite, which had features paralleled in his ethnographic data. In focusing on regional land use by groups specializing in domesticated animals, Hole's article provides both an interesting contrast with those of Jochim on hunter-gatherers and Lees on irrigation agriculturalists, and a number of useful observations about a subsistence strategy with worldwide distribution.

A generation has passed since Robert Braidwood's interdisciplinary teams began the first intensive search for sites that bear on the beginnings of agriculture in Southwest Asia (Braidwood 1951, Braidwood and Braidwood 1953, Braidwood et al. 1960). One of those teams counted among its members a graduate student, "who had begun his studies in physical anthropology and paleontology, made the field appraisal of the animal bones from the excavations and gave some attention to the general contemporary ecological situation'' (Braidwood et al. 1960:20). In retrospect, it is ironic that Fredrik Barth's direct contribution to the archaeological project was to look at bones and that when he began his study of contemporary Kurdish villages he was preoccupied with social organization rather than with aspects of life that might have been of more archaeological interest. It would be graceless to complain that Barth did not launch a fruitful study in ethnoarchaeology and that he has provided only indirect aid to prehistorians through his perceptive studies of tribal peoples; rather we should salute the first step in his distinguished career in social anthropology (Barth 1952, 1953, 1956, 1959–60, 1961).

When Braidwood took Barth to the field, ethnoarchaeology was an approach whose time had not yet come. Now the time has come. Now archaeologists realize that the study of human culture history requires more than just arranging artifacts in chronological sequences, and that there are circumstances when it is most efficient to study living people if we wish to rediscover the past. But isn't this old hat, a belated recognition of what the general anthropologists half a century ago were still doing routinely? In some measure it is, and it is a measure of how anthropology itself has advanced, that it isn't. In the older style of ethnography it was sufficient to record a culture's traits and to compare these tribe by tribe or area by area in much the same way that archaeologists compare artifacts. However, when anthropologists ask questions concerning how a society functions or how social organization relates to cognitive categories, they part company with the archaeologists and largely confine themselves to the less tangible aspects of culture which are the stuff of ethnographies but not of museums. Even in the most compulsive days of inventorying peoples' possessions, ethnographers seldom considered the social context or even, in many cases, the direct uses of the objects they assiduously noted down. Thus we have list after list that record that stone mortars occurred among acorn eating people of California and only a rare aside on how these tools were used. Perhaps in 1900 it was obvious that a deep bedrock mortar was used with an oak pestle for pounding up acorns, and that a shallow metate with a basket cemented to its upper surface served the same purpose. Unfortunately for archaeologists, it is no longer obvious and it may no longer be possible to find out, although the relevance of an answer is clear when archaeological analogs are found (Smith 1972:166).

It is not just a matter of simple analogy. We know that metates, manos, pestles, mortars, querns, and so on were used to smash and grind things. As an archaeologist I would like to know why we have some of each in an ancient site. If they were interchangeable, why did people bother with the variety; if they were for different purposes, what were they? Such questions are unlikely to stimulate most cultural and social anthropologists to investigate the material manifestations of a people. That task must be left to archaeologists who are interested in the behavioral contexts of the matter that is our subject. We must do our own ethnographies.

Discovering the Problem

Until 1950 there were only a handful of excavated sites in the Near East that bore directly on early stages of agriculture and animal husbandry, and none that provided evidence of their origins or incipient stages. Since the Second World War, however, there have been a great many such sites excavated either by design or by accident. Most of these sites seem to conform with the model that Childe proposed: the self-sufficient food producing community (Childe 1965:67). Some of these sites are too old for fully effective food production, whereas others display well developed or advanced stages of it. Taken together, however, the range of sites from many regions of the Near East seems to provide a reasonable and consistent picture of emerging and developing agriculture, and in consequence the search for early agricultural sites has lost much of its excitement. Most archaeologists have settled into a routine of filling in chronological and geographic gaps. Nevertheless, this picture leaves out a very important consideration. Were animals domesticated in the same set of events that led to the cultivation of wheat and barley? Although most archaeologists and zoologists have inextricably linked the two in their minds, there are a number of theoretical reasons why it may not be true and some archaeological evidence that suggests alternative possibilities.

Let us look at theoretical reasons first. We know that during the Pleistocene the wild counterparts of domestic sheep, goats, cattle, and pigs were in the region where villages dating to the early post-Pleistocene are found. The location of the cereals is more problematic but some evidence suggests that today's natural habitat was devoid of the relevant species (Wright 1968, 1976). Thus, people living in these regions could have begun a process of taming animals before they had access to grains. Second, at many epipaleolithic sites in lowland regions of the eastern Mediterranean, gazelles comprise nearly the total evidence of animal use among people who show no strong evidence of doing any cultivation (Ducos 1968; Legge 1972; Saxon 1974, 1976). At these sites we may ask whether the gazelles were under some sort of human management by people who had not yet adopted the arts of cultivation.

We can look at this picture, again theoretically, in the reverse. Is it possible that cereal cultivation began apart from animal domestication? Most authorities would answer affirmatively, especially if the cultivators could supplement their diets with hunted wild animals (Wright 1971). Such a position is supported in other parts of the world like Mesoamerica where agriculture began in spite of the lack of suitable livestock. Theoretically, then, there are plausible alternatives to the idea that the first domesticators automatically developed a mixed economy based on a suitable combination of plants and animals.

The archaeological evidence forces us to consider the alternatives even if we are unswayed by theory. In Iran, Ganj Dareh (Smith 1975), Sarab (Braidwood 1960 a, b), Guran (Mortensen 1972; Mortensen and Flannery 1966), and Chagha Sefid (Hole 1977) strongly suggest early and intensive attention to livestock, even to the extent of specialization on one species, and patterns of transhumance. Similarly, Zawi Chemi (Solecki 1964) in Iraq and Suberde (Bordaz 1970; Perkins and Daly 1968) in Anatolia are both early camps or villages which suggest the husbanding of animals more than farming. Indeed, if anything, the evidence points to such practices being older than any well-established farming community, in the sense of a Jarmo. In fact, by a curious turn of fate, it may turn out on closer examination that Jarmo is aberrant in its apparent balance of subsistence and degree of sedentism.

It hardly matters how one plays games with theoretical scenarios or even with the evidence; what should be strongly emphasized is that sedentary villages, old or young, have relatively little to tell us about pastoralism which, by its nature, occurs away from such settlements. Thus, it seemed imperative to devise a way of learning about the archaeological history of animal husbandry. There were three ways open: (1) to go blindly ahead with a survey in the hope of finding something; (2) to observe nomads to see what they do, determine whether these activities were applicable to the past, and then look for specific kinds of archaeological remains; or (3) to succumb to the temptation to write nomads off as a late specialization of no relevance to the origins of anything except predatory warfare.

Having spent a few years of my life wandering over the Iranian countryside in search of sites, I was reasonably confident that I was not going to find nomad camps without some special instructions (Hole 1962, Hole and Flannery 1967). Accordingly, the sensible thing was to study the modern people and learn what to look for. The success of this study has been told elsewhere (Hole 1974, 1975, 1977, 1978). Rather than reiterate these results, it is more useful here to consider some of the general implications of the study and to provide some specifically new information. The topics that I shall discuss are: (1) defining a geographic area of interest, (2) techniques of carrying out survey for nomad encampments, (3) uses of informants, (4) a brief review of the substantive results, (5) applicability of my results to other areas, and (6) the urgency of additional similar research.

Defining an Area

Ethnoarchaeology can be carried out in the absence of a particular archaeological problem in the expectation that the results will be of general theoretical interest. If we wish to discover in general how certain behavior is expressed in residues that archaeologists may find, or how behavior relates to *any* residue, then we might choose to study almost any living people. If we have a specific problem in culture history, however, it seems most expeditious to confine our ethnographic investigations to the geographic area in question or to the closest counterpart that we can find.

Only rarely will there be sufficient continuity between modern people and archaeological cultures in any particular area to warrant the assumption that much specific information relevant to prehistory will be gained. Explosive increase in the world's population, coupled with rapid technological change, has left us with few isolated regions where native peoples pursue anything like prehistoric patterns of behavior. For the most part such peoples are in places that are seldom visited by archaeologists. In any event, there is little reason to expect that there will still be "Stone Age" folk anywhere by the end of the century.

We must admit, therefore, that we cannot just go out into the world and find some people to question and observe who will provide us a vicarious glimpse into the past. Having admitted this, however, we are not conceding defeat. What we must do instead is look among modern peoples for examples that are analogous in important respects to our archaeological situations. Moreover, and equally important, the degree to which modern people are analogous must be as much an objective of our inquiry as the behavior we wish to observe. In other words, we must determine the relationship between observed modern behavior and prehistoric remains, and this must be done from the outset rather than as an afterthought. To do otherwise is simply to collect, mindlessly, miscellaneous, trivial, and anecdotal information in the hope that something useful may turn up.

Stated in these terms, ethnoarchaeology requires the same intellectual discipline which is expected in the planning and execution of any archaeological project. It may be voguish and even fun to go out and watch people doing things, but these factors do not ensure that the results of the observations will necessarily be useful in archaeology. In fact, it seems inevitable that ethnoarchaeology has as much potential to generate trivia as any other technique yet devised to inform us of the past.

Rarely one has the chance to relate a particular archaeological program to a particular modern lifestyle in a particular area. When the three converge, the elements are present which may make for successful and informative ethnoarchaeology. In such instances, one should seize the opportunity.

Each of these elements is noteworthy. First, the archaeological program. This implies a systematic and probably long-term commitment to a problem and to the culture history of a definite locale. Few regions have been investigated thoroughly and consistently enough to provide a good archaeological outline for any appreciable span of time. In fact, I can think of no area or period that has been investigated to the satisfaction of the specialists concerned. But we need not speak only of ideal situations. Let us take the broad problem of agricultural origins in Southwest Asia. We have many sites, and much data, from an area the size of the eastern United States. But compared with the area, and the time involved, we have an insignificant sampling. The problem is compounded by the facts that sites have been dug with a variety of techniques; that some have been reported in full and others only mentioned; and that most have been only tested. We find, then, that our assortment of sites is a pitiful foundation on which to build a historical narrative, let alone to test any theories.

We can alleviate these problems if we focus more narrowly. In Southwest Asia, only the Deh Luran plain has been systematically tested to provide consistent results for a long enough span to be informative (Hole and Flannery 1962, 1967; Hole, Flannery, and Neely 1969; Hole 1977); see figure 8.1. This is stated not to diminish the importance of other areas or excavations but rather to point up the essentially haphazard way in which chronologies and data have been acquired elsewhere, for the most part because an overall plan of operation was not implemented.

It must be pointed out, however, that we have established only enough of a framework in Deh Luran through our limited excavations to enable us to recognize change and variation insofar as they relate to agricultural practices and animal husbandry. Our results to this point are more like a list of key words in an outline than like a full exposition of the subject. In this key list, however, keeps occurring the notion of animal husbandry and the techniques of pastoral nomadism or transhumance.

Clearly, if we wish to discover the role of transhumance in the lives of the prehistoric Deh Luranis, or if we are interested in whether there were parallel developments of nomadism and farming, it is necessary to shift our attention away from the villages themselves. Until recently Deh Luran has been occupied chiefly by nomads, some of whom summer in the Zagros mountains, whereas others move between the Tigris River in Mesopotamia and the Deh Luran plain. It was logical, therefore, to look at these modern herders who occupy the same terrain that we are interested in for prehistory. Aside from being informative about nomadism, such an investigation allows us to examine the specific role played by geographic factors that have remained constant through the millennia. Such factors are topography, seasonality, overall climate, and to a lesser degree, vegetation.

What was required for an ethnographic study, then, was to iden-

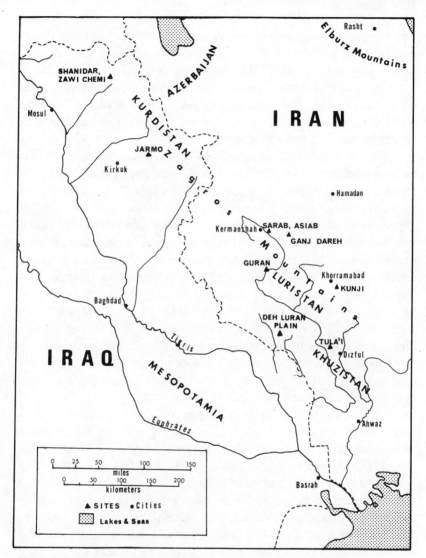

Figure 8.1. Location of sites in Iraq and Iran mentioned in the text.

tify a number of groups who could be visited for short periods of observation, and one or more groups with which we might live and
travel during migration. These are somewhat different problems. It is
relatively easy to observe tribal nomads if you just walk up to a
camp. Native hospitality will take care of the rest. It is less easy to

become part of a camp and to live with the people although this is necessary for gaining detailed information. In my view both kinds of information are essential. The former allows you to achieve broad areal coverage so that differences can be detected and responses to questions verified. The latter allows you to pursue topics in depth, observe infrequent activities, and record the relations between specific behavior and material residues.

The outcome of an ethnoarchaeological investigation might thus be a combination of specific information, and findings of general interest which are applicable to contexts wider than those encompassed by the immediate study. It would be foolish, however, to assume that any study is necessarily informative about an area or problem which was not directly investigated; until that hypothesis is tested, it must remain suspect. I stress this point because some may assume that a clearly worded illustration has general relevance. Thus I would categorically state that my study has definite geographic limitations and perhaps a good many others of which I am as yet unaware. In any case the ethnography has provided models for interpreting archaeology; it is not a substitute for it.

Furthermore, as Gellner (1973:6) says, it is an error to "combine an interest in the past with a disinclination to believe that it was discontinuous with the present." He refers to the problem that all of us face: that peoples in the Middle East today are at a stage of economic development and political integration which must be described as modern and hence "atypical." Our problem, then, is to factor out the modern elements which make pastoralists different from what they were under stable and more enduring conditions. We should also pay more than lip service to the question whether there has ever been a protracted period of stability during which pastoral life (and its contemporary settled and urban aspects) displayed some archetypical characteristics which it would be so useful to discern for heuristic purposes.

Techniques of Survey

The usual methods used in surveying for villages are not sufficient to discover campsites of pastoralists. There are two reasons: pastoral camps are usually sited away from arable land where village surveys are conducted, and the sites lack the accumulation of debris that results in village mounds. In practical terms, this means that surveys must be conducted over terrain that is difficult to reach, and they must be done on foot so as to discover the faint clues that may appear on the surface. Such survey is greatly aided by knowledge of where sites are likely to be found and this, in turn, relates back to ethnographic information.

Increasingly it has become apparent that our traditional mound-oriented surveys provide only a rough indication of what is present archaeologically. Robert Wenke's intensive survey of Khuzistan (1975), and James Neely's of Deh Luran (1974) are cases in point. They both found great numbers of archaeological sites, some of which could be mapped in elaborate detail, but they did not detect nomad camps, perhaps because they confined their search to arable land. Peder Mortensen's work in Hulailan is a better example of what is required (Mortensen 1972, 1974, 1975a,b). He and his team have attempted to cover literally *all* of the surface in certain transects of the Hulailan valley and its flanking hills and ridges. Slow and tedious as this work may be, it has provided us with the only substantial information on paleolithic campsites, and other similarly ephemeral surface scatters in Iran. The efficacy of such intensive examination is also attested by the work of many persons in the Negev (Marks 1971; Marks et al. 1972). There is no longer any mystery about how to find sites; it remains only to expend the time to do so.

Clearly one could not survey all of western Iran as intensively as Mortensen has small tracts of Hulailan. What we need is a set of guiding principles concerning where to look. This is where ethnoarchaeology is informative. Where do nomads put their camps? Why? At what seasons? What activities are represented at each? What auxiliary facilities do they have, and where are they to be found? Answers to such questions can enable one quickly to spot suitable places for camps and, on the assumption that nomadism is ancient and reasons for siting camps have not changed drastically, one should be able to find sites.

Belatedly (because I did not have access to them when I did my study), I discovered that aerial photos are a useful adjunct to ethnographic information. Aerial photos show trails, springs, nomad camps and facilities, cultivated plots, and forests; consequently, one can scan much ground economically and efficiently. Careful study of the photos enables one to plot patterns of settlement and densities of occupation much more effectively than is possible through on-the-ground survey or informants' testimony. In principle one could also use photos taken in successive seasons and over a number of years to chart minor variations and long term changes. Using a combination of good topographic maps, aerial photos, and informants' testimony, we should be able to tell where to look for sites.

We may not find them, however. Even with such excellent combinations of factors, ancient sites may be buried, they may have been eroded away, or they just may be elsewhere. If the latter, it is clear that we have misinterpreted our ethnographic data. The former problems, which may be confused with the latter, may be serious enough for us to require specialist help from geomorphologists. If either of these problems pertains we may presume that the environment itself has changed, and consequently our perceptions of its potential in ancient times may be wrong. Again, we may need specialist interpretation on these matters.

In summary, although we have the techniques at our disposal to find sites, we may still come up shorthanded as a result of factors beyond our control. In pursuit of prehistoric sites, as in any other deductive enterprise, an uncontrolled variable may confuse our results.

Uses of Informants

It is my experience that informants have both particular knowledge and an ability to generalize. Transhumant people live in a world which has few firmly fixed boundaries, and in the course of a long life a nomad has occasion to cover quite a lot of terrain and to question other people about places they have been. Thus a nomad's knowledge of geography is very good and is certainly far better than that of the average villager who tends to follow narrow paths with more limited geographic objectives. Nomads also possess an insatiable curiosity about the land and in particular about the quality of pastures and other resources. Visitors are always questioned about these matters, as well as about the location of other groups of people, political problems, and the like.

Information derived from a nomad in response to a query thus has an element of truth about it, but at the same time it should be recognized that a straightforward question may mean something quite different to the person questioned than it does to the questioner. Thus, in response to a question about the quality of a certain pasture or campsite, a person may answer that it is not good. What may be unstated is that some other camp is there, not that it is intrinsically of poor quality.

Rather than pose direct questions about particulars, it is often more useful to elicit information concerning the qualities in general that are desired in a campsite or pasture. Such queries directed to many groups of people throughout an area can be expected to yield consensus and accuracy. The underlying principles of behavior are thus exposed and we can then apply them ourselves in working up our survey plans. In this way we will not be misled by temporary factors that might have affected the assessment of a particular location by one informant.

Nomads are also able to give clear and concise answers to questions about sizes of tents and the relation between them and the people and activities that are carried out within: about the patterning of refuse; and similar matters that concern the structure of potential archaeological remains. Even though informants may think these questions silly, they do give useful answers, and they themselves perceive a timelessness in their way of life which makes such questions in the context of prehistory not at all out of place.

Native informants are also helpful in pointing out remains that they have seen. Herders are particularly good at this because they know nearly every square meter of terrain intimately. Although some herders are more perceptive than others, most would recognize flint tools, ancient pottery, tombs, and certainly terraces, check-dams and house foundations, all of which are frequently encountered in Luristan. Specific sites, which might be unrecorded on topographic maps and unseen in aerial photos, like caves and shelters, are also readily pointed out by informants. The major problem for the archaeologist lies in getting people to respond to the questions, not in finding people who know the answers.

Getting people to respond is partly a matter of asking the questions in the right way, and partly of asking the right people. In Luristan, and probably in most areas undergoing rapid modernization, the older people are usually more informative. It is not so much that the youth are ignorant, as the fact that they may see little future in their native way of life, and frequently they find it denigrated outside the tribal camps. Therefore, they often react with curt disdain to questions which a person brought up in the traditional manner would expand upon at length.

There are other reasons, however, for seeking out the elders. Tribal life today is much different than it was in the past, particularly because of changing political circumstances, most of which have taken place since 1930. The twentieth century has also seen a great increase in population, and the opening of communication, and motorable roads across Luristan. In turn, these have brought goods to the markets and enabled nomads to market their goods. Although these changes have had profound social and economic implications, many of the essential elements of tribal life, insofar as they pertain to herding animals, have remained very similar. This point is illustrated in the writings of the few western travelers who visited Luristan in the nineteenth and twentieth centuries (Curzon 1892; DeBode 1845; Stark 1933; Rawlinson 1839; Sheil 1856; Layard 1894; Morgan 1894–95; Wilson 1941).

The impressions recorded by these early travelers provide us with a base line against which we can measure change. Another way to measure change is to find informants whose memories reach sufficiently far into the past to be of value. We were fortunate in this regard to find Atawak, a man who was about 85 years old, an age we checked against events whose date we knew. The man himself thought he was more than 100 years old! What was interesting in his recollections was the degree to which the peoples of Luristan have been isolated from most of the major events of history. To a much greater degree than the Bakhtiari or the Kurds who occupy land to the southeast and northwest respectively, his particular group of Lurs has remained outside the mainstream of life. A measure of this isolation is that Atawak remembers when tea was introduced to the tribe at the start of the twentieth century (this was verified by old men in other camps). This means that beverages other than water or milk products were not consumed by these people until the twentieth century. Nor were sugar, cloth, shoes and other commodities, which most take for granted today, available until around 1900. Curzon, in reference to these people, aptly referred to ''the slow foot with which Time marches over the remote spots of the earth's surface'' (1892: part 2:288).

An aged informant who is still lucid can provide many details of changes as well as a useful perspective on how changes have affected the people. For example, Atawak could tell us in detail about changes in equipment, the landscape, and population, as well as what effect they had on the way of life and on relations between people. In short, he was able to factor out very modern features of nomadic life and leave us with a much sharper impression of the more timeless essentials. He maintained, for example, that the pattern of life as far as husbandry is concerned had not changed one bit; what has changed are the personal possessions, size of the population, and the quality of the landscape whose degradation is now a serious factor in the continued viability of nomadic life.

Informants may also be useful in defining the differences between neighboring groups. One of the problems in archaeology is to recognize boundaries between groups. Many such differences, which are extremely important to living people, are not preserved in archaeological evidence. Nevertheless, some may be, and it is useful to ask questions which may elicit relevant information. For example, details of tent construction and the styles of certain implements may vary between tribes, although variety in the style of dress is much more obvious. We might find archaeological evidence of the former, but rarely, if at all, of the latter.

Finally, informants may recall the meaning of certain symbolic remains which are no longer being produced but which can still be found. An example are the "houses of the dead" in Kurdistan. These simple house foundations are no longer being built and they had only symbolic meaning; they were not lived in (Hole 1978). Similarly, we were told during migration of a field full of wooden pigeons. Although we found no one who could provide us with a contemporary explanation for them, these birds have been described as expressive of religious beliefs among certain people (DeBode 1845, I:184) and the examples we were told of in Luristan probably served the same purpose. What our informants did was to provide us with clues about something that we would not have expected, let alone ever found, in the course of normal survey for campsites. It still remains, however, for us to find the birds and relate them in any direct way to cultural practices.

The example of the birds is illustrative of the problems as well as the advantages of working with informants. We were told about the pigeons only after it was too late to visit the pigeon site. This was an oversight rather than a matter of secrecy. We had expressed an interest in ancient campsites and the pigeon field was not a campsite. What this implies in terms of the strategy of interviewing is that we must make a deliberate effort to make our inquiry broad rather than excessively exclusive, and that discussions should be prolonged rather than perfunctory. Happily, among nomads, the social context of hospitality favors the rambling conversation.

Outline of Results

There are three results of the ethnoarchaeological project in Luristan that are especially notable in the present context. They concern the nature of pastoralism in antiquity as it can be inferred from study of modern tribal people; the nature of remains that pastoralists leave and the places where one may find them; and the excavation of an ancient nomad camp as a demonstration of some of the findings. Because of the orientation of this volume, my findings will be given in general rather than in very particular detail (see Hole 1974, 1975, 1978, for fuller documentation).

My study focused on people who live in and around Deh Luran, and practice transhumance. When I began, there was some doubt whether my findings would be directly applicable to antiquity but I hoped to determine this rather quickly when I could observe what husbandry entailed, learn what equipment was necessary, and find out whether nomads leave remains that we could hope to find archaeologically. I was never concerned that nothing would be applicable because the landscape has the same topographic features, the seasons are the same, and the species of animals require similar conditions as in the past. I reasoned that although some social and technological aspects might have changed, the environment and the need of the animals for food must have been essentially the same.

The ethnographic study was carried out very much according to plan. Its success was greatly enhanced by the participation of Sekandar Amanolahi-Baharvand, a member of one of the Luri tribes that I wanted to study. At the time, Amanolahi was a Ph.D. student at Rice University, and he later carried out research for his doctoral dissertation on other aspects of tribal life (Amanolahi-Baharvand 1975). Together we visited nomad camps, traveled widely through Luristan questioning people about herding, campsites, and pastures, and about changes that have taken place. We sought out elderly informants and cross-checked information by every means at our disposal. And we joined one camp of nomads while they made their annual migration from winter to summer pastures. This experience gave me a closeup view of many aspects of life which were not obvious from the many quick visits and sessions of questions elsewhere, and it gave me a more intimate feel for a territory that has coherence because it comprises the actual universe of a viable group of people. Through interviews with old men and women, we learned much about changing vegetation, changing dietary habits, changing social practices, changing technology, and influences from outside. We also learned about cyclical natural events of great importance that happen at unpredictable intervals, sometimes only once or twice in a lifetime. Such events are droughts, heavy snows, and sickness, all of which decimate tribes and herds.

After both observation and interrogation, I concluded that pastoral nomadism requires essentially the same equipment as used by villagers today, most of which was probably available by the time domestication began more than 10,000 years ago. The basic differences between tribal villagers and nomads today are in the amount of equipment and in the style of housing. Today people pack goods and supplies on animals, but the lack of beasts of burden hardly precludes movement. In the past, without pack animals, baggage could have been moved in stages by people and, in any case, it was much less bulky than is typical today. The availability of pack animals has encouraged people to accumulate baggage, much of which cannot be considered essential to the way of life.

My study also suggested that nomadic treks were usually short and took advantage of closely juxtaposed areas of environmental diversity. Deh Luran, at the base of the steeply rising Kabir Kuh, is a good example. The distance between summer and winter pastures there is only about 15 kilometers, an easy day's walk. The long migrations which characterize some tribes today are in part a response to population pressures and the presence of agriculturalists in some mountain pasturelands. We have no reason to suppose that either factor was important in early times.

My study and historic accounts also show that modern nomads may be entirely independent of agriculturalists; thus we may infer that specialized stock raising could have developed independently of, and at any time before or after, agriculture. There are two factors that make this independence possible: the use of acorns and the harvesting of wild cereals. Both activities are carried out today in times of economic stress and were formerly very important. In fact, several of the older nomads informed us that in their youth it was not the tribe's practice to do any farming. Instead, when they migrated into the mountains seasonally, the nomads took advantage of ripening stands of wild grains (which are dense enough in some places as to equal the productivity of planted fields), or of stands of acorns.

The ethnographic study convinced me that we could profitably look at the history of stock raising separately from the history of farming, although in some—perhaps in most—places they were complementary aspects of local subsistence. Thus, it reinforced my belief that we could gain only a partial picture of developing animal husbandry by continuing to rely on excavations of villages. Only a parallel study of sites in grazing areas promises to provide the answers to the questions of how and when animal husbandry developed.

Having established to my satisfaction that there is no theoretical reason why transhumance could not have begun as early as farming, it remained to establish that we could find evidence that will allow us to test the hypothesis.

It is usually thought that nomads leave few traces that might be found archaeologically. Conventional wisdom in this case runs exactly contrary to what we see everywhere in western Iran. Nomad camps are ubiquitous. They are not, however, conveniently mounded up like abandoned villages of mud houses are, and they tend to be scattered over broad tracts of land rather than nucleated in villages. But they contain (at least in western Iran) material which is as durable as anything used in antiquity: stone. The chief problem is that ancient remains of this kind are likely to have been robbed of their stones or buried under later deposition, and thus they may not be obvious on the surface.

It is also conventional wisdom among archaeologists, however, that if there is a site present, some material from it will show up on the surface. Routinely we base appraisals of ancient village sites on this principle and we even derive population estimates from evidence which is found on the surface of sites that have tens of meters of deposit. Thus, it would seem that our chief practical problem in finding nomad camps is to pick a spot on the surface of the earth to examine. If we can land on a site we ought to be able to find evidence of it.

This is precisely where ethnoarchaeology is important. By asking people in the area where you want to look for sites archaeologically why they camp where they do you can arrive at some general rules concerning where ancient camps should be (Stark 1933:253). It is then a simple matter to visit these locations. Luri nomad camps consist of clusters of individual (family) tent sites which are often outlined by stones or which have layers of stones filling in a rectangular area on which bedding, water bags and other equipment can be placed. There is usually a hearth in the center of the tent, and an area just outside the tent where ash and other trash is dumped. Often animals are penned in tents or kept in a kind of corral between tents so that layers of tightly compacted earth mixed with dung may occur within a camp. All of these features may be recognizable archaeologically. Sometimes nomads use caves or rock shelters as seasonal dwellings (Solecki 1955:402ff.), as pens for their animals, and for storage of fodder. That such practices may have been followed in prehistoric times is suggested by our excavation at Kunji Cave near Khorramabad where we found circular rings of stones that may have outlined impermanent structures, and a few sherds of early prehistoric pottery (Hole and Flannery 1967).

Nomads also construct facilities such as storage bins where grain is kept. Today such bins are built near farmed plots but they might also be located where acorns or wild cereals are harvested. These bins may be built of mud and stand above ground but often they are only pits in the ground lined with straw-tempered mud. Unfortunately, very often there are no artifacts in association with the bins to help in dating them. In areas where there are many oak trees, nomads often set up acorn crushers. These are heavy stones that can be rocked back and forth across a boulder or bedrock to crush the acorns into a meal that can be made into a variety of foods. In places where nomads use bedrock mortars for the same purpose, there may be several such depressions in a line. Finally, since Sassanian times (roughly since 200 B.C.) water-powered mills have been used where suitable sources of water can be found. Nomads still use these ancient installations. One can see, therefore, that there are various facilities which, by virtue of their location in areas suitable for nomadism, are indicative of human activity even though living or campsites may not be found. At least such installations may be useful clues that camp-sites are nearby.

The ethnographic study provided me with the necessary tools to find sites; it remained to demonstrate that it could actually be done. The demonstration came about in part by accident when my attention was drawn by Henry Wright to a small mound, Tula'i, in upper Khuzistan that had early prehistoric sherds on its surface. The mound was actually the bank of an old irrigation canal that had been cut through a buried prehistoric site. At the time I simply recorded the presence of the site and went back to continue with my nomad studies. By the time I had completed the ethnographic work it was apparent that the site was possibly interesting in regard to ancient transhumant patterns. In the meantime much of the land surrounding the site had been scraped down to a level surface in preparation for irrigating the once slightly rolling land.

When I began to investigate the mound through a small sounding, I saw in the newly leveled fields nearby large areas of ash, a few alignments of stones, and scattered bits of prehistoric pottery, flint tools and a piece of obsidian. Further inspection showed that a very large area displayed these signs, which were essentially what I would have predicted for a nomad camp. Moreover, the site was located precisely where I would have predicted that one should be. However, had there been no leveling of the land the site probably would not have been discovered by normal methods because it seems to have lain completely under the surface.

It took only one day's work to show conclusively that we were dealing with a nomad camp. Our workmen, former nomads themselves, testified to that point. What remained to demonstrate without question was the antiquity of the site. This we were able to do by thoroughly excluding any possibility of recency. We found prehistoric material stratified in the campsite, suggesting that it had been used for a long time, and we found no evidence whatsoever of modern artifacts. The latter had been shielded from the site by the overburden which had just been scraped off.

Interesting though the site may be, it still has not been adequately investigated in many respects because of circumstances beyond my control. Aside from the present limitations of the evidence, however, the site is a notable refutation of the idea that ancient nomad camps cannot be found and identified. Nonetheless, we have yet to dig another nomad camp and, in consequence, Tula'i stands in splendid isolation without the essential context that can be acquired only through further discoveries and digging.

During my surveys in areas of nomadism we searched diligently for evidence of ancient camps. We were almost always unsuccessful. One can adduce cogent rationalizations for this pervasive failure: we had too little time (and no permission) to dig in promising locales; Luristan is geologically unstable and erosion and deposition have been severe; and there has been an undetermined amount of other environmental change. The latter is the most interesting because it raises the question of whether we have yet managed to strip away enough of the present to really understand the past. In the particular case of Luristan the problem hinges on whether the mountain zone in which the nomads migrate today was pasture land 8,000 years ago.

Although today it is difficult to imagine it otherwise, we should remember that even though Luristan is wooded, most of the trees are so scrubby and scattered as to mock the term "forest." It is sobering, however, to read the few historic records of Luristan which emphasize the forests (e.g., Curzon 1892:281; Sheil 1856:226), and to hear Atawak tell how much of today's grazing land was so dense with trees that nomads did not penetrate it. One could make the case that Luristan was opened to grazing by farmers, woodcutters, and even herders who stripped trees of their leafy branches for use as fodder (Stark 1933:258). If that is true, we should not expect to find very early nomad camps there. Instead we should look outside the forest belt—on the upper Khuzistan plain where Tula'i stands, on the grassy foothills, or in valleys higher than tree line which have yet to be intensively investigated for early prehistoric sites of any kind.

As is usual in archaeology, our results have presented us with a problem which points us toward further survey and perhaps deeper into prehistory. Consequently, readers should beware. Tula'i does not prove that nomadism as we know it today existed in the seventh millenium B.C. It does show that some people lived at least part of the year in camps which are indistinguishable from modern nomad camps. We do not know that these people moved seasonally between the mountains and plains. The few hints of transhumance still consist solely of inference based on identification of bones of livestock in sites, and on a few occurrences of sherds equal in age to Tula'i that we have found in the mountains. Were these left by herders, traders, or gatherers of acorns? We are not yet in a position to say.

In spite of these caveats, the ethnoarchaeological project has shown how we may begin to study transhumant aspects of animal husbandry. In this study there is also the potential for understanding the relations between herders and farmers which were so important in the development of the early civilizations and in their subsequent political history. It now seems possible to investigate nomadism in its own right rather than simply inferring its presence from indirect evidence or from the relatively late and often ambiguous historical accounts.

Applicability of Results to Other Areas

The project described here shows that ethnoarchaeology is a useful tool when it is applied to a particular problem, and that it may generate principles which can be tested in other contexts or used as models for framing questions. In my view, a project designed to elucidate a particular problem should be used primarily for that purpose, although indirectly we might infer general rules of culture. In the present instance, that would be an afterthought and I would prefer that such studies use carefully planned procedures that are specifically tailored to the task.

In cases where particular aspects of human history are the issue, suitable ethnoarchaeological projects can often be designed, even when there are no people in the specific region who are living as they did in prehistory. In this sense my study has general applicability to an understanding of nomadic life throughout Southwest Asia, at least where the same animals are involved. It has lesser relevance to studies of mobile people, of other economic foundation, elsewhere. It is only in very elemental ways that all migratory or nomadic people share similarities.

Potentially there is a considerable range of uses to which a study of this kind might be put. As a guiding principle, however, it should be emphasized that the burden of demonstrating the applicability of any of the results should be on the person who uses them. As a general rule I should think that such uses need to be defended with suitable tests and in no instances should results or conclusions be used as decisive arguments for or against a position until such tests have been effected.

The Urgency of Further Research

The world is changing so rapidly that one is tempted to plunge back into ethnological fieldwork in the attempt to salvage what is left. Some of the Lurs whom I studied were out of business the following year owing to a combination of natural circumstances and increasingly burdensome social and economic factors over which they had no control. I understand that the long-standing policy in Iran of taking nomads off the land has been reversed but I have reasons to believe that it is too late for an effective reversal of the trends in Luristan. There *is* an urgency and we have precious little time to acquire useful information.

Nevertheless, there are compelling reasons why an immediate return to ethnographic fieldwork may be unwarranted. As I noted earlier, there is more to understanding the past than just observing people today. In particular, we need to assess what the effects of modern land use, changes in hydrology, vegetation, fauna, and soil cover have been. Until we do so our perception of what ancient sites should look like and where they should occur may be quite inaccurate. In short, we need much better base line information concerning the geographic context of today's people and of ancient sites before we can advance much farther in interpretation.

We also need to evaluate carefully all historical accounts—in this case, of tribal people in the Zagros. Although some of the travelers may have glossed over details and may even have misidentified certain tribes, their eyewitness records are our only hope of glimpsing Luristan during the golden era of tribal life. Most of us have a tendency to believe what we see and to think that today is normal. However, we have only to read about conditions in Luristan and Khuzistan during the nineteenth century to realize how incorrect this view is. To correct this tendency we need to continually juxtapose the historical, ethnographic, and archaeological lines of evidence. Surely we will be a step ahead if we make use of the few solid clues about our subject that the historical sources offer.

With that task as a prerequisite, the sensible course now is to record the variation among tribes. This requires an elicitation of tribal affiliation, an inventorying of equipment, and a recording of structural remains as Edelberg (1966–67) and Löffler and Friedl (1967) have done. These studies are helpful not to enable us to recognize specific tribes in antiquity but to tell us what kinds of differences are socially and culturally important (cf. Mortensen 1975a:191 and Wilson 1941:163–64). We would like to know the range of variation in scheduling the use of terrain, and specific information about mills, storage bins, and houses of the dead before knowledge of these matters disappears. Extensive surveys, perhaps employing standardized questionnaires, would be very helpful in providing an overview of a large area.

We may also put the fact of rapid social change to our own uses and study what happens when nomads take up farming and living in villages. How do their patterns of architecture, uses of artifacts, and maintenance of livestock change or become incorporated into new patterns? The interesting differences which Watson (1966) and Kramer (this volume) have found between villages in western Iran suggest that one can recognize traditions, reflecting a long history of social and economic differences, even among people who today might be dismissed as "typical" peasant farmers. The implications of such findings in helping us interpret differences in the structured remains of ancient sites are far reaching, and they seem to suggest that we may have the means at our disposal now to begin to infer how physical remains relate to the dynamics of demographic and social change (Parsons 1972). Other similar studies of villages which specifically elicit background information on the people's history are especially to be desired.

In summary, we need to fan out over the Zagros mountains (or elsewhere) with aerial photos, maps, and questionnaires and to gather and record information about nomad structures, facilities, and patterns of movement, *in extenso*. The archaeological problems we are concerned with are broad and clearly transcend any particular site or region. Our research then must likewise aim at an overall evaluation so that we can discover more quickly how to penetrate the past.

References Cited

Amanolahi-Baharvand, Sekandar

1975. "The Baharvand, Former Pastoralists of Iran." Ph.D. dissertation, Rice University.

Barth, Fredrik

1952. "A Preliminary Report on Studies of a Kurdish Community." *Sumer* 8:87–89.

1953. *Principles of Social Organization in Southern Kurdistan.* Oslo: Universitets Etnografiske Museum, Bulletin 7.

1956. "Ecologic Relations of Ethnic Groups in Swat, North Pakistan." *American Anthropologist* 58:1079–89.

1959–60. "The Land Use Pattern of Migratory Tribes of South Persia." *Norsk Geografisk Tidsskrift.* 8:1–11.

1961. *Nomads of South Persia.* Oslo: Universitets Etnografiske Museum, Bulletin 8.

Bordaz, Jacques

1970. "The Suberde Excavations, Southwestern Turkey: An Interim Report." *Türk Arkeoloji Dergisi Sayi* 17:43–71.

Braidwood, R. J.

1951. "From Cave to Village in Prehistoric Iraq." *Bulletin of the American School of Oriental Research,* no. 124, pp. 12–18. South Hadley and Baltimore.

1960a. "Preliminary Investigations Concerning the Origins of Food-Production in Iranian Kurdistan." *Advancement of Science* 17:214–18.

1960b. "Seeking the World's First Farmers in Persian Kurdistan: A Full-scale Investigation of Prehistoric Sites Near Kermanshah." *Illustrated London News* (October 22, 1960), 237:695–97.

Braidwood, R. J. and L. S. Braidwood

1953. "The Earliest Village Communities of Southwestern Asia." *Journal of World History* 1:278–310.

Braidwood, R. J., Bruce Howe, et al.

1960. *Prehistoric Investigations in Iraqi Kurdistan.* Oriental Institute, Studies in Ancient Oriental Civilization, no. 31. Chicago: University of Chicago Press.

Childe, V. G.

1965. *What Happened in History.* Baltimore: Penguin Books (first published 1942).

Curzon, G. N.

1892. *Persia and the Persian Question.* London: Longmans, Green.

DeBode, C. A.

1845. *Travels in Luristan and Arabistan.* 2 vols. London: J. Madden.

Ducos, P.

1968. *L'origine des animaux domestiques en Palestine.* Publications de l'Institut de Préhistoire de l'Université de Bordeaux, Mémoire 6. Bordeaux: Delmas.

Edelberg, Lennart

1966–67. "Seasonal Dwellings of Farmers in North-Western Luristan." *Folk* 8–9:373–401.

Gellner, Ernest
1973. "Introduction to Nomadism." In Cynthia Nelson, ed., *The Desert and the Sown*, pp. 1–10. Institute of International Studies, Research Series no. 21. Berkeley, Calif.

Hole, Frank
1962. "Archeological Survey and Excavation in Iran 1961." *Science* 137:524–26.
1974. "Tepe Tūlā'ī, an Early Campsite in Khuzistan, Iran." *Paléorient* 2:219–42.
1975. "The Sondage at Tappeh Tulā'i." *Proceedings of the Third Annual Symposium on Archaeological Research in Iran, 1974*, pp. 63–76. Tehran: Iranian Centre for Archaeological Research, Muzeh-e Irān-e Bāstān.
1977. *Studies in the Archeological History of the Deh Luran Plain*. Museum of Anthropology, Memoir No. 9. Ann Arbor: University of Michigan.
1978. "Pastoral Nomadism in Western Iran." In R. A. Gould, ed., *Explorations in Ethnoarchaeology*, pp. 127–67. Albuquerque: University of New Mexico Press.

Hole, Frank and K. V. Flannery
1962. "Excavations at Ali Kosh, Iran, 1961." *Iranica Antiqua* 2:97–148.
1967. "The Prehistory of South-Western Iran: A Preliminary Report." *Proceedings of the Prehistoric Society* 33:147–206.

Hole, Frank, K. V. Flannery, and J. A. Neely
1969. *Prehistory and Human Ecology of the Deh Luran Plain*. Museum of Anthropology, Memoir No. 1. Ann Arbor: University of Michigan.

Layard, Sir A. Henry
1894. *Early Adventures in Persia, Susiana, and Babylonia*, London: John Murray.

Legge, A. J.
1972. "Prehistoric Exploitation of the Gazelle in Palestine." In E. S. Higgs, ed., *Papers in Economic Prehistory*, pp. 119–24. Cambridge: Cambridge University Press.

Löffler, Reinhold and Erika Friedl
1967. "Eine Ethnographische Sammlung von den Boir Ahmad, Südiran." *Archiv für Völkerkunde* 21:95–207.

Marks, A. E.
1971. "Settlement Patterns and Intrasite Variability in the Central Negev, Israel." *American Anthropologist* 73:1237–44.

Marks, A. E., H. Crew, R. Ferring and J. Phillips
1972. "Prehistoric Sites Near Har Harif." *Israel Exploration Journal* 22:73–85.

Mortensen, Peder
1972. "Seasonal Camps and Early Villages in the Zagros." In P. J. Ucko, R. Tringham, and G. W. Dimbleby, eds., *Man, Settlement and Urbanism*, pp. 293–97. London: Duckworth.
1974. "A Survey of Prehistoric Sites in the Holailān Valley in Lorestān." *Proceedings of the Second Annual Symposium on Archaeological Research in Iran, 1973*, pp. 34–52. Tehran: Iranian Centre for Archaeological Research, Muzeh-e Irān-e Bāstān.

1975a. "The Hulailan Survey." *Iran* 13:190–91.

1975b. "Survey and Soundings in the Holailān Valley 1974." *Proceedings of the Third Annual Symposium of Archaeological Research in Iran, 1974*, pp. 1–12. Tehran: Iranian Centre for Archaeological Research, Muzeh-e Irān-e Bāstān.

Mortensen, Peder and K. V. Flannery
1966. "En af verdens aeldste landsbyer." *Nationalmuseets Arbejdsmark:* pp. 85–96. Copenhagen.

Neely, J. A.
1974. "Sassanian and Early Islamic Water-Control Systems on the Deh Luran, Plain, Iran." In T. E. Downing and M. Gibson, eds., *Irrigation's Impact on Society*, pp. 21–42. Anthropological Papers of the University of Arizona, no. 25. Tucson: University of Arizona Press.

Parsons, J. R.
1972. "Archaeological Settlement Patterns." In B. J. Siegel, ed., *Annual Reviews of Anthropology*, 1:127–50. Palo Alto: Annual Reviews, Inc.

Perkins, D. and P. Daly
1968. "A Hunters' Village in Neolithic Turkey." *Scientific American* 219:96–106.

Rawlinson, H. C.
1839. "Notes on a March From Zohab Through Luristan to Kirmanshah, in the Year 1836." *Journal of the Royal Geographic Society* 9:26–116.

Saxon, E. C.
1974. "The Mobile Herding Economy of Kebarah Cave, Mt. Carmel: An Economic Analysis of the Faunal Remains." *Journal of Archaeological Science* 1:27–46.

1976. "The Evolution of Domestication: A Reappraisal of the Near Eastern and North African Evidence." In IX Congrès, Union internationale des sciences préhistoriques et protohistoriques, 1976, *Colloque XX, Origine de l'élevage et de la domestication*, pp. 180–226. Nice.

Sheil, Lady Mary Leonora
1856. *Glimpses of Life and Manners in Persia*. London: John Murray.

Smith, P. E. L.
1972. "Ganj Dareh Tepe." *Iran* 10:165–68.
1975. "Ganj Dareh Tepe." *Iran* 13:178–80.

Solecki, R. L.
1964. "Zawi Chemi Shanidar, A Post-Pleistocene Village Site in Northern Iraq." *Report on the VIth International Congress on Quaternary, 1961* 4:405–12. Warsaw.

Solecki, R. S.
1955. "Shanidar Cave, a Paleolithic Site in Northern Iraq." *Smithsonian Institution Annual Report, 1954*, pp. 389–425. Washington, D.C.

Stark, Freya
1933. "The Pusht-i-kuh." *The Geographical Journal* 82:247–59.

Watson, P. J.
1966. "Clues to Iranian Prehistory in Modern Village Life." *Expedition* 8:9–19.

Wenke, R. J.
  1975. "Imperial Investments and Agricultural Developments in Parthian and Sassanian Khuzestan: 150 B.C. to A.D. 640." Ph.D. dissertation, University of Michigan.
Wilson, Sir A. T.
  1941. *S. W. Persia: A Political Officer's Diary 1907–1914.* London: Oxford University Press.
Wright, Gary
  1971. "Origins of Food Production in Southwestern Asia: A Survey of Ideas." *Current Anthropology* 12:447–77.
Wright, H. E., Jr.
  1968. "Natural Environment of Early Food Production North of Mesopotamia." *Science* 161:334–39.
  1976. "The Environmental Setting for Plant Domestication in the Near East." *Science* 194:385–89.

9/Catches and Caches: Ethnographic Alternatives for Prehistory

Michael A. Jochim
Department of Anthropology
Queens College,
City University of New York

Utilizing ethnographic and historic data, Jochim develops a set of predictive models in an effort to evaluate the hypothesis that salmon, a harvestable, abundant, and reliable resource, plays an important role in supporting high levels of population density, aggregation, and sedentism. Faunal remains, tool types, and site sizes and locations from Mesolithic Germany provide the data set against which the alternate models are compared, allowing him to select one as most useful in retrodicting some of the seasonal and demographic parameters of prehistoric land use. Jochim's analysis bears on the widely discussed role of abundant harvestable wild resources (in this case, anadromous fish) in the development of storage technologies and increasing sedentism, both thought to have contributed to the transition from food-gathering to food-producing economies. His methods may be applied to comparable data pertaining to this question in other geographic regions and, with modifications, might be effectively utilized in exploring other hypotheses based on causal relationships between subsistence resources, demographic variables, and settlement pattern.

A recurrent theme in North American Indian ethnographies is that an economic reliance on salmon seems to be directly related, perhaps causally, to high levels of population density, aggregation, and sedentism. An early formulation of the relationship is found in Osgood's division of northern Athapaskans into those of the Pacific

The author gratefully acknowledges the National Endowment for the Humanities, whose Summer Stipend Program supported part of this study.

(salmon) and Arctic drainages; the former are not only more sedentary, but they are also characterized by greater complexity of ceremonial life (Osgood 1936). McKennan has challenged this formulation on two points, arguing (1) that the importance of salmon in the economies of some of the groups in the Pacific drainage has been overestimated, and (2) that many of the features distinguishing the two groups are in no way related to the taking of salmon (McKennan 1969a, 1969b).

Nevertheless, an emphasis of this single economic factor as a major causal variable has persisted in the literature, and the existence of a general association between a salmon-based economy and certain aspects of demography and settlement behavior does, in fact, seem to be well-documented. Perhaps the clearest evidence of this associaton is found in a recent discussion of Alaskan Athapaskans, which may be summarized in table 9.1.

Table 9.1 Northern Athapaskan Economies

	Intensive Riverine & Maritime Emphasis	Inland Riverine Emphasis	Inland Hunting-Snaring Emphasis
Salmon resource	Abundant	Present	Absent
Salmon use	Primary	Important	None
Macroband size	>500	>250	150–200
Largest camps	>100	<100	<65
Settlements	Dual Pattern	Trilocal Pattern	Frequent Moves

After Graburn and Strong 1973:75–76.

Salmon, therefore, may be a singularly predictable and productive resource, which somehow permits or causes relatively high levels of population sedentism, density, and aggregation, and possibly of social and ceremonial complexity as well. This ethnographic generalization is provocative. It postulates that any region with salmon runs might be characterized by hunter-gatherer adaptations significantly different from those of neighboring areas without this resource. Specifically, it suggests the hypothesis that those regions of Europe which had annual runs of Atlantic salmon may have witnessed distinctive economies and settlement patterns in prehistoric times. The purpose of the present study will be in part to investigate the possibility for one area of Central Europe during the Mesolithic. In addition, the structure of the hypothesized relationships, which has been largely unexplored in the ethnographic literature, will be examined.

Until recent times, salmon were plentiful in most European rivers entering the Atlantic Ocean and the North Sea. Among these rivers, the most productive was the Rhine (Netboy 1968). Each year, thousands of salmon ascended to spawn in its headwaters and tributaries deep in Central Europe. The Rheinfall by Schaffhausen formed a barrier to this migration, so that the spawning grounds were concentrated primarily in the drainage basin of the Upper Rhine between Basel and Schaffhausen. As a result, this Upper Rhine was a center for the inland salmon fisheries. In 1893 the reported catch between Basel and Laudenburg totaled 16,000 kilograms (Kopp 1968). Records stretching back to the 1500s demonstrate the consistent productivity of this region, which provided the major support for local monasteries and regularly provided salmon for the court at Innsbruck (Vetter 1864). Today, salmon have disappeared from the Rhine as a result of pollution, canalization, and the construction of hydroelectric dams.

This documented historical significance of the Upper Rhine salmon fisheries suggests that these fish may have formed a significant resource in prehistoric times as well, with possibly great ramifications for human demography and settlement patterns. The Mesolithic, roughly 8000 to 4000 B.C., was the last period in which a purely hunting and gathering economy was practiced in this area, and will form the focus of this investigation. For this period, the Upper Rhine watershed seems to have been an area of significant occupation. In Switzerland, Mesolithic sites occur in two concentrations: a number of cave and rock shelter sites in the hilly Jura region of the northwest (principally in the Birs Valley), and open-air sites along the Aare and other rivers and lakes of the flatter central Switzerland to the east (Wyss 1973). In adjacent parts of Germany, the focus of known Mesolithic sites consists of open-air sites along the Rhine itself between Basel and the Aare confluence. Such concentrations of settlement in an area of historical salmon fishing demand an investigation of the role of salmon in the prehistoric economy.

Unfortunately, few of the sites in this area have preserved faunal materials, and for those that do, the excavations either yielded no fish remains or reported an inability to identify those that were found. On the basis of this evidence alone, then, there is no reason to believe that salmon were present during the Mesolithic. There are, however, other pertinent considerations. For the subsequent Neolithic, salmon formed one of the principal fish resources in central Switzerland (Hartmann-Frick 1969). Furthermore, in the preceding Late Magdalenian there is one reported find of salmon remains in the Birs Valley (Sarasin 1918). Archaeological evidence, consequently, suggests that salmon were present at least before and after the Mesolithic.

Climatic and geomorphological evidence indicate that this was a period of great changes which may have affected the Rhine salmon. The low sea level and massive ice sheets of the last glaciation probably forced the Rhine drainage not into the North Sea (which may have been a ponded lake), but into a Channel River flowing to the Atlantic, with an additional 700 kilometers to its course (Flint 1971: 594–605). During deglaciation, the mouth retreated with the rising sea level, and ultimately drained into the reformed North Sea (Dejong 1967). The change in location and elevation of its mouth, together with melting of glaciers in its Alpine headwaters, resulted in increased downcutting of its upper bed, including the formation of the massive waterfall at Schaffhausen in the late glacial or early postglacial (Heim 1931). By around 5000 B.C. at the latest, the Rhine attained the pattern characteristic of historic times until recent canalization and damming.

These changes in the river, coupled with probable changes in salmon distribution caused by alterations in water temperature and salinity (Netboy 1974), render difficult any reconstruction of salmon occurrence. Recent biological studies of salmon have been interpreted as indicating salmon presence in the Rhine since late glacial ("Würm III") times, but this interpretation is based on the assumption of a North Sea water body large enough to support the fish—an assumption as yet unverified (Payne, Child, and Forrest 1971). Consequently, any reconstruction of the environment of the Upper Rhine drainage during the Mesolithic should consider the alternative possibilities that salmon were absent or present.

Not only environmental, but also technological alternatives must be considered. Kroeber and Barrett (1960) have drawn a useful dichotomy between methods of mass fishing (weirs, nets, traps) and methods of taking fish individually (harpoon, bow and arrow). All of the groups that form the basis for the ethnographic generalizations about salmon fishing practice the former, and thus are able to take huge harvests during the periods of concentrated aggregation of this resource. Moreover, all of these groups practice some means of food storage, allowing them to spread out these harvests over leaner periods. Clearly an investigation of prehistoric salmon exploitation must consider the available technology and its effects on realized harvests.

The archaeological evidence for Mesolithic fishing technology in this area is scant and ambiguous. The presence of bows and arrows is presumed from the abundance of microliths, but only elsewhere in Europe have they been preserved mounted as barbs and points (Clark 1958). Double-barbed bone and antler harpoon points are one of the outstanding features of the Mesolithic of the Birs Valley, but their use in fishing has not been proven. Except for one grooved stone, interpreted as a possible netsinker (Bandi 1964), no remains of nets, weirs, or traps have been found in this region for this time period, although they occur in the Scandinavian Mesolithic. Similarly, while there is no evidence for food storage in this area, hints of such practices have come from Mesolithic and Paleolithic sites elsewhere in the form of pits and depressions with concentrations of bones or nutshells (see, for example, Taute, n.d.). Thus, all these technological alternatives remain as possibilities for the area and time under study.

Finally, it must be realized that salmon are not totally reliable resources: a periodicity of about eight to eleven years in runs of Atlantic salmon has been noted (Mills 1971). Thus, no group can or does rely solely on this resource. Even in years of good runs, a variety of other resources are available and utilized. Consequently, in dealing with prehistoric salmon fishing, an entire set of alternatives must be considered—in salmon abundance, harvesting efficiency, storage ability, and use of other resources. The entire focus of this study as well as these alternative considerations have been suggested by ethnographic studies; it remains now to translate these alternatives into implications for the archaeological record.

Resource Exploitation: Ethnographic and Historical Models

Previous work in this translation process resulted in the construction of a model of hunting and gathering economies (Jochim 1976). The objects of this model were to construct and organize explicitly a set of generalizations about how such economies are structured ethnographically, and to enable the generation of an expected system of exploitation in reconstructed environments of the past. Economic and settlement behavior were viewed as the result of rational decisions with the often conflicting goals of security and efficiency, and the most significant criteria relevant to these decisions were seen in the seasonally changing behavior and distribution of the resources themselves. Simple numerical means of evaluating the resources and of reconciling the goals led ultimately to a set of predictions about relative settlement size, location, and component activities. The archaeological application of this model was to the later Mesolithic of the Upper Danube Valley in southwestern Germany. This application did not comprise a true test of the model's hypotheses, because the archaeological data did not constitute a truly representative sample of the region (but rather comprised all discovered sites), and because comparability of the various sites was uneven (due to differential excavation, collecting, and reporting). Nevertheless, the model did suggest a likely set of interrelationships among these sites, which previously had been discussed only in isolation, and provided a set of implications that can be tested with additional fieldwork.

A similar modeling procedure will be used here to investigate one portion of the Upper Rhine watershed, and because this is adjacent to the previous Danube study area (which had no salmon), a comparison of the two regions would be possible and interesting. While the initial application of the model considered only simultaneous alternatives of resource use, with the environment and technology held constant, the present study will have to consider environmental and technological alternatives as well, with the result that four separate models—differing according to their initial assumptions—will be constructed. In short, the models (I to IV) considered here are as follows:

```
                                                        ┌PRESENT (IV)
                                    ┌MASS────────STORAGE┤
              ┌PRESENT──HARVEST─────┤                   └ABSENT (III)
SALMON────────┤                     └INDIVIDUAL (II)
              └ABSENT (I)
```

Since the evidence for the primary criteria distinguishing these models is practically nonexistent, it is hoped that the models will differ sufficiently in their implications for settlement locations, size, and contents to allow a comparison with the archaeological materials. Again, since the archaeological data consist of all known sites, gathered with no underlying research design or sampling considerations, this comparison cannot constitute a test of the hypotheses, but rather may suggest which of the four models is most probable. Furthermore, the value of such models for translating ethnographic alternatives into archaeological implications should be demonstrated.

The study area chosen includes only part of the Upper Rhine drainage: a naturally constricted corridor of the watershed below the Aare confluence defined by the heights of the Black Forest and the Swiss Jura (figure 9.1). Above the Aare, the Rhine flow is much less (the Aare actually contributes more water than does the Rhine) and the valley is much wider. Below Basel the immediate Rhine Valley widens into the flat, wide "Rheingraben plain" (up to 40 kilometers wide), the watershed widens considerably to include the headwaters of lower tributaries in France and Germany, and the river gradient drops rather sharply. With a total area of about 3,300 square kilome-

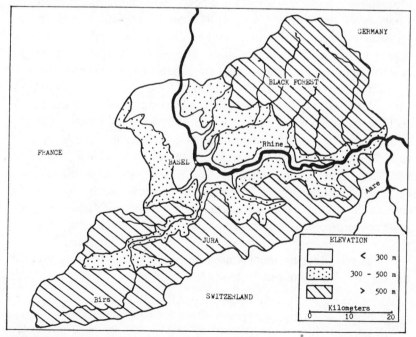

Figure 9.1. Study area along the Upper Rhine.

ters, this region includes the Swiss Mesolithic sites of the Birs Valley and the German sites along the Rhine itself.

The time period chosen for study is the late Boreal and early Atlantic of the Postglacial, roughly 6000 to 4000 B.C. This period was characterized by temperatures somewhat warmer than present and by gradually increasing moisture. Reforestation of Central Europe was far advanced, dominated by trees of the mixed-oak forest—oak, elm, and maple—with widespread undergrowth of hazel. Pine and birch were restricted to poorer soils and higher elevations (Firbas 1949). Of the diverse animal species, those large and abundant enough to serve regularly as human resources included: red deer, roe deer, aurochs, wild boar, chamois, beaver, numerous smaller mammals like marten and otter, a variety of migratory waterfowl, and a number of fish species including cyprinids (such as carp and bream), pike, and trout. Potential plant foods are virtually unknown, but may have included hazelnuts and a variety of roots, greens, and berries.

Each of the resources shows a pattern of changing attributes through the year which would have been important to its exploitation. Changes in resource weight, fat content, aggregation, and spatial location are all noted and evaluated by hunters and gatherers in organizing their economic activities. The model used here tries to approximate this evaluation process by converting this attribute behavior into expressions of relative ranking of the resources according to each of two major economic goals: (1) security of income, which seems to increase with resource weight (w), non-food yields (n, skins, antlers), and density (d), and to decrease with resource mobility (m), and (2) net yield, which increases with resource weight, non-food yields, and aggregation (a), and decreases with resource mobility. Thus, each resource may be assigned a score for each month according to each of these goals: wnd/m (security) and wna/m (net yield). An estimate of the projected importance of each resource in the diet is accomplished by averaging the proportional scores according to each goal.[1]

The modeling techniques used here differ from those applied to the Danube Valley in three ways:

1. By the inclusion of additional resources (aurochs, chamois)
2. By the calculation of the overall yearly importance of each resource as the average of its monthly proportions (rather than by using figures for

yearly averages of the attributes; this change was necessary in order to deal with salmon, which are present only part of the year)
3. By expressing technological differences in terms of differences in "perceived" resource attributes (i.e., the use of nets would increase the perceived aggregation size of fish)

With these alterations, the techniques are applied to the first three forms of the model; the implications of Model IV (with storage technology) will be discussed in the "Conclusions."

In modeling the utilization of salmon, a number of considerations are necessary. Salmon are present in the Rhine much of the year; they enter the mouth of the river from fall to the following summer. Spawning occurs mainly in the tributaries above Basel from November through January (Netboy 1968). In the Upper Rhine the first salmon of the year traditionally appeared in May, and runs fluctuated in intensity through January; the fish were virtually absent from February through April, and their weight and aggregation size dropped precipitously in this period as well. In recent times the peak of the Upper Rhine fishery occurred from October through December, but earlier the summer runs were equally important, before the downstream fishing blocked these runs (Koch 1927). Salmon will be considered present in the main river from May through December, and in the tributaries from December through January.

Historically, the fishing was conducted with a variety of weirs, nets, traps, and spears; baited hooks would not be taken by the salmon (Herbster 1919). In considering prehistoric technology, ethnographic observations are informative (Kroeber and Barrett 1960; Post 1938). Spear, harpoons, and arrows require clear and shallow water; in the main river these conditions would be found most commonly from October through April, when the water level is low (Heim 1931). Tributaries would provide these conditions for a greater part of the year. Weirs together with traps, dipnets, and spears similarly require relatively low water and moderate flow. Larger nets, on the other hand, require high and murky water and would be most useful from May through September, or at restricted pools at other times. The combination of salmon distribution, water level, and technological requirements leads to some much simplified generalizations for the models. Salmon fishing with spears, harpoons, and arrows (Model II) should be restricted primarily to the period of October

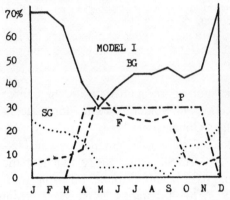

SEASONS					
RESOURCE	DJFM	A	M	JJAS	ON
Fish	8	12	36	25	8
Big Game	68	41	31	43	45
Small Game	21	17	4	4	14
Plants	-	30	30	30	30

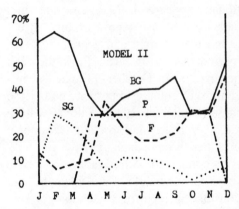

SEASONS						
RESOURCE	JFM	A	M	JJAS	ON	D
Fish	9	10	36	21	30	45
Big Game	63	38	29	41	32	53
Small Game	21	17	5	10	3	2
Plants	-	30	30	30	30	-

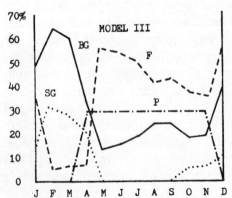

SEASONS						
RESOURCE	JFM	A	MJJ	AS	ON	D
Fish	16	8	53	43	36	54
Big Game	58	33	17	26	20	39
Small Game	26	22	-	1	7	10
Plants	-	30	30	30	30	-

Figure 9.2. Predicted seasonal resource use.

through January in the main river and tributaries. More intensive fishing with nets, weirs, and traps would occur from May through January: in the main river from May through December, and in the tributaries in December and January. Salmon abundance is approximated from historical sources (Koch 1927; Kopp 1968; Vetter 1864).

The projected seasonal resource utilization is presented in figure 9.2. Without salmon, fishing is a decidedly warm weather occupation (Model I). Salmon fishing with spears provides an additional fish emphasis in fall and early winter (Model II). Elaboration of the fishing technology increases the importance of fishing from May through January (Model III). These changes of resource emphasis determine seasonal patterns of economic activities, and the resulting "economic seasons" with their expected percentages of resource use are also presented in figure 9.2.

It is expected that seasonal changes of activities may require changes of settlement in order to obtain the desired resources with the least effort. The seasonal distribution of each resource can be estimated through a consideration of topography, temperature, rainfall, soils, and reconstructed vegetation patterns in the study area. It is expected that camps would be placed in zones of overlapping distribution of resources for each season; in the event that there is no single area offering all the necessary resources, then it is assumed that camps would be situated closer to the less mobile resources (Jochim 1976:60). These areas of probable settlement location can be presented in the form of potential catchment areas around the overlap zones using a radius of ten kilometers (Jochim 1976:125). The topographic hindrances to mobility are temporarily ignored.

Crucial to the construction of resource distribution maps in the case of salmon is again a consideration of the implications of technology. The use of different techniques depends, not only on general water level, but also on the configuration of the river bed. In major rivers, at least, spearing will tend to be confined to areas of accessible shallows and low rapids; in tributaries such areas may be more common. Weirs can be used most easily at natural fords and low rapids at relatively narrow regions of the river, and probably not at spots with a rock bottom preventing the sinking of posts. Deep water nets tend to be most productive at pools at the foot of falls or high rapids, and at eddies adjacent to sand bars and projections of the river bank (Kroeber and Barrett 1960; Post 1938). Such characteristics of the Rhine bed have long been destroyed or flooded by modern canalization and damming, but their location can be determined from historical documents. One source in particular, a study of historic fishing and shipping in the Upper Rhine, has been especially useful (Vetter 1864). These locations, together with technological requirements and the salmon distribution, have been used to determine the locations of potential salmon procurement in the various models.

The projected cycle of seasonal catchments for each model is presented in figure 9.3. A distinction has been made between "probable" and "possible" catchments. In Model I, for example, it is projected that winter camps, over a period of four months, would be located along the uppermost portion of the Rhine. In the early spring month of April, the potential catchments include both the Upper Rhine and the valley of the Birs. Potential resource depletion (including firewood) during the previous winter along the Upper Rhine, however, together with a possible desire to change locations after a four-month residence, would render a shift of settlement to the Birs Valley more probable.

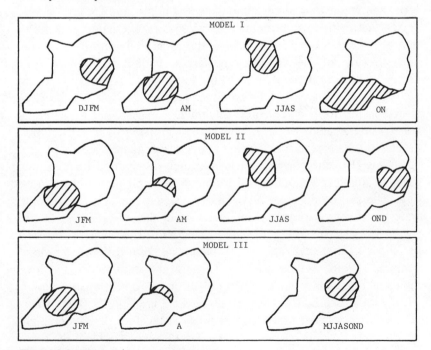

Figure 9.3. Probable seasonal catchments.

A number of differences in projected settlement locations among the three models can be seen. The Upper Rhine Valley is expected to be the location of winter sites in Model I, of spring and late fall/early winter sites in Model II, and of spring, summer, and late fall/early winter sites in Model III. The Birs Valley is expected to have spring and fall settlements in Model I, and winter and spring settlements in Models II and III. The lower Rheingraben is expected to have summer occupations in Models I and II, and none in Model III. These differences derive primarily from the changing location of the most productive fishing spots in relation to the distribution of other game. A clear and dramatic feature of these maps is the great difference in potential sedentism expected among the models. For Models I and II, the longest stay in one region is about four months; in Model III, however, an occupation of the Upper Rhine Valley of eight months is projected. A technological, not environmental, factor is responsible for this restriction of preferred settlement locations.

Having constructed a set of predictions about economic activities and settlement patterns, attention can be given to demographic factors. In each model, a specific percentage contribution to the yearly diet has been calculated for each resource. Estimating a low daily need of 2,000 kilocalories per day, one person's yearly diet comprises 730,000 kilocalories, to be supplied in specific proportions by different resources. The caloric biomass (weight × density × percent edibility × caloric content) of each resource per square kilometer can be calculated, and given its percentage contribution, the number of people per square kilometer that can be supported by each resource can be determined. Since the specified contributions of *all* resources must be obtained, then the lowest population estimate should represent the maximum possible. Furthermore, since these figures assume a 100 percent harvesting efficiency of each resource, they must be reduced by some factor to estimate actual rates of procurement. As in the study of the Danube Valley, the present formulations of Models I and II will estimate harvesting efficiency at 20 percent for all resources, based on ethnographic estimates. For the technology of Model III, the efficiency of salmon fishing is estimated to approach recent figures, and a figure of 60 percent is used; since this technology should influence the harvest of other, smaller fish as well, the same figure is used for these.

Calculations performed for the three model economic systems

suggest that non-anadromous fish are the limiting resource in Models I and II, while salmon are limiting in Model III. The figures for maximum carrying capacity reveal an interesting pattern:

Model	People/Square kilometer
I	.11
II	.12
III	.26

The simple presence of salmon in the environment is not sufficient to permit significantly higher population densities. The technology of intensive harvesting, however, allows for a doubling of the possible density in this case, not so much because of its higher yields, but because it provides for salmon procurement over a longer time period, and thus decreases the necessary reliance on the less valuable other fish. According to these figures, the maximum population in the study area is 363 (Model I), 396 (Model II) and 858 (Model III).

Another aspect of the demography that needs to be investigated is the arrangement of population, that is, the seasonal patterns of coresident group size. Many factors influence human settlement size: those that are considered here include the degree of resource clustering, size of catchment area, variety of economic activities, and necessity of cooperative labor. A measure of resource clustering, weighted according to size and density of the resource, might be expressed as $\Sigma\, wnad/m$; the greater the sum of this measure for all resources, the greater may be the potential for low-cost human aggregation. Of course, such a measure does not take into account the degree of spatial overlap of the various resources. The sum of these measures for each month is presented in table 9.2 for each of the models.

To judge from these figures alone, the potential group size in Model I is remarkably stable, with possible fission indicated only in April and October. The figures for Models II and III suggest an increasing potential in the salmon fishing months, as might be expected with this concentrated resource. Model III shows especially large seasonal discrepancies.

A factor crucial to human aggregation is the catchment area exploitable from a settlement. Beginning with an assumed average catchment with a 10 kilometer radius, or 314 square kilometers, it is postulated that topographic features (such as steep valley walls) and snow cover (especially in the absence of snowshoes, for which there

Table 9.2 Population Aggregation Potential ($\Sigma wnad/m$)*

Month	Model I	Model II	Model III
J	55,435	76,435	163,435
F	50,279	50,279	50,279
M	53,030	53,030	53,030
A	29,363	29,363	29,363
M	56,253	56,253	128,253
J	41,129	41,129	105,125
J	43,816	43,816	107,812
A	46,555	46,555	102,559
S	52,919	52,919	122,915
O	32,094	60,894	122,094
N	43,242	79,242	151,242
D	50,212	86,212	158,212

*w: weight; n: non-food yields; a: aggregation size; d: density; m: mobility

is no archaeological evidence) will reduce considerably the area of exploitation. Assuming a constant energy expenditure in movement, a summer catchment in a narrow valley may approach 200 square kilometers, while that in winter may be as little as 18 square kilometers (Jochim 1976:138). Calculation of resource biomasses available in the catchments of each of these two extreme seasons, coupled with estimates of human caloric needs, may suggest estimates for the expected magnitude of settlement sizes. These population ranges are as follows:

Model	Winter	Summer
I	6–12	43–86
II	11–21	50–100
III	32–64	80–240

From these figures, there is a pronounced difference between the estimated populations of winter and summer camps in all three models. Model III shows significantly larger camps in both seasons.

An additional factor that may affect settlement size is the degree of economic specialization. Given the fact that any resource may fail, a seasonal concentration upon any one activity is potentially insecure. One possible response to such a situation would be to increase settlement size, thereby increasing the number of resource procurers and helping to insure that some food will be brought into camp. A dominance index borrowed from ecological research can be calculated for the economic activities of each season; the higher this index, the greater the specialization upon one or a few resources. The index used is $\Sigma (ni/N)^2$, where ni/N is the proportional use of each resource (Jochim 1976:75). These seasonal indices are:

	DJFM	A	M	JJAS	ON	
Model I	.18	.18	.25	.20	.17	

	JFM	A	M	JJAS	ON	D
Model II	.17	.17	.24	.19	.21	.27

	JFM	A	MJJ	AS	ON	D
Model III	.20	.18	.38	.30	.24	.34

Thus, the indices are highest in those seasons emphasizing fishing, and if considerations of security affect group size, then these seasons should have the largest aggregations.

Finally it must be asked whether any specific seasons require larger groups for cooperative exploitation. Technology has not been considered here in any detail, but most resources can be procured by individuals or small groups (albeit perhaps not most efficiently—as in the case of game drives). Certainly the spearing of fish requires no large groups. The construction, maintenance, and operation of weirs and large nets, however, is often a communal endeavor (Kroeber and Barrett 1960), and hence it might be expected that aggregation would be a feature of the salmon fishing seasons of Model III.

In summary, the probable patterns of group sizes for Model I might include the largest aggregations in summer, the smallest in early spring, and groups of intermediate size in fall and winter. Model II should show the largest groups in late fall/early winter, the smallest in early spring, and those of intermediate size in other seasons. The largest aggregations of Model III may occur in summer and late fall/early winter, the smallest in late winter/early spring, and intermediate groups in early fall.

As a result of these various calculations, a number of specific predictions have been generated for comparison with the archaeological record. The assumptions and estimates built into the three models have resulted in distinctive differences in projected economic activities and seasons, settlement locations, population density, and settlement size. Because of the nature of the available archaeological materials, many of these predictions cannot be checked, but it may be possible to suggest which of the hypothetical models is best supported. Additional fieldwork could be aimed at investigating these

Table 9.3 Predictions of Site Characteristics

Model I	DJFM	A	M	JJAS	ON
Location	Rhine	Birs	Birs	Rheingraben	Birs
Shelter need [a]	+++	++	+	+	++
Population	Medium	Small	Medium	Large	Medium
Big game	68%	41%	31%	43%	45%
Fish	8%	12%	36%	25%	8%

Model II	JFM	A	M	JJAS	ON	D
Location	Birs	Birs	Birs	Rheingraben	Rhine	Rhine
Shelter need [a]	+++	++	+	+	++	++
Population	Medium	Small	Medium	Medium	Large	Large
Big game	63%	38%	29%	41%	32%	53%
Fish	9%	10%	36%	21%	30%	45%

Model III	JFM	A	MJJ	AS	ON	D
Location	Birs	Birs	Rhine	Rhine	Rhine	Rhine
Shelter need [a]	+++	++	+	+	++	++
Population	Small	Small	Large	Medium	Large	Large
Big game	58%	33%	17%	26%	20%	39%
Fish	16%	8%	53%	43%	36%	54%

[a]The number of +'s represent the relative degree of need for protection from winter cold and precipitation.

predictions. A summary of the predictions for each of the models is presented in table 9.3.

Resource Exploitation: The Archaeological Evidence

In dealing with the archaeological materials of this region, a number of significant problems have to be considered. Some areas have undergone tremendous alterations since Mesolithic times, especially the low Rheingraben plain. Modern canalization and damming have lowered the water table appreciably, so that the area today is quite dry. Formerly, however, this area contained numerous natural channels and backwaters and thousands of islands. High annual floods occurred and resulted in the deposition of much silt (Kriegsmann 1969). As a result, archaeological materials of any period are rare in this area, presumably because they lie deeply buried. Some Mesolithic sites have been found in the plain along the Middle Rhine farther to the north, but these occur on high dunes that, further south, are lacking or have been buried. Early in this century a number of "Meso-lithic" sites were reported from a series of small caves above the eastern edge of the Rheingraben (Mieg 1901, 1904, 1910; Lais 1929), but the circumstances of their recovery, the identification of their materials, and the probable mixing of sites and levels have led to doubts about their exact nature. The only candidate for consideration, a cave called Isteiner Klotz, was partially excavated after an earlier disturbance, and contained artifacts of both stone and organic materials.

In the area of the Upper Rhine, twenty-four sites have been found and attributed to the Mesolithic (Gersbach 1969), including twenty-three open-air sites and one small cave which yielded from 5 to 1,055 stone artifacts each; none shows preservation of organic materials. All of the sites seem to contain mixed occupations, and most, if not all, have been seriously disturbed by plowing, quarrying, construction, and burrowing. The only approach possible for dating of these sites is through a stylistic analysis of the geometric microliths in conjunction with known stratigraphic sequences of the Danube and Birs Valleys (Taute, manuscript; Wyss 1973). Ten of the sites are thus excluded at the outset because they contain no microliths (these yielded from 5 to 29 total artifacts each). A further seven sites are excluded because their microliths include no types of known chronological significance. Thus there are only seven sites that can be assigned to stages within the Mesolithic on the basis of certain diagnostic microliths. Of these, only two seem to have had an occupation during the Late Mesolithic with any certainty. One of these, Säckingen, is by far the largest site, having yielded 1,055 artifacts. The other, Öfflingen, contained only 56 artifacts. Both of these open-air sites were apparently also occupied in earlier stages of the Mesolithic as well as during the late Paleolithic, a fact that will render comparison of artifact frequencies difficult.

The Birs Valley contains a number of rock shelters and caves in the limestone cliffs along the river and its tributaries. Most of these were found and excavated quite early; by modern standards the techniques of excavation and stratigraphic control, as well as the preservation of excavated materials, are seriously deficient. Early in this century, most of these materials were assigned to the Azilian, which in many cases was poorly separated from the underlying Magdalenian (Sarasin 1918). A later reanalysis of these materials attributed Mesolithic occupations to most of these sites (Ludin 1961). Four more recently discovered sites, on the other hand, were investigated with excellent techniques of excavation; three of these (Birsmatten, Liesberg VI, and Tschäpperfels) achieved good stratigraphic control of materials and a firm dating, and are published in full (Bandi 1963; Sedlmeier 1968; Wyss 1957). The fourth, Wachtfels, has been only summarily reported and the materials are inaccessible (Ludin 1961). Many of these sites in the Birs Valley contained organic materials, but they differ in their preservation and analysis.

It is obvious that the archaeological materials of the study area are tremendously uneven in quality. No conclusions based on these can be considered statistically reliable. In fact, any attempt to explore their interrelationships at all can be seriously questioned. It should be realized, however, that archaeology in Europe has been practiced for many years. Many of the most obvious or accessible sites have been disturbed, trenched, collected, or excavated, and their materials lie scattered in a variety of national and regional museums, or in private hands. If some understanding of European prehistory is to be at-

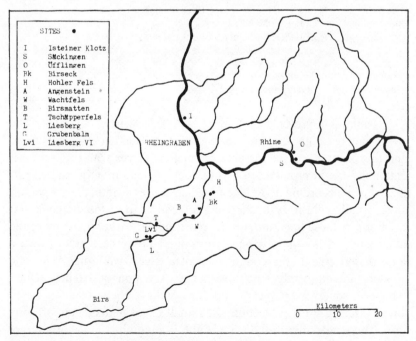

Figure 9.4. Late Mesolithic sites in the study area.

tained, it is not sufficient to rely upon new excavations: some means of evaluating the older materials in their present condition must be devised. It is hoped that the techniques used here can aid this evaluation.

The distribution of sites is presented in figure 9.4. Lithic artifacts can be compared among some sites in all three regions, as long as the problems of chronology and mixing are kept in mind. Quantified faunal materials are present only in some of the sites in the Birs Valley; these will be investigated for similarities and differences. Finally, characteristics of location and size can be considered for all of the sites to some extent.

Table 9.4 Site Characteristics

Site	Location	Nature	Area (m²)	Orientation
Säckingen	Upper Rhine	Open-air	18,000	—
Öfflingen	Upper Rhine	Open-air	?	—
Birseck	Lower Birs tributary	Rock shelter	40	S
Hohler Fels	Lower Birs tributary	Rock shelter	29	S
Angenstein	Lower Birs	Rock shelter	c.20	E
Wachtfels	Birs Valley	Rock shelter	?	S
Birsmatten	Upper Birs Valley	Cave	33	S
Tschäpperfels	Upper Birs tributary	Rock shelter	37	S
Liesberg VI	Upper Birs Valley	Cave	48	S
Liesberg Cave	Upper Birs Valley	Cave	23	WNW
Grubenbalm	Upper Birs Valley	Rock shelter	c.40	S
Isteiner Klotz	Rheingraben Edge	Cave	.75	SSE

Table 9.4 presents a number of characteristics of sites. The caves facing south should offer the most protection and insolation, and thus should provide the greatest shelter. Caves with different orientations should provide less, while rock shelters may be ranked further down according to orientation and valley width. The open-air sites would seem to offer the least protection from the elements. At least one of these open-air sites is tremendously larger than any of the other sites (as is to be expected from overlapping occupations over a long period outside the confinement of a cave), while the caves and shelters are uniformly small (with the exception of Isteiner Klotz, which is somewhat larger). The Birs Valley, then, contains small caves offering great protection, and small caves and shelters offering less. The single site on the edge of the Rheingraben is slightly larger

and relatively sheltered, while the Upper Rhine sites may represent still larger settlements providing the least shelter.

Functional interpretations of lithic assemblage differences among the sites are hampered by a lack of knowledge regarding specific functions of artifacts and by purely chronological changes in the frequencies of artifact categories. It has been suggested previously that among contemporaneous sites, microliths should vary directly with the importance of big game hunting, that scrapers and borers were used, at least in part, for hide working which should be predominantly a fall activity, and that if burins were used partly to work antler, then these should occur with greatest frequency in fall settlements when red deer antlers are in best condition (Jochim 1976:179f.). These statements allow the translation of the economic and seasonal predictions of the models into terms allowing comparison with lithics. For all models, late winter sites should show the highest proportion of microliths, followed by fall, early spring, and summer, while fall sites should have the highest frequencies of scrapers, borers, and burins.

Complicating these expectations are observed chronological changes in tool frequencies which have no obvious functional significance, and may derive from functional replacements. From late Paleolithic to Early Mesolithic there is a general decrease in burins, retouched blades, and borers, and an increase in microliths. From Early to Late Mesolithic there is an increase in notched and retouched blades and a decrease in burins and microliths (together with the appearance of barbed bone and antler harpoons). Unless sites are contemporary, therefore, their assemblages can be expected to differ with no necessary functional significance. Partial control should be provided by comparisons matched as much as possible in chronology. Table 9.5 presents these matched comparisons.

The two open-air sites show remarkable similarities in tool frequencies, despite their great difference in assemblage size. Birsmatten, by contrast, differs in having more microliths and notched blades and fewer scrapers, burins, borers, and retouched blades. How much of this difference is due to the lack of a Paleolithic component, and how much to varying activities, is not clear. In comparison with Birsmatten, then, Isteiner Klotz contains fewer microliths and notched blades and more scrapers, burins, borers, and retouched

Table 9.5 Comparison of Site Lithics

	Säckingen	Öfflingen	Birsmatten 1–5	Isteiner Klotz
Date: Paleolithic	X	X		
Early Mesolithic	X	X	X	X
Late Mesolithic	X	X	X	X
Microliths	33%	32%	51%	42%
Scrapers	25	27	19	28
Burins	10	14	5	8
Borers	12	11	1	4
Notched blades	1	—	15	3
Retouched blades	18	16	10	15
Total artifacts	1,055	56	1,024	72

	Birsmatten 1–2	Tschäpperfels	Liesberg VI
Date: Late Mesolithic	X	X	X
Microliths	37%	10%	4%
Scrapers	18	15	4
Burins	4	1	15
Borers	1	2	—
Notched blades	23	48	31
Retouched blades	17	24	46
Total artifacts	428	151	26

blades. Within the Birs Valley, the clearest differences among the three Late Mesolithic sites are that Liesberg VI shows fewer scrapers and more burins and retouched blades, while Birsmatten has more microliths. Despite the probable influence of chronological variation, it would seem that Birsmatten may contain more evidence for big game hunting, Isteiner Klotz and the open-air sites for hide working, and Liesberg VI and the open-air sites for antler working. These tentative suggestions must be considered in light of the other evidence.

A final class of evidence is provided by faunal materials. Since quantitative information is available only for some of the sites in the Birs Valley, its applicability is most restricted. Furthermore, for two sites (Birsmatten and Tschäpperfels) only bone counts per species are available, while for the more problematic materials of two older sites (Birseck and Hohler Fels), estimates of the minimum number of individuals have been reported. Each of these two methods of reporting species frequencies can be converted into estimates of meat yields, but the comparison of results of the two methods may be suspect. Fish remains (unidentified) were recovered only at Birsmatten, and

Table 9.6 Predicted Percentages of Big Game Diet

	Model I		Model II		Model III	
Resource	Fall	Spring	Winter	Spring	Winter	Spring
Red Deer	31%	42%	51%	43%	51%	50%
Boar	34	21	25	22	22	14
Aurochs	28	28	19	28	21	30
Roe Deer	7	9	6	7	6	6

bird remains were not quantified at any site. Consequently, only mammalian remains can be considered. Since small mammal bones can be expected to have undergone greater post-depositional disintegration than those of large mammals, the latter may be over-represented in the archaeological collections. To help compensate for this differential preservation, only the relative percentages of such larger mammals will be initially examined. In order to derive any applicable predictions from the models, just those seasons that are expected to show occupation in the Birs Valley can be considered, and for these seasons the amount of meat represented by various large mammals can be calculated as percentages of the total. These predicted percentages, based on calculations of the models, are presented in table 9.6, and can be compared to those calculated for the remains of the four sites (table 9.7).

These calculations suggest a degree of similarity between Birsmatten and Tschäpperfels on the one hand and between Birseck and Hohler Fels on the other, primarily in the combined importance of the two major resources, red deer and boar. Moreover, the pattern of differences between these two pairs of sites comes closest to approximating that predicted by Model II. Additional faunal evidence sup-

Table 9.7 Archaeological Big Game

	Birsmatten 1–2		Tschäpperfels		Birseck		Hohler Fels	
Resource	No. Bones	% Meat[a]	No. Bones	% Meat	MNI[b]	% Meat	MNI[b]	% Meat
Red Deer	397	56%	16	47%	5	44%	4	35%
Boar	315	38	17	45	4	30	3	23
Aurochs	17	5	1	7	1	20	2	40
Roe Deer	20	1	1	1	4	6	1	1

[a]Weighted according to body weight and percentage edibility.
[b]Minimum number of individuals.

ports this interpretation. The only known piglets occur at Birseck and Hohler Fels; in Central Europe today, most piglets are born from March to May. Birsmatten contained both shed and unshed red deer antlers; since shedding usually occurs between February and April, and because shed antlers do not usually survive long under natural conditions, this suggests an occupation at Birsmatten at least at some time during this period and possibly earlier as well. These seasonal indications are compatible with the designation of Birsmatten and Tschäpperfels as late winter sites, and of Birseck and Hohler Fels as spring sites, as suggested by the agreement of large mammal percentages with the pattern of Model II. Furthermore, the patterns of shelter, lithics, and relative size of the sites in the study area are most compatible with the expectations of Model II. The evidence indicates a substantial disagreement with Model I in terms of faunal percentages and seasonal needs for shelter. Model III is contraindicated by faunal percentages and by the relative impermanence of the Upper Rhine sites (which should be occupied for up to eight months, according to Model III).

Conclusions

As a result of these comparisons it would seem that the best approximation to the Mesolithic economic and settlement system in the study area is provided by Model II. The salmon fishing season at the end of the year would have been spent along the Upper Rhine, and since technology required shallow water, the clustering of sites around a natural ford between Säckingen and Öfflingen is understandable. The more intense cold of late winter saw a shift of settlement to the Upper Birs, with later movements downstream to spend summers in the Rheingraben flood plain. The probability of population fission and fusion, and the resulting relative number of sites of different seasons, suggest that base camps along the Upper Rhine should be least abundant, those of spring most numerous, and those of late winter and summer of intermediate frequency. The relative abundance of rock shelter sites compared to caves occupied in the Birs Valley may reflect the differential frequency of spring over winter camps. Future work to investigate these hypotheses could include explorations along the Upper Rhine away from shallows, on the heights of the Black Forest and Jura, and in the Rheingraben plain.

In conclusion, however, the aims of this study are not so much to claim that the hypotheses of Model II are necessarily the "correct" explanation of these archaeological materials, but rather to emphasize the value of ethnography and models to archaeology. Ethnographic sources can suggest a number of alternative assumptions about prehistoric economies. The translation of these assumptions and their ramifications into statements about archaeological materials can be effectively accomplished through the simplified system of relationships that constitute a model. The nature of these relationships—for example, the environmental requirements of different technologies—again can be suggested by ethnographic studies.

A significant benefit of such models is that they permit the recognition of a variety of implications of the initial assumptions that are not readily obvious. In the present study, the importance of both environment and technology in influencing settlement locations, demography, and mobility is obvious. Moreover, the models permit some statements about the ethnographic generalizations regarding salmon-based economies. The observed higher levels of population density, aggregation, and sedentism would seem to be possible only with the development of a technology of intensive harvesting. Furthermore, the development of this technology, even though it may seem to enrich the economic base, may paradoxically increase selection pressures favoring the development of storage techniques. As the importance of salmon increases in magnitude and seasonal distribution, those seasons without this resource became relatively less productive by contrast. This trend is obvious in the figures of population aggregation potential for Model III: the leaner seasons became relatively leaner. One response would be to increase resource procurement during the richer seasons in order to provide greater security for the periods of scarcity—a response that would require storage techniques. In addition, the increased sedentism characteristic of Model III could conceivably lead to serious local depletion of non-salmon resources. Again, one possible response would be to intensify the salmon harvest beyond immediate consumption desires, and storage would allow a flexibility in the temporal distribution of this increased harvest. In other words, the models suggest how one technological innovation may not only lead to, but also require another, to create what appears to be a positive feedback loop of cultural evolution.

Notes

1. The procedure was as follows: (a) For each resource, numerical estimates of five attributes (weight, non-food yields, density, aggregation size, and mobility) were made for each month. These estimates were based on paleontological and ethological literature. (b) The attributes were then combined in simple formulas to express the relative security (wnd/m) and net yield (wna/m) of each resource. (c) For each of these two goals, the scores of all resources of each month were totaled. (d) Each resource score was converted into a percentage of the total. (e) The two percentage scores of each resource were averaged to yield one percentage figure, which is taken here to represent the relative importance of that resource in the food quest for that month. For further details, see Jochim (1976).

References Cited

Bandi, H. G.
     1963. *Birsmatten-Basisgrotte* (Acta Bernensia I). Bern: Stämpfli.
Clark, J. G. D.
     1958. "Blade and Trapeze Industries of the European Stone Age." *Proceedings of the Prehistoric Society* 24:24–42.
Dejong, J. D.
     1967. "The Quaternary of the Netherlands." In K. Rankama, ed., *The Quaternary*, pp. 374–77. New York: Interscience Publishers.
Firbas, F.
     1949. *Waldgeschichte Mitteleuropas*. Jena: Fischer.
Flint, R. F.
     1971. *Glacial and Quaternary Geology*. New York: Wiley.
Gersbach, E.
     1969. "Urgeschichte des Hochrheins." *Badische Fundberichte*, Sonderheft 11.
Graburn, N. H. H. and B. S. Strong
     1972. *Circumpolar Peoples: An Anthropological Perspective*. Pacific Palisades: Goodyear.
Hartmann-Frick, H.
     1969. "Die Tierwelt im Neolithischen Siedlungsraum." *Archäologie der Schweiz*, vol. II.
Heim, A.
     1931. *Geologie des Rheinfalls*. Schaffhausen: Kühn.
Herbster, K.
     1919. *Die Rheinfischerei zwischen Säckingen und Basel*. Blätter aus der Markgrafschaft.

Jochim, M. A.
1976. *Hunter-Gatherer Subsistence and Settlement: A Predictive Model.* New York: Academic Press.
Koch, H.
1927. "Lachsfischerei im Rheine." *Badische Fischerei-Zeitung* 4/10:85–96.
Kopp, W.
1968. *Laufenburg: Von der Salmenfischerei zur Internationalen Schaltanlage.* Aarau: Hauszeitung Sprecher & Schuh, Sonderdruck.
Kriegsmann, F.
1969. "Die Oberrheinfischerei zwischen Karlsruhe und Basel." *Welt am Oberrhein* 9/1:8–19.
Kroeber, A. L. and S. A. Barrett
1960. "Fishing Among the Indians of Northwestern California." University of California Publications, *Anthropological Records 21,* no. 1.
Lais, R.
1929. "Ein Werkplatz des Azilio-Tardenoisiens am Isteiner Klotz." *Badische Fundberichte* 2(3):97–115.
Ludin, C.
1961. "Mesolithische Siedlungen im Birstal." *Jahrbuch der Schweizerischen Gesellschaft für Urgeschichte* 48:52–70.
McKennan, R. A.
1969a. "Athapaskan Groupings and Social Organization in Central Alaska." National Museum of Canada, Bulletin 228, pp. 93–114.
1969b. "Athapaskan Groups of Central Alaska at the Time of White Contact." *Ethnohistory* 16:335–43.
Mieg, M. M.
1901. "Note sur une Station de l'Époque Paléolithique Découverte à Istein." *Bulletin de la Société des Sciences de Nancy,* series 3, 2:101–7.
1904. "Stations Préhistoriques de Kleinkems." *Bulletin de la Société des Sciences de Nancy,* series 3, 5:47–63.
1910. "Note sur l'Age et l'Industrie Paléolithique des Grottes d'Istein." *Bulletin de la Société des Sciences de Nancy,* series 3, 9:60–69.
Mills, D.
1971. *Salmon and Trout: A Resource, Its Ecology, Conservation, and Management.* New York: Macmillan.
Netboy, A.
1968. *The Atlantic Salmon.* Boston: Houghton Mifflin.
1974. *The Salmon: Their Fight for Survival.* Boston: Houghton Mifflin.
Osgood, C.
1936. *The Distribution of the Northern Athapaskan Indians.* New Haven: Yale University Publications in Anthropology, no. 7.
Payne, R. H., A. R. Child, and A. Forrest
1971. "Geographical Variation in the Atlantic Salmon." *Nature* 231:250–52.
Post, R. H.
1938. "The Subsistence Quest." In L. Spier, ed., *The Sinkaietk or Southern Okanagon of Washington,* pp. 11–33. General Series in Anthropology, no. 6,

Contributions from the Laboratory of Anthropology, no. 2. Menasha, Wis.:
Banta.

Sarasin, F.
1918. *Die Steinzeitlichen Stationen des Birstales zwischen Basel und Delsberg.*
Zurich: Zürcher & Furrer.

Sedlmeier, J.
1968. "Der Abri Tschäpperfels." *Jahrbuch des Bernischen Historischen Museums* 48:117–41.

Taute, W.
n.d. "Untersuchungen zum Mesolithikum und zum Spätpaläolithikum in südlichen Mitteleuropa: Chronologie." Tübingen. Manuscript.

Vetter, J.
1864. *Die Schiffahrt, Flösserei und Fischerei auf dem Oberrhein.* Karlsruhe:
Braun'schen Druckerei.

Wyss, R.
1957. "Eine Mesolithische Station bei Liesbergmühle." *Zeitschrift für Schweizerische Archäologie und Kunstgeschichte* 17:1–13.
1973. "Zum Problemkreis des Schweizerischen Mesolithikums." In S. K. Kozlowski, ed., *The Mesolithic in Europe,* pp. 615–49. Warsaw: University of
Warsaw Press.

10/Cultivation and Cognition: Plants and Archaeological Research Strategies

Ellen Messer
Department of Anthropology
Yale University

In her discussion of plants in Mexico's Valley of Oaxaca, Messer provides valuable information about contemporary utilization of both cultivated and unsown plants. She suggests some ways in which evidence of plant utilization may be reflected in the archaeological record, and reviews some of the available paleobotanical evidence from the region. Messer's observations about contemporary plant use and folk taxonomy are relevant to the interpretation of the functions of particular archaeologically retrieved plants; her "case study" of the avocado, a significant New World plant whose history is less completely documented than are those of corn, beans, and squash, underscores this point. Messer's article, like Hardin's, suggests some of the ways in which knowledge of a contemporary native taxonomy can be used to refine archaeological approaches to classification and interpretation. Her suggestions about archaeological methods of botanical sampling and retrieval are pertinent to Mesoamerica as well as to other regions; the data which she provides are relevant not only to the analysis of individual archaeological sam-

A shorter version of this paper was presented under the title "Ethnobotanical Implications for Archaeology: Examples from the Valley of Oaxaca, Mexico," at the American Anthropological Association Annual Meeting, Washington, D.C., November 19, 1976. I would like to thank symposium members and Harry Merrick for their comments.

Ethnobotanical data were collected by the author during twelve months of ethnobotanical fieldwork over the period 1971–74, as part of the project, Prehistory and Human Ecology of the Valley of Oaxaca, directed by Kent V. Flannery, University of Michigan, Museum of Anthropology. This research was supported in 1971 by a National Science Foundation Traineeship and in 1972–74 by a Junior Fellowship in the Michigan Society of Fellows. Additional travel funds were provided by a Ford Foundation Travel Grant in 1971.

ples, but bear on the broader issues of reconstructing prehistoric
land use systems and understanding the process of plant domestication.

Almost every archaeologist today collects and analyzes botanical remains as a routine procedure. With the aid of a paleobotanist or ethnobotanist, he records plant remains represented at his excavation
sites. With them, he tries to answer economic and ecological questions, such as "what range of plants were being exploited for food,
fuel, and shelter? What different botanical zones were being used?
Were floral communities changing, and if so, why?" Questions about
the origins of horticulture and agriculture have been of particular interest.

While paleobotanists can analyze the archaeological data and
provide insights into the processes of cultural manipulations of
plants, current ethnographic analyses of plant distribution and use
have much to contribute to the interpretation of plants recoverable
from archaeological sites. Ethnobotanists, working in contemporary
settlements, can combine data on folk plant classifications, native
conceptions of plant-animal-human ecology, and economic botany to
give the archaeologist ideas for both research design and (plant) artifact interpretation. This paper will suggest how ethnobotanical studies can help structure the interpretation of plant remains from archaeological sites in two ways. First, ethnobotanists can provide
ethnographic models for how and why plant remains recovered from
particular archaeological loci were deposited. Second, observing current patterns of plant distribution and use, ethnobotanists can formu-
late hypotheses about prehistoric plant use, and suggest strategies of
archaeological collection and analysis to test them.

In the sections that follow, archaeological and ethnobotanical
data from the Valley of Oaxaca, Mexico, will be used to illustrate
these points. The paper will discuss (1) potentially edible plants from
different vegetation zones; (2) how and why these plants reach households; and (3) what refuse one might expect to find from their exploitation. Archaeological data are drawn from the Valley of Oaxaca
Human Ecology Project, directed by Kent V. Flannery (cf. Flannery
et al. 1970; Kirkby 1973; Drennan 1976; Whalen 1976). Ethnobotanical data come from the author's ethnobotanical fieldwork in San

Sebastián Abasolo and San Pablo Mitla, which formed part of the Project. In the sections treating "Gathering," "Weeds," and "Cultivator's Wisdom," ethnobotanical data will be used to show how plants from three principal ecological zones—the uncultivated hillsides, agricultural fields, and house gardens/orchards—are represented in modern household sites. These ethnobotanical insights will then be used to comment on the archaeological remains and to suggest new questions and interpretations for understanding plant-based subsistence activities.

Setting

The Valley of Oaxaca is located in the southern highlands of Mexico, with altitudes ranging from 1,600 to 1,850 meters (figure 10.1). Climate is temperate all year around, and relatively frost free. There is a pronounced rainy season-dry season alternation within which farmers space their crops. Timing and spacing of rains, as well as absolute quantity of precipitation, affect both sown and unsown vegetation growth. According to the pollen record, climate and vegetation have not varied very significantly since the Early Formative (1200–900 B.C.; Flannery and Schoenwetter 1970), though the introduction of agriculture and extensive firewood cutting have altered the floral communities in many locations.

Zapotec Indians, who comprise the bulk of current village populations in the valley, exploit the various plant products from the river alluvium, piedmont, and mountain zones. The valley alluvium, drained by the Río Salado and its tributaries, is cultivated. It supplies agricultural maize, beans, and squash along with unsown edible herbs. Some wild plant foods, medicinal herbs, and cultivated cane also come from this zone. Moving upward from the higher alluvium toward the piedmont, cactus and thorny legumes have been partially cleared for agriculture and house sites, but wild products, including edible fruits and fuel, are still economically important. Higher elevation zones are important chiefly for firewood, though wild fruits are still seasonally important. Finally, the distinctive vegetation of household lots comprises a botanically distinct "cultural zone" unconsciously (through refuse) and consciously (through cultivation) modified by man.

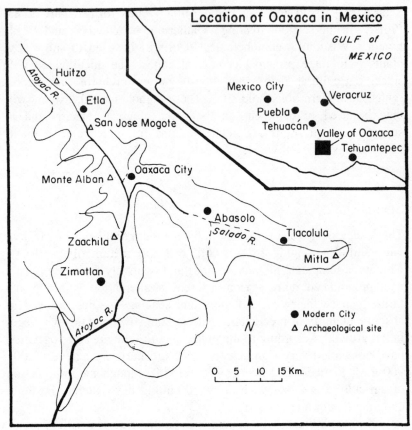

Figure 10.1. The Valley of Oaxaca, Mexico.

Gathering

We know as much as we do about "pre-agricultural" gathering strategies because people have continued to gather along with their other subsistence activities. From the ethnohistoric, recent historic, and ethnographic literature, it is obvious that wild foods have continued to play an important role alongside cultivation in the subsistence of Middle American Indians (cf. Messer 1975).

Current observations show that considerable gathering is done outside of cultivation zones (see table 10.1). In modern Mitla, people gather wild legumes and fruits from the river alluvium; cactus fruits, other fruits, nuts, and pod legumes are gathered from the surrounding

Table 10.1 Edible Wild Plants from Non-Agricultural Zones: Mitla, Oaxaca

Generic Name	Spanish (English) Common Name	Eaten Now	Found in Caves
Agave spp.	maguey (century plant)	x	x
Allium sp.	cebolla (onion)	x	x
Arctostaphylos polifolia	shobnid	x	
Arctostaphylos pungens	manzangish	x	
Asclepias sp.	gueto, binya		x
Cassia polyantha	tepeguaje		x
Celtis sp.	rompecapa	x	x
Condalia mexicana	shobinyi	x	x
Echinocactus sp.	biznagre	x	
Jatropha dioica	suzí	x	x
Lantana velutina	sapotilla	x	
Lemaireocereus sp.	pitaya	x	x
Leucaena esculenta	guaje	x	x
Lysiloma divaricata	guaje	x	x
Malpighia sp.	nanches	x	x
Opuntia spp.	nopales, tunas (prickly pear)	x	x
Oxalis spp.	camotito, agriodulce	x	
Prosopis laevigata	mesquite		x
Quercus sp.	bellotas (acorns)		x

Sources: Messer 1975:172; Flannery et al. 1970:10–19; Flannery, personal communication.
Note: Identifications of plant remains from the Mitla preceramic caves by C. Earle Smith.

higher elevation zones. They are eaten as field snacks, and taken back to house sites for domestic consumption. Certain people, particularly those of limited economic means, carefully watch for the inflorescence of the century plant (*Agave* spp.). It is cut and brought home, where it is slowly roasted and then ground with maize dough to form tortillas. Remains of all these wild plants, which may originate ten minutes to several hours' walk from the house site, are found in modern household refuse. Many of these wild plant genera—*Agave,* Cucurbits, *Leucaena/Lysiloma, Malpighia, Opuntia,* and *Phaseolus*— have been cultivated, and are now found in the gardens, orchards, or field borders of Mitla and other Mesoamerican towns. These cultigens are more convenient, if not more productive, than their wild counterparts. But the old, unchanged wild specimens also continue to be gathered. Thus, a reserve of edible material, as well as gathering knowledge, continues in the cultural environment.

In addition, Mitleños know a number of genera which are "edible" though they do not currently eat them. These include milkweed pods, the heart of the century plant, and the flesh of *biznagre* cactus. All are food which elderly people remember having eaten during famines of the recent past. Mitleños also recognize a number of other plant foods, like mesquite pods, as "not poisonous," since they see other people (including archaeologists) eating them, but Mitleños do not classify them as edible, and prefer to eat other foods. Both the famine foods of the past and the latter class of "not edible" but "not poisonous" plants are potential starvation foods. Between the older generation, which has known famine, and marginal members of local populations—shepherd boys who eat anything potentially edible in the environment—and non-local people who have different rules for culturally classifying foods as edible or nonedible, an extensive body of reserve knowledge about the edible potential of the environment is maintained.

Turning to the archaeological record, one finds that most of the wild foods currently available were also represented in prehistory. Evidence of food gathering in the pre-ceramic period comes from the Mitla caves (cf. Flannery et al. 1970) about three kilometers from the Mitla town center. Plant remains include *Agave* (*maguey,* century plant), *Leucaena* and *Lysiloma* (*guajes,* pod legumes), and *Quercus* (*bellotas,* acorns), from the cave area and *Celtis* (*rompecapa,* hackberry), Cucurbits (*calabaza,* squash), *Jatropha* (*suzí,* nuts), *Malpighia* (*nanche,* cherrylike fruit), *Opuntia* (*nopales,* cactus stems; *tunas,* prickly pear), *Phaseolus* (*jicamita,* beans), *Prosopis* (*mesquite,* leguminous pod), and wild onions from the plain and lower hills below. All are eaten or known to be edible by contemporary Mitleños. Fruits of *Lemaireocereus* and *Myrtyllocactus,* the seeds of which are also found in the archaeological debris, also are picked in season by those venturing nearby today. Only four plants found in the caves and presumed to have been eaten are *not* currently gathered for food by Mitleños. These are *Cassia* pods, which are never selected, even as supplemental foods; *Acacia* pods, which are occasionally referred to for medicinal use but never eaten; and *Diospyros* (wild black *zapote*), which was never mentioned as food. *Pinus* (pinyon pine), the fourth plant, is not currently found in the Mitla area at all.

On the other hand, several plants currently eaten are not represented in the caves. *Arctostaphylos pungens* and *Arctostaphylos poli-*

folia, found in the hills surrounding Mitla, both produce edible berries gathered in the early fall by small expedition parties. At lower
elevations, the flesh of *Echinocactus* (which is candied into sweets)
and berries of *Lantana* spp. (*sapotillas*) are gathered. Their absence
in the archaeological record may indicate that they were (1) not
present in the environment, (2) not classified as "edible," or (3) by
chance not preserved in the archaeological record. Future archaeological work may provide data to support one hypothesis over another.

In addition to learning the range of potentially edible plants in
the environment, ethnobotanists can also provide a more complete
model for how single plants are used over the course of their life
cycles. These observations, by way of analogy, may also aid the interpretation of archaeological remains. For example, *Agave,* while it
has been cultivated for *pulque* (a mildly alcoholic beverage fermented
from the raw juice) and more recently for *mescal* (a liquor distilled
from the cooked heart), still exists in a number of wild forms used in
various ways. *Maguey del monte,* a wild *Agave* which grows in the
Mitla vicinity, has a six-year life cycle over which it provides food in
each of its stages. In its pre-inflorescence stage, outer leaves can be
stripped to expose the tender inner stalk, which is boiled with brown
sugar into a kind of preserve. After five years, the plant "flowers,"
sending up its reproductive stalk (*quiote,* inflorescence), which may
reach more than a meter in height. It is processed into tortillas. Finally, one year after the inflorescence, the underground heart is ready
to be excavated and roasted. It can be cooked into a high energy,
fibrous sweet meat or alternatively sold to a *mescal* factory for high
energy liquor.

Such close studies of plant use can be valuable for the archaeologist. In this case, utilizing analogical reasoning, the archaeologist
can suggest why both inflorescence and the heart of the century plant
were found in the Mitla caves—they are both "edible." Generally,
the more ethnobotanical data the archaeologist has, the more complete his functional interpretation of paleobotanical remains. Ethnobotanical reports of native classifications, observations, and uses of
plants at different points in their life cycles also suggest why certain
plants become candidates for cultural manipulation and cultivation, a
topic to which we return in the next section.

In summary, wild plants continue to be found with cultigens

among household refuse. In spite of the agricultural transformations which gave Mesoamericans a staple diet of maize, people have continued to gather. Contemporary ethnobotanical data show that food gathering either supplements normal harvests or provides starvation foods in times of minimal harvests. People in Mesoamerica up to the present continue to know about and use wild foods because they have been forced to exploit them periodically to avert famine, and because they see others exploiting wild foods. The seasonal and supra-annual life cycles and ecology of wild plants continue to be noted by at least some members of current populations; and they provide models for understanding how wild flora were classified and used for food in the past.

Weeds

Field weeds comprise a second category of unsown food. Modern cultivation practices in many parts of Mesoamerica, as in other parts of the world, include production and gathering of edible weeds in addition to the harvest of the sown crops (cf., e.g., Wilken 1970, Messer 1973). From the disturbed, fertilized, and sometimes irrigated soils supporting maize, beans, and squash come a variety of edible greens eaten early in the rainy season, before the sown crops are ripe, and for the remainder of the wet months. Edible weeds both add to the productive potential of the sown environment and may supply vital nutrients otherwise lacking in the staple (maize) diet (Messer 1972, 1973).

In both the Mitla and Abasolo field systems, several herbs are gathered for food (cf. table 10.2). *Amaranthus hybridus, A. powellii* (and possible hybrids between the two),[1] *Anoda cristata, Crotalaria pumila, Galinsoga parviflora,* and *Portulaca oleracea* are species picked, cooked, and eaten by contemporary Zapotec Indians and mestizos. All may be eaten in their young, tender stages of growth— all except *Amaranthus* spp. in more mature growth as well. Leaves of *Chenopodium ambrosioides,* another weed, provide a condiment for beans. The entire plant may also be boiled into a concentrated brew used to purge intestinal worms; and the dried leaves, mixed with chile, are believed to act as an insect repellent when scattered with stored maize and beans. Thus, *Chenopodium ambrosioides* has sev-

Table 10.2 Most Common Edible Herbs from Field Systems: Linnaean Identification

	Part Used		
Name	Tender greens	Mature greens	Seeds
Amaranthus hybridus L.	x		x [a]
Anoda cristata (L.) Schlecht	x	x	
Chenopodium ambrosioides L.	x	x	x [a]
Crotalaria pumila Ort.	x	x	
Galinsoga parviflora Cav.	x	x	
Portulaca oleracea L.	x	x	

[a]Seeds of these species not eaten by modern population, but seeds of other species within the genera edible.

eral uses. All of these edible herbs reach the household when they are brought in purposefully for a meal. Seeds of any of these weeds may also accidentally reach households when carried along with the maize harvest.

Besides these edible weeds, other field plants are recognized by natives as medicinally significant, and others as integral parts of the field environment that are not otherwise useful. Native and anthropological ethnobotanists can describe field systems on the basis of certain expectations as to which species will be represented, some of them useful, some of them not. Seeds of medicinal and non-useful weeds also reach households when cultigens are harvested. Cultural practices, which prohibit gathering in field borders (since this is where humans and now animals defecate), ensure the continuation of all these herbs in the field system, even though most within fields are weeded out over the course of the agricultural cycle.

Microfossil and macrofossil evidence from the archaeological record indicates that certain of these weed genera have long been part of local field systems. The Chenopod-Amaranth pollen index has been used to show cycles of increasing-decreasing moisture conditions over the period when agriculture developed (Flannery and Schoenwetter 1970), but it may also be an indicator of field clearing and agricultural activities. In other areas, palynologists have shown that increases in certain weed pollens may be associated with human cultivation activities, not simply climatic fluctuations (Davis 1965). This may be the case for the Valley of Oaxaca as well (Messer 1973).

Macrofossils, including carbonized seeds of several "edible

weed" genera and other unidentified "weed" seeds, also provide evidence for the interpretation of early agricultural conditions in the Valley of Oaxaca. From bell-shaped storage pits at the site of Tomaltepec, *Amaranthus, Chenopodium,* and *Portulaca* seeds were recovered (J. Smith 1976) and from Fábrica San José, seed of *Crotalaria* (Ford 1976). Both *Amaranthus* and *Chenopodium* provide edible seeds as well as leaves and might have been exploited for food at two stages in their life cycles (cf. Messer 1973). Particularly large quantities of *Chenopodium* seeds from the Middle Formative level of Tomaltepec (J. Smith 1976) favor this interpretation, though *Chenopodium* ripen along with maize at the end of the rainy season, and could have been accidentally introduced into ancient households along with the maize harvest.

Chenopodium, Amaranthus, and *Crotalaria* in these early sites are also intriguing since all are currently cultivated, though people continue to gather unsown specimens. Small bushes of *Chenopodium ambrosioides* are uprooted from their natural habitats and transplanted into house gardens; alternatively, seeds from wild or cultivated specimens are saved and sown. The spice is highly desirable and people like to have it close at hand. Also, the leaves may be sold to others who do not have their own plants, and have neither the time nor the knowledge about where to gather.

Amaranthus (*alegría*), sown in household gardens, is an ornamental as well as a food plant. The seeds are popped, mixed with sugar, and made into a sweet which is particularly popular at the end of the rainy season (the beginning of November). This species of *Amaranthus,* unlike *Chenopodium ambrosioides,* does not currently grow in the wild, though other species of *Amaranthus* do. *Crotalaria pumila,* the other potential cultigen, is a rainy season herb of cultivated fields and other disturbed environments. When it is fully mature, people carefully collect both seeds and leaves. The seeds are stored until early spring and sown as soon as the slight danger of winter frost has passed, before the rains begin. People sow the herb in their gardens in order to eat fresh greens at a time when there are not yet any in the fields. Thus, they expand both the geographic and temporal range of *Crotalaria pumila* and produce garden greens "out of season."

Current selective manipulations of field weeds provide a good description of, and rationale for, cultivation. Field weeds are classified and named in the folk taxonomy and recognized to fit into particular niches in the field system. Noting their habitats, limited season of growth, and growth cycles, people take weeds from their natural habitat to home gardens and extend their productivity in space and in time. This may be one way in which early cultivation began.

While it is not possible to say with certainty why particular weed seeds are represented in particular site locations, recovering these seeds archaeologically indicates at least that certain kinds of field conditions were present. Ethnobotanical descriptions of possible field systems and the ways in which weed seeds would reach household refuse can provide archaeologists with ideas for data collection as well as data interpretation. Many of these weed seeds are almost microscopic in size. To find these field systems indicators, archaeologists can screen flotation samples with micromillimeter mesh to recover very small seeds (such as *Portulaca*) that would otherwise escape notice. With attention to the ethnobotanical evidence of what they might expect to find as remains from given field systems, archaeologists will be able to collect more data significant for describing land use and calculating total edible productivity. Existing excavation procedures, if they include fine screening of soil samples from house floors, storage, and refuse areas, should recover this evidence.

In addition, the archaeologist who recovers paleobotanical weed evidence can contribute to the research interests of other disciplines. For historians of medicine and diet, information on *Chenopodium* is highly desirable, since the native practice of consuming *Chenopodium ambrosioides* as spice and occasionally as medicine effectively kills intestinal worms (cf. Kliks 1975). Though we cannot say how people on Early and Middle Formative sites of Oaxaca were consuming *Chenopodium,* the seeds recovered from living floors and storage pits show that the plant was present in the environment and reached household sites. This suggests possibly great antiquity for such beneficial dietary practices with their by-product of intestinal medication.

There are also other non-edible weeds found in archaeological contexts that are noteworthy for other studies. At Tomaltepec, *Dalea* and *Argemone mexicana* were recovered from Early Formative materials outside of storage pits; *Mollugo* from a Middle Formative context. Ethnobotanical studies showed that all are present in the modern environment, and that all have some medicinal use. Specimens of

Dalea (*D. capitulata* (Rydb.) Harms., *D. citriodora* (Cav.) Willd., D. spp.) grow in the Mitla hillsides. People say they rub the leaves on hives and other skin rashes. *Argemone mexicana,* a common poppy, exudes a milky sap, which is used as a salve for sore eyes. One species of *Mollugo* was considered by some to be a stomach remedy for *empacho,* a common intestinal complaint. Though it cannot be said that any of these plants were being used medicinally in antiquity, it is interesting that they were at least represented in the prehisto⸱ic field environment and either intentionally or unintentionally introduced into living areas.

Finally, finding seeds from weeds such as *Mollugo* and *Portulaca* are also important, since they give the paleobotanist evidence of the antiquity of such genera in the New World (cf. Chapman, Stewart, and Yarnell 1974).

In summary, knowing what plants had nutritional and medicinal uses is important for both cultural anthropologists and economic botanists. In addition, archaeologists can advance our understanding of cultivation, domestication, and the evolution of cultigens and weeds in field systems (cf. de Wet and Harlan 1975). Though weeds have traditionally been looked upon as "plants growing out of place" (King 1966), it is certainly true that "There will be weeds for a long time to come, and it may be that the most important evolutionary studies in the future will concern the evolution of ecosystems in which weeds play a regular part" (Baker 1974:18).

Cultural evolution at particular sites can contribute to this more general ecological evolutionary study. Ethnobotanists, by providing a corpus of data on field systems, weed incidence, and uses, can provide the archaeologist with an index of what weeds to look for, hypotheses about environmental use, and research strategies to test them.

Cultivator's Wisdom: Avocados

Gathering from the hillside and reaping both sown and unsown food products from the fields provides Mitleños with some, but not all, of their most useful plant foods. Though the traditional Mesoamerican diet is usually described as maize, beans, squash, and chili peppers, avocados (*Persea americana*) are a very important native food as well. In Mitla, the small fruits of the native avocado (*Yeswí, aguacate criollo*) yield from May through August, and are a favorite food. Many households have one or two trees in their yard, and avocados are also acquired through the marketplace from other valley or nearby mountain towns. Stones of all of these are discarded in the general household refuse, though stones of particularly delectable fruits— savored for the texture or taste of the flesh, or for small stone size relative to the quantity of flesh and thin skin—may be planted and nurtured close to the house.

Avocados are also an important food because they are both highly productive and highly nutritious. Trees begin to yield within five years, yield for up to fifty years, and may produce hundreds of fruits per season. Nutritionally, the Mexican avocado is also favorably composed. Fruits average 9 to 15 percent fat (Kester 1951:44) with the Mexican race (the small, thin-skinned anise-scented fruits— those found in Mitla and other Valley of Oaxaca towns) having a higher fat content than any of the other races (Hodgson 1950:287). They are high in calories, essential fatty acids and B vitamins, and vitamins A and E. Their high energy value but relatively low carbohydrate content also gives them digestive-aiding properties—"as if fruit and olive oil had been chemically combined by nature" (*ibid.*).

In addition to the nutritious flesh, Mitleños also value the avocado for its leaves and stones. The anise-scented leaves are a condiment used to flavor beans, *tamales,* and *Opuntia* stems. They are sold by households having the trees, and also in the marketplace, to those who have none. The stones are traditionally used medicinally to treat wounds. Hence, having the avocado close to the household is advantageous for a number of reasons.

Though it is not at all certain at what point avocados began to be cultivated in Mesoamerica (C. Smith 1967; J. Smith 1976), avocado seeds appear very early in Mesoamerican sites. In Tehuacán, seeds appear from the hunting and gathering Coxcatlán horizon (8000–7000/6500 B.C.) onward (C. Smith 1966) and in the Valley of Oaxaca definitely by the Early Formative at Tomaltepec (J. Smith 1976). They are represented in the Formative levels at Huitzo, Tierras Largas, Abasolo, and Fábrica San José as well (Flannery et al. 1970:37, 68, 74; Ford 1976). Thus, avocados appear as early as or along with cultivated maize, beans, and cucurbits. The question of domestication and cultivation, however, remains open. Though botanists have generally assumed that seed size will increase along with increasing fruit size, they have been unable to produce evidence of a clear break in seed size from one period to the next at any of these sites. If there was a selection for larger fruits (with larger stones), smaller fruits continued, and are represented up to the most recent levels in the archaeological record (C. Smith 1967, 1969; Ford 1976; J. Smith 1976). Seeds may be from wild, protected (but not sown) or domesticated (sown) trees, but it is difficult to distinguish definitively among them.

Both C. E. Smith and R. I. Ford have also considered where ecological conditions would have permitted the avocado to grow without intentional human propagation. C. E. Smith has convincingly shown that in the vicinity of the Tehuacán caves, the same spiny vegetation has continued since 10,000 B.C. and that avocado trees were not native to the semi-desert Tehuacán valley floor. Along with *Capsicum annuum* and *Spondias mombin,* avocados were one of the fruits probably "imported," planted, and enabled to survive by artificial irrigation (C. Smith 1966). At Formative sites in Oaxaca, by contrast, moisture was sufficient to support natural growth, but avocados may have been domesticated to meet the increased consumption needs of a larger population. Ford (1976) argues that numbers were artificially increased through human propagation. In neither case, however, is there a compelling argument that people could not have imported increasing quantities of avocados from non-local sources to meet increasing local demand. Up until very recent times, large quantities of avocados have continued to reach town and urban markets from outlying rural areas and have been carried by tumpline.

At present neither the seed size nor local ecological evidence derived from archaeological settings provide convincing data for when and where avocados were domesticated or cultivated. Ethnographic analogy provides a model for why and how people sow particular crops. Contemporary people are constantly planting seeds of fruit trees and vegetables. They save the seeds of fruits they like, including avocados, plant them, and nurture them in small gardens near their homes. In this regard, avocados are cared for analogously to *Crotalaria pumila,* the field herb mentioned earlier. Seeds of avocados, like those of *Crotalaria,* are saved and planted so the product will be close to home. Though for avocados there is obviously a wait for return to seed, people express a desire to have choice avocados available near them, and so individually plant trees. This is different, however, from planting orchards—purposeful, large-scale cultivation, which is still not practiced to any great extent in the towns studied. People also note that cultivated avocados have a more extensive production season than wild trees. They begin to yield earlier in the season, and may fruit late into August. As with *Crotalaria* cultivation, one expressed purpose of caring for avocado trees is to extend their yield seasonally beyond what is available in nature.

One further consideration is that of production efficiency. Avocado domestication might serve not only to meet the consumption needs of a larger population (cf. Ford 1976), but also to reduce the amount of time and effort expended in avocado gathering. With trees nearby, one can gather avocados without sacrificing time to other activities, and there is little risk involved if one never leaves the local area. Trees close to home also contribute shade, leaves, and avocado stones. For all these purposes, it would have been useful to domesticate avocados in prehistory, either from the seeds from wild trees or from trees already sown. Some gathering may have continued as it does now, along with domestication and careful cultivation, which might account for the persistence of seeds of different sizes.

Summary

The preceding discussion has demonstrated how certain products from the uncultivated hills, the cultivated fields, and household gardens contribute significantly to the subsistence of modern Zapotec Indians and mestizos in the Valley of Oaxaca towns. Recent studies show that plant gathering strategies have in many cases continued alongside agricultural practices; and studies of contemporary plant use may offer reasonable bases for inferences on how particular genera and species, found in the archaeological record, were being classified and used in prehistory. Knowing what plants are available in the contemporary environment and how they are used can provide the archaeologist with botanical data pertaining to field systems. With such data, he can adjust his collection procedures to save, for instance, almost microscopic weed seeds which may contribute to his interpretation of environmental use.

In addition, contemporary ethnobotanical studies offer new ideas for interpreting the origins of cultivation and other cultural practices. They may be of interest to the botanist studying the evolution of genera such as *Amaranthus* and *Chenopodium* in conjunction with the archaeologist. The ethnobotanist's data on medicinal weeds which are found in the archaeological record, and any additional data, may interest the social anthropologist who is tracing the antiquity of certain patterns of plant use. While one cannot say with certainty that any of the plants recovered were being used in the particular ways observed in the ethnographic setting, the locations of finds within households or in storage pits make some possibilities more probable than others. For the ethnobotanist, the archaeological data are very significant in that they show the antiquity of certain patterns of plant distribution as well as possible plant use.

Notes

1. *Amaranthus* identifications by E. L. McWilliams. All other identifications by Rogers McVaugh, University of Michigan Herbarium.

References Cited

Baker, Herbert G.
    1974. "The Evolution of Weeds." *Annual Review of Ecology and Systematics* 5:1–24.
Chapman, Jefferson, Robert B. Stewart, and Richard A. Yarnell
    1974. "Archaeological Evidence for Pre-Columbian Introduction of *Portulaca oleracea* and *Mollugo verticillata* into Eastern North America." *Economic Botany* 28:411–12.
Davis, Margaret B.
    1965. "Phytogeography and Palynology of Northeastern United States." In H. E. Wright, Jr. and David G. Frey, eds., *The Quaternary of the United States: A Review Volume for the VII Congress of the International Association for Quarternary Research,* pp. 377–402. Princeton: Princeton University Press.
de Wet, J.M.J. and J.R. Harlan
    1975. "Weeds and Domesticates: Evolution in the Man-Made Habitat." *Economic Botany* 29:99–107.
Drennan, Robert D.
    1976. *Fábrica San José and Middle Formative Society in the Valley of Oaxaca.* Museum of Anthropology, Memoir No. 8. Ann Arbor: University of Michigan.

Flannery, Kent V., et al.

1970. "Preliminary Archaeological Investigations in the Valley of Oaxaca, Mexico, 1966–69." A report to the National Science Foundation and the Instituto Nacional de Antropología e Historia. Mimeo.

Flannery, Kent V. and James Schoenwetter

1970. "Climate and Man in Formative Oaxaca." *Archaeology* 23:144–52.

Ford, Richard I.

1976. "Carbonized Plant Remains." In *Fábrica San José and Middle Formative Society in the Valley of Oaxaca, Mexico.* Appendix XIII, pp. 261–68. Museum of Anthropology, Memoir No. 8. Ann Arbor: University of Michigan.

Hodgson, Robert W.

1950. "The Avocado: A Gift from the Middle Americas." *Economic Botany* 4:253–93.

Kester, Ernest B.

1951. "Minor Oil-Producing Crops of the United States." *Economic Botany* 5:38–59.

King, L. J.

1966. *Weeds of the World: Biology and Control.* London: Hill.

Kirkby, Anne V.

1973. *The Use of Land and Water Resources in the Past and Present Valley of Oaxaca, Mexico.* Museum of Anthropology, Memoir No. 5. Ann Arbor: University of Michigan.

Kliks, Michael

1975. *Paleoepidemiological Studies on Great Basin Coprolites: Estimation of Dietary Fiber Intake and Evaluation of the Ingestion of Anthelmintic Plant Substances.* Berkeley: University of California, Department of Anthropology, Archaeological Research Facility.

Messer, Ellen

1972. "Patterns of 'Wild' Plant Consumption in Oaxaca, Mexico." *Ecology of Food and Nutrition* 1:325–32.

1973. "Sown and Unsown Aspects of Productivity in Agricultural Systems in the Valley of Oaxaca, Mexico." Paper prepared for the symposium on Cultural Ecology, Society for American Archaeology Annual Meeting, San Francisco, Calif.

1975. "Zapotec Plant Knowledge: Classification, Uses, and Communication About Plants in Mitla, Oaxaca, Mexico." Ph.D. dissertation, University of Michigan.

Smith, C. E.

1966. "Archaeological Evidence for Selection in Avocados." *Economic Botany* 20:169–75.

1967. "Plant Remains." In Douglas S. Byers, ed., *Environment and Subsistence: The Prehistory of the Tehuacan Valley,* 1:220–55. Austin: University of Texas Press.

1969. "Additional Notes on Pre-Conquest Avocados in Mexico." *Economic Botany* 23:135–40.

Smith, Judith
    1976. "Formative Botanical Remains at Tomaltepec." Ann Arbor, Michigan.
Whalen, Michael
    1976. "Excavations at Santo Domingo Tomaltepec; Evolution of a Formative Community in the Valley of Oaxaca, Mexico." Ph.D. dissertation, University of Michigan.
Wilken, Gene
    1970. "The Ecology of Gathering in a Mexican Farming Region." *Economic Botany* 24:286–95.

11/Ethnoarchaeology and the Interpretation of Community Organization

Susan H. Lees
Department of Anthropology
Hunter College,
University of New York

Like other contributors to this volume, Lees discusses contemporary and prehistoric features of a system of land use. Outlining ethnographic data from the anthropologically well-documented Valley of Oaxaca, Mexico, she discusses some of the relationships between political organization and irrigation. Framed as a theoretical and cautionary note, Lees' argument is that a diachronic and regional approach is of greater utility than is a community (or site-) oriented study for the investigation of changing political organization and its relationship(s) to irrigation technology. Lees' discussion has interesting implications for the archaeological investigation of settlement patterns; her provisional finding of a lack of association between variations in form of local administration, community size, location, and irrigation technology, for example, might be tested against data from other irrigating societies. Lees' review is relevant not only to Mesoamerica, but to other areas in which the relationships between subsistence technology and the development of state systems of organization are being explored.

The fieldwork on which this discussion is based was done primarily in 1969, in association with a long-term project, the Prehistoric Cultural Ecology of the Valley of Oaxaca, directed by Professor Kent Flannery and funded by the National Science Foundation and the National Institute of Mental Health (e.g., Flannery et al. 1967). This article is based on a paper delivered at the annual meeting of the American Anthropological Association in Washington, D.C., in November 1976.

I profited considerably from discussions long ago with Kent Flannery, and more recently with Carol Kramer, Gregory Johnson, Stephen Kowalewski, Daniel Bates, and Gary Feinman. They bear no responsibility, however, for the opinions expressed in this paper.

Some of the most serious problems that preoccupy archaeologists reconstructing the emergence of complex societies lie in interpreting the organization of economic and political activities on the basis of material remains. Ethnoarchaeology, which may be broadly conceived as the study of contemporary societies using the time and space perspectives central to archaeological research, offers the potential for gaining useful insights about ancient social systems. If a contemporary society is viewed as representing one segment of a long evolutionary sequence, the question becomes: what can be learned about previous segments of that sequence from an observation of a more recent one? Some of the insights to be gained may initially appear to be negative ones; for in the process of discovering what we can infer on the basis of material remains, we also learn what we cannot infer. But these observations may also prove constructive.

In order to illustrate several points related to archaeological inference on the basis of contemporary observations, I refer here to my own research in the Valley of Oaxaca, Mexico. The objective of this research was to elucidate archaeological inferences about the relationship between technology—in this case, canal irrigation—and political organization. This research was carried out with the express purpose of complementing archaeological research on the process of state formation during the Late Formative period in the valley. The following discussion focuses on three main points emerging as a consequence of that research.

First, it is not fruitful to make archaeological inferences about the nature or determinants of local administrative organization on the basis of an isolated community study, whether ethnographic or archaeological. Second, the role of a particular technological feature or device in community-level political organization may be subject to dramatic changes over relatively short periods of time. The methodological implications of these two points are the basis for the third, namely that spatial (regional) and temporal sampling are of immeasurable utility in the interpretation of any particular organizational configuration. The value of such sampling for strictly archaeological research has been amply and convincingly documented in a publication edited by Kent Flannery, *The Early Mesoamerican Village* (1976). Though regional, not to mention temporal, sampling in ethnographic research is at a far more elementary level, I hope to make clear their potential importance for future ethnoarchaeological studies.

Setting

While there have been major historical changes during the millennia that have intervened between the Late Formative and the present, there seems to be sufficient continuity at the level of local communities and their agricultural practices to warrant some inferences about the past from contemporary observations. The contemporary settlement pattern seems similar in many respects to that which emerged at the end of the Formative: nucleated villages along the valley floor and the piedmont slopes, regional towns and a central urban complex which lies today at the foot of the hill on which Monte Albán, the great Late Formative/Classic site, was constructed (figure 11.1). Sev-

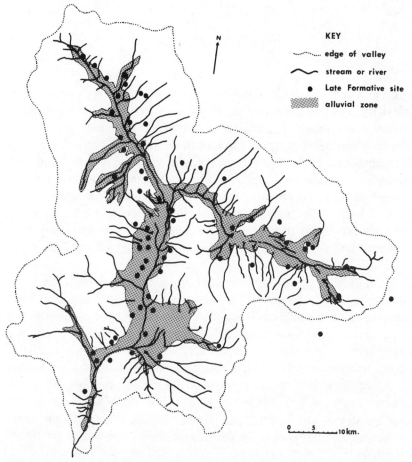

KEY
- ········· edge of valley
- ～ stream or river
- ● Late Formative site
- ▨ alluvial zone

0 ___5___ 10 km.

Figure 11.1. Late Formative sites in the Valley of Oaxaca, Mexico.

eral years of research have provided evidence for considerable continuity in climate, geography, and irrigation technology from the Late Formative to the present.[1] It was the apparent convergence in time of three factors, the expansion of permanent settlements into the piedmont zone near tributary streams,[2] the use of canal irrigation,[3] and the emergence of a new form of socio-political integration represented by the founding of Monte Albán, that initially stimulated the inquiry under discussion here. Was there a relationship between use of canal irrigation technology and the rise of the state in the Valley of Oaxaca? Would a direct connection between water control and general political structure in communities be evident in canal-irrigating villages today? It was hoped that an answer to the second question might shed some light on the first.

Sampling

The first and sometimes the most important decisions to be made in devising a research strategy in ethnography involve determining how many cases should be studied, and how they should be selected. More often than not, when the unit in question is a community, the ethnographer is restricted to a sample of one, due to time and manpower limitations. And, because preliminary surveys may be costly and time-consuming, the community chosen for intensive research is likely to be selected on a rather arbitrary basis, often for reasons exogenous to the problem at hand. The researcher may then have difficulty gauging the extent of regional variability in the characteristics under study.

In order to circumvent the latter difficulty, I decided to begin my own study with a survey on the basis of which I could form a selected sample of communities to study more intensively. The ideal course to take at that point would have been the construction of a random sample of all communities in the valley, or at least of those practicing canal irrigation. Unfortunately, at the time the study was done, this was not feasible. The only practical alternative was to drive to as many villages as possible in the limited time available, observe, and ask questions. The fact that this sample did not have a random basis limits the reliability of statistical manipulations of the data obtained. Nevertheless, it was a highly instructive starting point for making important discoveries about variability in community organization. The survey covered some 22 canal-irrigating communities and 2 others which did not depend on canal irrigation. Villages included in the sample were located in all three arms of the valley (Lees 1973).

The advantages of making a systematic survey became apparent as I discovered the extent to which communities differed in the ways they organized control over and access to canal irrigation. In some communities, administrative control was vested in a single high-ranking official, while in others, it was divided among several low-ranking officials. The survey provided an opportunity to ask, at least on a preliminary level, whether this variation was associated with variation in community size, location on the piedmont slope, irrigation technology, and other factors. No such associations were apparent. While a firm conclusion on this matter will await a broader survey based on a probability sample, a tentative interpretation of the results was possible. That is to say, the sources of administrative variation were not to be found in local technical, topographical, or demographic factors. Rather, the existence of a relatively high level of variability represented a characteristic of the larger unit, the region, or an even larger one, the state. This variability was in part the product of a kind of state policy, in this case, of nonintervention in certain community administrative affairs. This fact became clear through contrast, because the previous policy had recently been reversed. With a state level policy of intervention in local level administrative practices, there would be far more uniformity in village organization of water use (Lees 1974). I return to this point below.

To recapitulate up to this point: the results of a village-to-village survey of the administrative form of water control indicated that isolated community study would be an insufficient basis on which to understand or interpret the nature and determinants of local organization. A regional approach may prove useful not only to show just how representative one community may be of the rest, but to suggest how and why communities may appear different or similar with regard to particular attributes.

Interpreting Inequality and Power

To describe a formal administrative organization is not to show how it works. Showing how it works would be crucial in relating political organization to the technology of canal irrigation. In order to investigate the internal operation of community organization, I selected three communities from my sample for more intensive study.

The problem of operationalizing the concept of "power" was apparent from the start. One index of relative power might be unequal access to resources such as irrigation water. Another would be unequal participation in the formal administration of the community. Thus, I tried to discover whether those whose homes and fields were located upstream on the canals were also those who received more water and who served more frequently in higher political office. After I gathered data on house and irrigated field locations, actual allocations of water, and public careers by individuals, I found that people held irrigated land in scattered plots often distant from their homes, that water was allocated not on the basis of location but on extent of the holdings, and service in higher office seemed neither to be directly related to location of home or fields nor to amounts of irrigation water received. These negative findings were useful in eliminating from consideration a number of direct and simple relationships which might otherwise form the basis of archaeological inferences about technology, unequal access to resources, and political power.

The administrative structure of each community, whether irrigation-based or not, was hierarchical. The basis for this hierarchy was not in the intrinsic administrative needs or consequences of local technologies or environments, but rather in external governmental policy, which had long dictated local administrative forms and modes of selection of administrators. There were some material manifestations of the presence of administrative centralization, even hierarchy, at the village level, including staffs of office and civic buildings. There were also churches containing considerable material wealth. These structures and their contents were clearly distinct from residences and other utilitarian structures of ordinary households. At any one time only a few individuals from the community had a direct connection with these civic and ceremonial symbols of power; these were civil and religious officials.

What was not evident from these material manifestations of differential power was that tenure in high office was restricted to short terms: three years for civil offices and one year for ritual ones. Responsibility for office-holding was circulated among adult males of the community, each individual becoming eligible for a higher level as he matured through time, having filled lower offices. High officials, then, tended to be older men.

Holding high political office did not appear to be grounds for special influence over others, though the reverse might be true, that individuals with more influence might be chosen for office more frequently. On the whole, community members saw public service as a duty, a heavy burden, and did not seek such public honor. Decisions were made on a consensus basis in any case, so that holding office generally entailed little actual power.

A possibly significant difference between community members was that of wealth in land. Unlike access to higher office, access to land was not public and circulated. Those who owned more land had more money, more secure lives, and more influence because they could hire others to work for them. But in fact, differences in landholding tended to be relatively slight, or of relatively little political significance, for reasons I discuss below.[4] What is important here is that the differences in landholding were rarely evident in the homes or dress of individuals; wealthier individuals were called upon more frequently to sponsor ephemeral ceremonial displays which ate up their surpluses. The material evidence of this surplus, when it existed, was concentrated not in the homes of the wealthier, but in the church, for high prestige was associated with giving gifts to the saints as well as sponsoring fiestas. Furthermore, there were strong social sanctions against the private display of wealth.

While greater wealth in land and service in high administrative office were roughly correlated, both factors correlated best with age. That is, older men tended to serve in high office and to have larger landholdings. There may have been a slight tendency to retain wealth and tenure in high office in some households over more than one generation, but partible inheritance practices tended to mitigate such tendencies.

Thus, there was some contradictory material evidence. While on the one hand, it was clear that there was some centralization of administrative authority in the community, and there was accumulation of wealth, these differentials did not apply significantly to community members as individuals. If there had been any basis for power differentials in the local environment, particularly in the characteristics of the water source and technology needed to use it, the connection had long ago been obliterated by subsequent events, the most recent of which may have been the Conquest and its system of rule which produced closed corporate communities, and the Revolution which had reinforced significant elements of the previous pattern. For it had become clear that egalitarian community relationships, as well as the form of administrative structure, were a consequence of and adaptation to the organization of the larger polity.

The results of the intensive studies thus reinforce the point that isolated community studies may prove inadequate for interpreting local events. It seems reasonable to assume, furthermore, that this situation applies to the Late Formative just as much as to the present.

Interpreting Processes of Change

A realization of the importance of recent historical events in the shaping of local community political organization led me to a search for historical data about the region. Records from the colonial and immediately post-colonial period are sketchy and incomplete, but it was possible to get at least some notion of continuing processes of change in the past. Putting these materials together with an even more incomplete archaeological record, one can see a suggestion, at least, of recurrent patterns of relationships. It is perhaps in the identification of such repeated patterns that ethnoarchaeology can make its greatest contribution to archaeological reconstruction of organizational change, rather than in the detailed description of community behavior in a minute slice of time.[5]

In this case, where the focus of research was on the relationships of water resources to political organization, I was most fortunate in being able to observe the impact of both technical and political change on certain communities in my sample, while other communities were as yet untouched. That is to say that my survey of villages afforded an opportunity to survey not only spatial variation, but a kind of temporal variation, in that some villages were beginning to be altered in a certain direction which others were likely to follow later on. Those communities involved directly in the process of change were ones which had received state government aid in the installation of new irrigation devices. (In terms of formal attributes, this generally meant that they had larger cement dams, tanks, or wells with diesel pumps.) Along with this aid came government intervention in community organization, particularly that related to control over water resources. These communities were in the process of becoming less autonomous, less locally diverse, and less stable. That is to say, they were becoming increasingly responsive to non-local events in the central government and the national market situation, as their participation in commercial agriculture intensified (Lees 1976). While the source of this change was not all regional, but at a national or even international level, its impact on local political, market, and ecological factors led to what might be called a chain of mutual causation. With a change in the marketing activities of some villages would surely come changes in the activities of others—and so forth.

It became clear that a focal point for change in the piedmont irrigating communities was the water supply system. This was often the point at which technical and organizational intervention from outside was initiated. As increasing pressure was placed on their resources thanks to intensification of production, communities became increasingly dependent upon the centralized power of higher government to supply advanced technology and technicians as well as higher administrative coordination of the shared resources (Lees 1974).

What was important about these observations was not the obvious point that political centralization, productive intensification, and technological development all seemed to be connected with one another, but that this process was only one segment of a larger one. For such developments had apparently occurred in the past and had been followed by periods of decentralization, lower levels of production, and decline of technological expertise. Documentation of a relatively recent decline was easy to find: abandoned stone dams and mills from the pre-Revolutionary period attested to a previously higher level of intensification of resource use in several areas of the valley (Lees 1973).

While I had set out initially to discover a connection between the technology and the organizational requisites of irrigation, I came to see that if there was a connection, it was subject to dramatic alterations in time. At certain points in time, irrigation played a key role as a locus for change in the linkages between villages and central governments, while at other times it seemed to have little or no importance in those linkages. An explanation for change was not to be found in the local government at all, except to the extent that intensified resource use by one community affected resource availability in another.

Conclusions

It may have been simply a fortuitous accident that the area I was investigating was at that time undergoing significant changes that were directly pertinent to my own research. But it is difficult to imagine any area of the world which is not also undergoing change. Ethnoarchaeology can benefit considerably from viewing each contemporary case as an example of adjustment to ongoing changes whose characteristics might lead to insights about past processes. The question is, then, what is the nature of the changes that are happening or have occurred most recently; and how can observed behavior patterns be related to those changes? Many of the problems that face the archaeologist also face the ethnoarchaeologist. These concern, in particular, determining what part of a larger whole is represented by the small sample one is able to observe and describe. Considerations of temporal and spatial variability must play a critical role in interpretations, whether the observations are archaeological or ethnographic in nature.

It is becoming increasingly clear from ethnoarchaeological studies that observations of contemporary behavior can help us to learn not only what we can infer from certain types of material remains, but also what we cannot infer. The latter sort of understanding can be useful not simply as a warning not to jump to unwarranted conclusions, but to guide us in the use of ethnographic research for providing different sorts of insights. If the expected material correlates of an observed pattern of behavior seem to be absent, obscure, or deceptive, we can begin to ask why this is the case, and learn something from that. In the course of contributing to the interpretation of material remains, ethnoarchaeology holds the potential for making substantial contributions to the documentation and explanation of processes of changing patterns of behavior.

Notes

1. Much of the information on this continuity has been published in a monograph by Anne Kirkby (1973).

2. The archaeological survey of the valley which suggested this expansion into the piedmont zone during the Late Formative was initiated by Ignacio Bernal and continued by Kent Flannery. Since the time that the ethnoarchaeological study under dis-

cussion was completed, considerably more intensive surveys of parts of the valley have been carried out by Richard Blanton, Stephen Kowalewski, and others. When these are published, we will have much more complete information about numbers of sites and approximate numbers of people inhabiting these zones. The initial observation of expansion, however, seems to be supported by these later studies. I include a map of the Late Formative sites as we knew them at the time the study under discussion was done.

3. At the time of this study, only one Late Formative canal system had been excavated, that of Hierve el Agua (Neely 1967). It was primarily on the basis of site location that we assumed the use of canal irrigation facilities during this period. Since that time, however, more Late Formative canals have been discovered and excavated in the valley. Neely found one at the base of Monte Albán; S. Kowalewski found one in the eastern arm of the valley near San Sebastián Tutla, and M. Whalen found one at Tomaltepec (S. Kowalewski, personal communication).

4. I should note here that while differences in private wealth, as well as differences in political influence, could be observed at the village level, the scale of these differences renders them virtually insignificant in the context of the larger system, in which wealth and power differentials are extremely pronounced. Amount of irrigated land owned by an individual was considered indicative of his "wealth." In the Oaxacan communities I studied, land owned by individuals varied from 0 to about 1.25 hectares. One extremely unusual individual held just under 7 hectares (Lees 1973:45–81). On the whole, average differences between larger and smaller landholders came to approximately .5 hectares.

5. Examples of the ways in which recurrent patterns of relationships identified ethnographically may be utilized in archaeological interpretation may be found in Flannery (1972).

References Cited

Flannery, Kent
    1972. "The Cultural Evolution of Civilizations." *Annual Review of Ecology and Systematics* 3:399–426.
Flannery, Kent, M. S. Kirkby, A. V. T. Kirkby, and Aubrey W. Williams, Jr.
    1967. "Farming Systems and Political Growth in Ancient Oaxaca." *Science* 158:445–54.
Flannery, Kent, ed.
    1976. *The Early Mesoamerican Village.* New York: Academic Press.
Kirkby, Anne
    1973. *The Use of Land and Water Resources in the Past and Present Valley of Oaxaca.* Museum of Anthropology, Memoir No. 5. Ann Arbor: University of Michigan.
Lees, Susan H.
    1973. *Sociopolitical Aspects of Canal Irrigation in the Valley of Oaxaca Mex-*

ico. Museum of Anthropology, Memoir No. 6. Ann Arbor: University of Michigan.

1974. "The State's Use of Irrigation in Changing Peasant Society." In Theodore E. Downing and McGuire Gibson, eds., *Irrigation's Impact on Society*, pp. 123–128. Anthropological Papers of the University of Arizona, no. 25. Tucson: University of Arizona Press.

1976. "Hydraulic Development and Political Response in the Valley of Oaxaca, Mexico." *Anthropological Quarterly* 49:197–210.

Neely, James

1967. "Organización Hidráulica y Sistemas de Irrigación Prehistóricos en el Valle de Oaxaca." Instituto Nacional de Antropología e Historia, Bulletin 27. Mexico, D.F.

12/The Idea of Ethnoarchaeology: Notes and Comments

Patty Jo Watson
Department of Anthropology
Washington University, St. Louis

Assuming the role of constructive critic, Watson comments on each of the articles in the volume, adding pertinent comparative data as well as observations of a more general nature. Coming as they do from a leading practitioner of ethnoarchaeology, her caveats regarding the nature, utility, and limitations of this approach are welcome.

The theoretical basis for ethnoarchaeology is the use of analogies derived from present observations to aid interpretation of past events and processes. The reason we archaeologists do this—make observations in contemporary communities—is to provide ourselves with as many and as varied interpretive hypotheses as possible to help us understand (explain and predict) archaeological remains. Archaeological remains, of course, are the sole means of describing and explaining human behavior throughout those vast reaches of time and space where there are no written records.

Logically speaking, it does not matter where these interpretive hypotheses come from; what matters is how they stand up when tested against the archaeological record. I say *logically* it does not matter, but—as is so often the case—*practically* it does matter. It is most rewarding to search for suitable analogies (trial explanations for

Much of the substance of this paper was first presented as discussant's remarks at the symposium, "Ethnoarchaeology: Implications of Ethnography for Archaeology," held November 19, 1976, at the seventy-fifth annual meeting of the American Anthropological Association in Washington, D.C. The symposium was organized and chaired by Carol Kramer. The title for this published version of my comments is chosen with apologies to R. G. Collingwood.

excavated archaeological data, or trial predictions about sites or portions of sites as yet unexcavated) in settings as much like the prehistoric ones as possible. If one's archaeological work is being done in a part of the world (like the southwestern United States or some parts of Latin America or the Near East) where cultural continuity is great, then ethnoarchaeological research is bound to be highly productive. In fact, the flow of insights resulting from immersion in an ethnographic situation that resembles one's prehistoric situation in a number of fundamental ways can be so overwhelming that at times it verges on a mystical experience. The archaeological ethnographer in a Near Eastern community watching a *tauf* or *chīneh* (puddled adobe) wall being built, observing an old woman spinning goat hair with a wooden spindle and whorl, following the shepherd boys and the sheep and goat flocks into the hills above the mud village on a winter morning *"knows"* he or she is witnessing patterns that are in every detail many millennia old in this part of the world. No matter how strong this "You are there!" feeling becomes, however, it is essential to resist the temptation to make wholesale transfers from the ethnographic to the archaeological. Relationships, techniques, functions, etc., that can be observed in detail ethnographically and that appear to be highly appropriate to the archaeological remains are no more than hypotheses that must be tested before being accepted as explanatory of those archaeological remains.

Comments on the Papers

Many of the papers in this book rely largely if not completely on the direct-historical approach, which I have just been discussing. Frank Hole's paper is a particularly clear example of this. His presentation, as well as a number of his recent writings, represents an ethnoarchaeological attack on the problem of the origins of pastoralism in western Asia. To get empirical evidence relevant to this problem (which, in turn, is relevant to the origins of a food-producing economy), he immersed himself in a contemporary pastoral nomadic society so that he would know what the prehistoric evidence might comprise (what do the remains of nomads' camps look like archaeologically?) and where to look for it. As he notes, the success of his project was in no small part owing to the strength of traditional lifeways in this part of western Asia. The remains of the 8,000-year-old nomadic encampment he excavated were sufficiently comprehensible to contemporary nomads in the same area that they accurately predicted the locations of such features as fireplaces. This is an excellent example of the possible rewards resulting from the practice of ethnoarchaeology in a region where cultural continuities are numerous and extraordinarily long-lived. As a result of his ethnographic observations, Hole now knows where to look and what to look for in surveys devoted to tracing the origins and development of pastoral nomadism, which probably go farther back in time than we thought. As he makes clear, the purpose of his study was to derive behavioral regularities pertaining to sheep and goat pastoralists in the Zagros terrain that would enable him to predict where prehistoric pastoralists might have camped in that terrain and what the camps might have looked like.

There is another obvious line that can be pursued utilizing ethnographic data, and that is a search for broadly generalizable regularities in the relationship between tangible materials and their distributions on the one hand, and the intangible behavior that produced the materials on the other. Kramer's and Jacobs' papers and the paper by DeBoer and Lathrap exemplify this procedure, in part. Kramer and Jacobs are concerned with relationships between architectural plans and features and the size and nature of the occupying human population. If general approximations can be made for these space-size relationships (i.e., how many people are implied by how much space), then our understanding of prehistoric demographic patterns in the Near East will be much advanced. Readers familiar with recent research on and discussion of agricultural and state origins know that possible fluctuations in population size have figured largely in such discussions. It is interesting to find that the average amount of dwelling space per person in Shāhābād is very close to Naroll's figure of 10 m^2 per person (Naroll 1962; see also LeBlanc 1971), whereas at Tell-i Nun, there are about 30 m^2 per person of living space in the old walled village. At Hasanābād, the Iranian village in which I worked sixteen years ago (Watson 1979), the figure per person is 7.3 m^2, but with a large standard deviation.

It is perhaps worthwhile to note one of the other contrasts between Kramer's results and mine: as Kramer notes, the Shāhābād household complexes contain separate kitchens with ovens. This is not the case at Hasanābād, where all food preparation is done on or around a stone-lined firepit in the same room where the family sleeps, eats, and entertains. The Hasanābādis, in this respect as in various others, give every indication of being recently settled nomads whose domestic arrangements are significantly more similar to those of people like Hole's Baharvand than like the longtime peasants Kramer studied.

One of the points Jacobs makes about domestic arrangements at Tell-i Nun is something that should be followed up there and elsewhere: although men's equipment is communally owned, women's equipment is individually owned; hence, redundancy in women's possessions indicates a multi-family compound. Jacobs suggests that this may often be the situation in virilocal societies: if so, that would have significant implications for archaeologists attempting to derive social organization from archaeological remains.

A few other comparative figures for Shāhābād, Tell-i Nun, and Hasanābād are as follows: the average family size for Shāhābād is 6.2, for Tell-i Nun it is 8.8, for Hasanābād it is 4.4. Shāhābād village includes about 420 people and covers 3.0 hectares so there are 140 people per hectare. Tell-i Nun covers 4.2 hectares (within the wall of the old village) and was occupied by 490 people so there were 85.9 persons per hectare maximum (with gardens), or 116 persons per hectare minimum (if gardens are excluded). Hasanābād village (including the dung and trash midden area immediately surrounding the walls) includes 180 people and covers 2.4 hectares, so there are 75 people per hectare. If the dung and ash midden areas are excluded and only the land enclosed within an imaginary wall around the dwelling compounds is included, then the Hasanābād figure is closer to 1.5 hectares (120 people per hectare).

Kramer's and Jacobs' papers include exactly the sorts of data archaeologists working in western Asia must have if they are to approach prehistoric demographic problems with sufficient sophistication to obtain valid and increasingly detailed results. Further, some of the information they provide can be generalized to aid knowledge of cultural formation processes that have affected the archaeological record in other times and places.

Sumner's discussion of a population estimate for Tall-i Bakun is an excellent example of how to use ethnographic data to illuminate an archaeological situation. Further, the information he obtained for the relationship between area and population in 110 Iranian villages is a very valuable addition to the small but growing corpus of empirical information on this topic. Like the Shāhābād and Hasanābād data, the figures Sumner presents for human density per hectare of settlement area indicate that an estimate of around 100 people per hectare for prehistoric farming villages in the Zagros region is probably more nearly correct than the higher figure of 200 people per hectare which is sometimes used.

DeBoer and Lathrap provide some very valuable detail on the ceramic industry of the Amazonian group they studied. Their general concern is that of most archaeologists: to understand the relationships between particular kinds of behavior and the products of that behavior. Hence, I would amend one of their introductory statements (the second sentence in paragraph two of the paper) to read: "We compare ethnographic observations of contemporary behavior *and the results of that behavior* with archaeological observations on the remnant by-products of past behavior." (The italicized words are my suggested addition.)

As operating archaeologists we do assume the basic isomorphism between relationships we can observe now (between present behavior and the material result of present behavior) and relationships we infer for the past (between archaeologically observable remains and the past behavior that produced them). But, until now, we have not done nearly enough work on the left-hand side of the equation.

There is a wealth of information in the paper to which a brief commentary cannot do justice, but one body of data I found especially interesting is the distance table for procurement of raw materials. Average distance to the nine resources listed (clays, pigments, resins, polishing stones) is no less than 8 kilometers and several (six of the nine) are over 100 kilometers. I assume this must reflect relative ease of communication on the river (as one not very familiar with Amazonian ethnography, I would have appreciated some details on how the Shipibo-Conibo move around and transport these materials), but it is something site-catchment enthusiasts ought to consider carefully.

The other data of exceptional interest were those having to do with discard and refuse. This information in combination with that of Stanislawski for the Hopi (Stanislawski 1969) and David for the Fulani (David 1972) provides an exceedingly valuable corpus on life expectancies and disposal patterns relative to pottery as a whole and to different ceramic forms. Use of prehistoric sherds by the Shipibo-Conibo for temper is directly paralleled in the southwestern United States.

The doughnut shaped Shipibo-Conibo middens are similar in general form to those around Hasanābād where stable cleanings and household refuse, including firepit ashes, are dumped at the most easily accessible point outside the village walls. I certainly agree with DeBoer and Lathrap's concluding remarks about archaeological attention to refuse: we are all, by definition, middenophiles.

Margaret Hardin's data lie within the general comparative realm rather than the direct historical, and provide a very welcome supplement to Bunzel's study of Pueblo pottery design. In particular, Hardin's information on conceptualization of designs seems to contradict some of Bunzel's. Bunzel stresses—or relays her informants' stress—on having in mind a complete picture of the design before beginning to paint:

> I always know the whole design before I start to paint. (Zuni.)

> When I have finished with the shape, my thoughts are always on the design that I shall put on. Generally I have the whole design in my head before I begin to paint. (Laguna.)

> All the time when I am not working, I am thinking about what designs I shall make, and when I start to paint, I have it all in my mind. (Hopi.)

> . . . I think this is sufficient to show that the whole scheme of decoration is most carefully planned and is fixed in the mind of the artist before she begins on any part of her design. (Bunzel 1972:49)

Often the working out of a design seems to be rather traumatic, or at least a matter of considerable concern to the artists:

> They all speak of sleepless nights spent in thinking of designs for the pot to be decorated in the morning, of dreams of new patterns which on waking they try and often fail to recapture, and above all, the constant preoccupation with decorative problems even while they are engaged in other kinds of work. (Bunzel 1972:51)

According to Hardin the behavior of the San José potters is quite different from that of the Pueblo potters in this regard. They do not work from a mental template of the complete design, but go from decision to decision during the actual painting process. Unlike the Pueblo case, the final result is one that was not envisioned in its entirety in the artist's mind before he put brush to pot, but is the result of a series of decisions, each of which (except the very first) was partially constrained by those made previously.

One may ask, in the context of the preceding discussion, what is the significance of mental templates, anyway? Archaeologists are concerned with them because the existence of a mental template held in common in the minds of prehistoric artisans is thought to be the reason why standardized types of artifacts are produced, why bell-shaped curves are derivable from artifact analysis; because artifact makers in any one culture have common, culturally imposed ideas about the size and shape of the things they make. However, archaeologists' typologies may use attributes not necessarily meant to reflect those presumed mental templates, but rather meant to serve purely archaeological purposes such as determination of chronological relationships. What is usually most important to archaeologists is not the templates themselves, but the fact of that patterned behavior (whether or not verbalized or realized by the potters) which can be put to various uses, chronological ones being of great importance traditionally.

Clearly, two studies of this sort (Hardin's and Bunzel's) are not enough. We need much more of this kind of information before we can reach some semisecure understanding of living ceramic design systems and their origins.

James Ebert considers chipped stone tools from both an archaeological and an ethnographic viewpoint. With regard to the brief general discussion that prefaces his paper, I have the following comment. Regardless whether a simple form/function analogy is being made—i.e., the archaeological form (a particular kind of chipped stone tool for instance) is the same as an ethnographic form (an Eskimo end scraper) so the archaeological object probably functioned much like the ethnographic one—or a form/process analogy—i.e., the archaeological form (marked differentiation in quality and quantity of grave goods) is the same as an ethnographic form (marked differentiation in burial goods that correlates with a particular process observable ethnographically: status differentiation among the individuals in question before death) so the archaeological form probably resulted from a process much like the ethnographic one—the logical structure of the procedure is the same. The analogy is an hypothetical construct to be tested against the archaeological record.

The analytical approach to chipped stone artifacts advocated by Ebert is a refreshingly simple one that seems to have considerable promise. However, his argument would have been much stronger had he examined the defining characteristics of the quadrats within the ethnographic context as well as in the archaeological one. That is, I wish he had measured ethnographically known chipped stone hunting kits and secondary tools, etc., and counted the edges to see whether the distributions do indeed plot out as he suggests they should.

Carneiro, in his paper on tree felling with a stone ax, offers a combination of ethnographic and quantitative documentation for a technique that must have been ubiquitous from 10,000 B.P. until 5000 B.P. in much of the Old World, and down to the time of Columbus and later in the New World. His account can be added to that of the Danish archaeologists who chopped down trees with stone axes in a replication of prehistoric slash-and-burn cultivation (Iversen 1956), to Carneiro's own Peruvian data (Carneiro 1974), and to the data he refers to for the Heve of New Guinea (Townsend 1969), but the total corpus of detailed information on the subject is still exceedingly small compared to the growing literature on the manufacture and use of chipped stone tools.

With respect to the experiment Carneiro describes, one wonders how a person as young as Dobrabewä (only about 19 years old) knew anything at all about stone tools and their use. Was he making up the techniques of hafting and chopping as he went along, or was he somewhat guided by lingering traditions about stone tool use? How did Dobrabewä's manner of using the stone ax differ from the Yanomamö technique of felling a tree with a steel ax? Carneiro's formula for tree-felling time is ingeniously derived, but, of course, should be checked against more cases before being relied upon too heavily. Nevertheless, Carneiro's (and Dobrabewä's) work has established a basis for more precise assessments of the labor costs implied by prehistoric slash-and-burn cultivation than has hitherto been attainable.

In her paper on ethnobotanic research in the Valley of Oaxaca, Messer relates the value of detailed botanical and agronomic information obtained from contemporary societies for application to archaeological problems centering on plant use, agriculture, and paleoenvironment. I am especially interested in her statements about the feasibility of predicting archaeological plant remains and field systems on the basis of ethnographically known practices, and in her discussion of medicinal, ritual, and symbolic uses of plants. These latter uses might not show up clearly, if at all, archaeologically, but might nevertheless be explanatory of some plant distributions that *are* detectable. Such an explanation would be difficult to test, but insofar as it *is* testable, means for checking it would have to derive primarily, if not solely, from ethnographic data. Fortunately, there is a fairly substantial body of such data going back at least to the 1920s and 1930s' interest in ethnobotany of scholars such as Frances Densmore, Melvin Gilmore, and Volney Jones, and continuing to the contemporary work of ethnobotanists and paleoethnobotanists such as Leonard Blake, Hugh Cutler, Richard Ford, Earle Smith, Richard Yarnell, and Jean Black Yarnell.

Susan Lees, in her paper on "Ethnoarcheology and the Interpretation of Community Organization," seems to be saying that in the ethnographic situation she studied in Oaxaca, she did not find it useful to try to delineate direct correspondences among environmental factors, technological traits, and specific forms of political organization. Rather, when the state was strong and aggrandizing, centralizing technologies (like canal irrigation) were encouraged; when influence from the state center was weak, diversity developed in local water-control systems and in socio-political structures as well. In other words, what was happening at the state center rather than changes in the environment dictated what sort of subsistence technology was used. This seems fairly straightforward (and is even closely parallel to some developments in our own state-based, centripetal society: the press for nuclear energy—a highly centralizing technological system—at the expense of decentralizing systems like solar energy). When the archaeological situation is one of a state center and its hinterland, events in the hinterland are often more directly dependent on events in the state center than on the local (hinterland) social and physical environment. This seems to me to provide a good way of keeping track of success or failure in overall control by those in power at the state center. The "keeping track" consists of assessing the nature and intensity of perturbations in the hinterland caused by events at the state center. Contrariwise, if your concern is not with the state center, then you have to subtract those perturbations as best you can, and Lees has some suggestions about that.

Michael Jochim applies published data (ethnographic and other) on relevant contemporary topics to an archaeological problem. His paper on "Catches and Caches" expands an earlier study (Jochim 1976) of Mesolithic hunter-gatherers in the Danubian region of Europe. To understand fully how he arrived at the figures in various tables of the present Rhine Valley study (such as table 9.2), the reader should refer to Jochim's earlier and more detailed presentation. He relies upon a variety of detailed information about contemporary animal species and human hunting-gathering groups to construct a subsistence-settlement model for the Mesolithic hunter-gatherers of the Rhine Valley. He then compares the expected (derived from the model) with the observed (archaeological remains). In spite of many grave (some nearly insuperable) difficulties with the available archaeological data, Jochim is able to draw some interesting conclusions about the possible nature of Mesolithic subsistence-settlement systems along the Rhine Valley. I wish he had been more explicit and detailed in discussing tests of these conclusions, but he has at least provided another demonstration of the heuristic value for prehistorians of detailed, quantified models derived from contemporary data of a variety of different kinds (ethnographic, zoological, geological, and so on).

Concluding Remarks

In closing I should like to repeat and reinforce the point made earlier about the probationary status of information derived ethnographically by archaeologists. We are confronted with a paradox or conundrum in that the only way we can comprehend the past is via our knowledge of the present, but the past is, of course, not necessarily isomorphic with the present and, in fact, probably differs in many significant ways from the present. How can we get at the "real past" as distinct from our possible erroneous reconstructions or recreations of it? We get at it in the same basic fashion we acquire knowledge about anything: by formulating hypotheses about the real past and testing them in every way we can. Ethnoarchaeology is a wonderful means of generating such hypotheses, but if they are meant to be included in valid explanations of portions of the archaeological record, then the hypotheses must be tested in other ethnoarchaeological situations and against the archaeological record itself. Intense contact with a particular contemporary lifeway can result in a potentially dangerous identification with that lifeway—an archaeological version of one of the traditional *bêtes noires* of the ethnologist: "going native" and losing analytical perspective—so that one is tempted to impose the ethnographically familiar lifeway on the archaeological remains without further scrutiny. Hence, I temper my own great enthusiasm for ethnoarchaeological research and my admiration for present-day ethnoarchaeologists with a closing note of caution: Accepting knowledge claims always involves a leap of faith (we have known that for more than 200 years, at least since the time of David Hume). But there is a very important difference between a *tested* and an *untested* leap of faith.

References Cited

Bunzel, Ruth
    1972. *The Pueblo Potter: A Study of Creative Imagination in Primitive Art.*
    New York: Dover Publications; published 1929 by Columbia University Press.
Carneiro, Robert L.
    1974. "On the Use of the Stone Axe by the Amahuaca Indians of Eastern
    Peru." *Ethnologische Zeitschrift Zürich* 1:107–22.
David, Nicholas
    1972. "On the Life Span of Pottery, Type Frequencies, and Archaeological In-
    ference." *American Antiquity* 37:141–42.
Iversen, Johannes
    1956. "Forest Clearance in the Stone Age." *Scientific American* 194:36–41.
Jochim, Michael
    1976. *Hunter-Gatherer Subsistence and Settlement: A Predictive Model.* New
    York: Academic Press.
LeBlanc, Steven A.
    1971. "An addition to Naroll's Suggested Floor Area and Settlement Population
    Relationship." *American Antiquity* 36:210–11.
Naroll, Raoul
    1962. "Floor Area and Settlement Population." *American Antiquity* 27:587–89.
Stanislawski, Michael
    1969. "What Good is a Broken Pot? An Experiment in Hopi-Tewa Eth-
    noarchaeology." *Southwestern Lore* 35:11–18.
Townsend, William
    1969. "Stone and Steel Tool Use in a New Guinea Society." *Ethnology*
    8:199–205.
Watson, Patty Jo
    1979. *Archaeological Ethnography in Western Iran.* Viking Fund Publications
    in Anthropology, no. 57. Tucson: University of Arizona Press.

Index